DOING HARM

DOING HARM

How the World's Largest
Psychological Association
Lost Its Way in
the War on Terror

ROY J. EIDELSON

MCGILL-QUEEN'S UNIVERSITY PRESS

Montreal & Kingston | London | Chicago

© McGill-Queen's University Press 2023

ISBN 978-0-2280-1861-2 (cloth)
ISBN 978-0-2280-1862-9 (ePDF)
ISBN 978-0-2280-1863-6 (ePUB)

Legal deposit third quarter 2023
Bibliothèque nationale du Québec

Printed in Canada on acid-free paper that is 100% ancient forest free
(100% post-consumer recycled), processed chlorine free

LIBRARY AND ARCHIVES CANADA CATALOGUING IN PUBLICATION

Title: Doing harm : how the world's largest psychological association lost its way
   in the war on terror / Roy J. Eidelson.
Names: Eidelson, Roy J., author.
Description: Includes bibliographical references and index.
Identifiers: Canadiana (print) 20230175821 | Canadiana (ebook) 20230175872
   ISBN 9780228018612 (cloth) | ISBN 9780228018636 (ePUB) | ISBN 9780228018629 (ePDF)
Subjects: LCSH: American Psychological Association. | LCSH: Operational
   psychology—Moral and ethical aspects. | LCSH: Operational psychologists—
   Professional ethics—United States. | LCSH: Psychologists—Professional ethics—
   United States. | LCSH: Intelligence service—Moral and ethical aspects. | LCSH:
   Terrorism—Prevention—Moral and ethical aspects. | LCSH: War on Terrorism,
   2001–2009.
Classification: LCC BF636.3 .E33 2023 | DDC 174/.915—dc23

This book is dedicated to the dignity,

resilience, and memory of all who needlessly suffer,

and to all who try to alleviate their pain.

CONTENTS

ACKNOWLEDGMENTS

There are many people who deserve recognition and thanks for their diverse contributions in bringing this book into the world. Foremost, my years as a member of the Coalition for an Ethical Psychology have been transformative for me, offering camaraderie, purpose, and an intellectual and activist home of the rarest sort. I will always value the friendship, insights, and inspiration that Jean Maria Arrigo, Trudy Bond, Yosef Brody, Brad Olson, Steven Reisner, Stephen Soldz, and Bryant Welch have provided. Without them, *Doing Harm* would never have been written.

I've also learned a tremendous amount and found invaluable support from my involvement with Psychologists for Social Responsibility and the broader community of dissident psychologists who refused to be sidelined or silenced. Colleagues to whom I owe a debt of gratitude, both for their efforts and for their example, include Dan Aalbers, Neil Altman, Ghislaine Boulanger, Martha Davis, Serdar Degirmencioglu, Sarah Dougherty, Diane Ehrensaft, Ruth Fallenbaum, Sharon Gadberry, Rebecca Gordon, Gerald Gray, Ian Hansen, Michael Jackson, Jeffrey Kaye, Paul Kimmel, Jeanne LeBlanc, Alice LoCicero, Jancis Long, Brinton Lykes, Kathie Malley-Morrison, Tony Marsella, Jack O'Brien, Susan Opotow, Robert Parker, Mary Pelton-Cooper, Marc Pilisuk, Ken Pope, Deborah Popowski, Nathaniel Raymond, Gil Reyes, Alice Shaw, Frank Summers, and Michael Wessells (and more).

Doing Harm benefited considerably from countless engaging discussions, as well as specific feedback and recommendations from close colleagues and other experts. In addition to three anonymous readers who were generous with their time and knowledge, particular thanks for reviewing the manuscript – in whole or in part – go again to my Coalition colleagues, as well as Dan Aalbers, Mandy Conrad, David Frakt, Ellen Gerrity, Ian Hansen, Susan Opotow, and Jake Romm.

From draft manuscript to published book, the dedicated staff at McGill-Queen's University Press brought their expertise and enthusiasm to *Doing Harm*. I extend my appreciation to all of them, including those whose names I do not know. Emily Andrew, my editor at MQUP, has been extraordinary, an expert guide and teacher, and a staunch advocate throughout the entire process; I thank Peter Agree for helping me find my way to her. Jared Toney was a painstaking copyeditor, never blanching at the necessity of re-reading the manuscript, again and again. Managing editor Kathleen Fraser coordinated all the moving parts without a hitch. My thanks go as well to attorneys Carolyn Schurr Levin and Julius Grey for their thorough legal vetting of the book.

I also want to express my deep admiration for the essential and courageous work of the individuals and groups that, for years, have persisted in revealing and challenging the US government's decision to engage in abuse and torture as part of its so-called war on terror. Among others, I recognize here the journalists who were steadfast in their coverage of these horrors, the attorneys who were tireless in defending the due process rights of detainees, and the organizations that fearlessly placed their commitment to human rights above considerations of politics or popularity.

Last, but certainly not least, I thank members of my family for their immeasurable support and encouragement throughout this project. And as with so many other endeavors – of all sorts – over the past five decades, I can never adequately express my gratitude to my wife Judy, whose consistent engagement and well-timed reassurances kept me going, and whose commitment to repairing the world continues to inspire me every day.

AUTHOR'S NOTE

In addition to the author's personal views, this publication is based largely on publicly available records, reports, and court documents. Where public meetings are referenced, all quotations are derived from the transcripts of those recorded meetings. Where individuals have disputed the findings in public reports, the author has made efforts to include or acknowledge those publicly available responses. A complete list of sources can be found in the endnotes.

DOING HARM

INTRODUCTION

In January 2002, the first of hundreds of prisoners in the "war on terror" – many of them swept up and sold into captivity in exchange for US bounty payments – were brought from Afghanistan to Guantanamo Bay, Cuba.[1] Shaved from head to toe, they were shackled to their seats for the entire twenty-hour flight. Upon arriving on the island, they were led away in orange jumpsuits to outdoor cages. Few of them had any connection to international terrorism.[2] But that didn't matter. At a press conference, General Richard Myers, the chairman of President George W. Bush's Joint Chiefs of Staff, described the new prisoners as "people that would gnaw hydraulic lines in the back of a C-17 to bring it down ... These are very, very dangerous people, and that's how they're being treated."[3] Standing by his side, Secretary of Defense Donald Rumsfeld chimed in, "To be in an eight-by-eight cell in beautiful, sunny Guantanamo Bay, Cuba, is not inhumane."[4]

This was a time when the United States was stunned by the carnage of the 9/11 terrorist attacks just a few months earlier, and distraught over the frightening prospect of new attacks in the days ahead.[5] So a high premium was placed on the collection of information that might protect Americans from further harm. Vice President Dick Cheney bluntly told a national television audience that it would be necessary to "work the dark side," "spend time in the shadows," "use any means at our disposal," and not tie the hands of US military-intelligence operatives.[6] Cofer Black, the director of the Central Intelligence Agency (CIA) Counterterrorist Center, told a congressional committee: "After 9/11 the gloves come off."[7] In short, it was hardly a secret that the Bush Administration was prepared to toss aside international law, human rights standards, and perhaps even basic human decency in pursuing its agenda. And that's exactly what it did.[8]

Something else, however, wasn't nearly so obvious: that members of my own profession – fellow psychologists – would play facilitating roles in this unconscionable descent. Nor was it initially so clear that the world's largest organization of psychologists – the American Psychological Association (APA) – would fail to forcefully challenge the barbaric enterprise of abuse and torture as it unfolded. The APA could have joined with other human rights groups seeking to constrain a White House set on unbridled and far-reaching retribution that brutalized prisoners and diminished the country's moral standing around the world.[9] For the APA, however, that seemingly proved to be the road not taken.

In this book, I recount a disturbing story: the apparent betrayal of a healing profession's most cherished values. My primary focus is on key episodes and developments within the APA over the past two decades. As I write this introduction in mid-2022, the final page on this ugly era has not yet been written. Powerful forces within and beyond the APA remain committed to defending the involvement of psychologists in harsh national security operations and ensuring that these same opportunities will be available in the future. Across both major political parties, the US government's refusal to hold perpetrators of torture accountable for their actions further increases the likelihood that similar debates and decision points will arise again – possibly much sooner than we would like to believe. And those outcomes are far from certain.

Until resigning over the so-called torture scandal, I was an APA member for more than twenty-five years. For most of that time, like the vast majority of APA members my membership in the association was largely an inconsequential choice. Once having joined, continuing as a member was done with little further thought, except for a brief pause each year when it came time to pay the annual dues of a few hundred dollars. But the general membership's lack of active engagement doesn't mean that the APA is unimportant. Rather, the APA is recognized as the leading voice of and for US psychology, and few would dispute that the organization often effectively champions the career interests of psychologists. Moreover, the APA's Ethics Code has served as the basis for sanctioning professional misconduct – not only by its own members, but also by non-member psychologists subject to licensing laws in many states.

The APA is also important because it's part of the larger network of civil society organizations that contribute to a well-functioning democracy through expert analysis, education, the provision of services, and public advocacy. These are especially critical roles when such groups act independently of government and corporate interests – and when they hold these powerful actors accountable for negligence and wrongdoing. So, taken altogether, what an organization like the APA does or doesn't do can matter a lot, even if most members, and the general public, know little about how it operates and have little interest in learning more.

After the 9/11 attacks, my own involvement in the APA was initially still mostly limited to attending the annual convention on an occasional basis. That changed for me at the 2007 convention in San Francisco. I went that year primarily to give a presentation about war propaganda, with a focus on the psychological appeals that were used to garner and maintain Americans' support for the invasion and occupation of Iraq. Thankfully, Jancis Long and Tony Marsella, two leaders of the non-profit organization Psychologists for Social Responsibility whom I had not previously met, found their way to my early morning talk. Thereafter, they nurtured and mentored me – shy by nature – in taking on leadership responsibilities in that organization.

At the same August 2007 convention, I attended an informative three-day symposium on "Ethics and Interrogations: Confronting the Challenge." It was there that I heard Jean Maria Arrigo describe how she was deceived and manipulated as an unsuspecting member of a 2005 APA task force that endorsed the continuing involvement of psychologists in war-on-terror interrogations. Dominated by representatives from the military-intelligence establishment, and with strong support from key APA insiders, the task force's purportedly open-minded deliberations were actually an illusion, Arrigo explained to the large audience of conventioneers. Her descriptions lifted the veil, and along with it came the realization that the APA had arguably lost its independent ethical compass. Later that day, I also joined an outdoor protest organized by Psychologists for an Ethical APA.

I think of that weekend as lift-off for my own dedicated engagement in challenging the APA on its failure to adequately uphold the profession's fundamental ethics in the war-on-terror context. I soon became president of Psychologists for Social Responsibility, and not long after a member of the Coalition for an Ethical Psychology, where I began a years-long close collaboration with Jean Maria Arrigo, Trudy Bond, Brad Olson, Steven Reisner, Stephen Soldz, and Bryant Welch. I was very fortunate to find these and other like-minded colleagues, and we collectively came to be known as "the dissidents."[10] The strength of their commitment to countering the self-serving, misleading statements from APA leaders – seemingly false claims that psychologists were consistently valuable and ethical contributors to the detention and interrogation operations of the Defense Department and the CIA – was an inspiration to me.

For many years, it felt as though our efforts were routinely met with denials, stonewalling, and retaliatory personal attacks. In public forums, the APA's ethics director dismissed reports of detainee abuse as "long on hearsay and innuendo, short on facts."[11] One APA president condemned dissident voices as "opportunistic commentators masquerading as scholars."[12] Another advised us to "turn down the temperature on outrage."[13] And a military operational psychologist who had been stationed at Guantanamo boasted in his self-congratulatory memoir, "I confronted one of my critics and threatened to shut his mouth for him if he didn't do it himself."[14]

But gradually, over time, our persistence paid off. We were able to gain ground and support in challenging both the APA's narrative of blamelessness and the suspect foundations of its misguided policy stances. We were helped along by the ever-mounting evidence of psychologists' grievous conduct as part of a national security apparatus run amok. Like rising floodwaters, one new revelation followed another, and they eventually breached the makeshift dam built on apparent double-talk from the APA's leadership.

Grudgingly, the APA's Board of Directors eventually commissioned an extensive independent review. The findings, released in 2015, confirmed dissidents' allegations of significant wrongdoing over the preceding decade.[15] In letters to the membership, the APA's president-elect and past president apologized for the association's "actions, policies and lack of independence from governmental influence," and acknowledged that "what happened never should have."[16] Shortly thereafter, the APA reversed its ill-conceived course and rescinded its support for psychologist involvement at Guantanamo and similar sites.

Still, what lies ahead for the APA and for the profession of psychology in the United States is far from settled. Even now, the military-intelligence establishment and some of its psychologists seemingly prefer to deny or disguise the past. And those who have dared to cross them have felt their wrath as the targets of character attacks, ethics-related complaints, and defamation lawsuits. Their courage animates my own, and I am convinced that telling this story is something that is owed to those who have suffered at psychology's hands, and to the next generation of psychologists that follow us.

The progression of chapters in *Doing Harm* is as follows. In Chapter 1, "Embracing the 'War on Terror,'" I examine the APA's immediate response to the 9/11 attacks and to the so-called war on terror that quickly followed. The APA's embrace of the Bush Administration's agenda led to key decisions that increasingly tied professional psychology to ethically fraught operations – even as credible reports emerged in the media alleging that prisoners, many of whom were innocent of any wrongdoing, were being abused and that health professionals were involved in their mistreatment. As this chapter shows, throughout this period it seemed that the APA's focus was almost always on promoting what psychologists were capable of doing, and hardly ever on warning what they should *not* do.

Chapter 2, "The Perversion of a Profession," reviews key policies adopted by the Bush Administration – including explicit reliance on health professionals – in its effort to justify the use of detention and interrogation practices that diverged from long-established human rights norms and international law. This overview is followed by a discussion of the characteristics and consequences of torture, along with descriptions of the roles that were allegedly played by several individual psychologists who worked at the CIA's clandestine "black sites" and at the Defense Department's Guantanamo Bay detention facility.

The focus of Chapter 3, "The Pretense of Deliberation," is an in-depth discussion and analysis of the APA's 2005 task force on "Psychological Ethics and National Security" (PENS). Conceivably the most consequential of all the steps taken by the association, this task force concluded that it was ethical for psychologists to participate in war-on-terror detention and interrogation operations – despite the profession's do-no-harm foundations and the growing evidence of prisoner abuse by US forces. I delve into the many problematic aspects of the PENS Report and the process that led to it. The chapter concludes with a description of reactions to the report from dissident psychologists and the human rights community at large, along with a discussion of the public relations tactics used by APA leaders in an effort to defend the PENS Report and quell the growing outrage.

In Chapter 4, "Revelations and Resistance," I describe the emergence of organized dissident opposition to the APA's support for the involvement of psychologists in war-on-terror detention and interrogation operations. Faced with this growing resistance, some APA leaders took extensive measures to obstruct reform efforts. These reform efforts included calls for strengthening the association's Ethics Code as well as its policies prohibiting abuse, removal of psychologists from Guantanamo Bay and other unlawful military-intelligence facilities, and investigations and possible sanctions against psychologists alleged to have been involved in the mistreatment of prisoners.

Chapter 5, "The Reckoning," recounts how the claims of dissidents were validated and magnified in the public eye by confirming revelations that appeared in *Pay Any Price: Greed, Power, and Endless War*, a 2014 book by Pulitzer Prize–winning investigative journalist James Risen.[17] The book and the greater awareness it brought finally led the APA Board of Directors to authorize an independent investigation of the association. The "Hoffman Report," which included thousands of pages of key documents and previously private email exchanges, concluded that APA leaders had secretly collaborated with military-intelligence personnel to ensure that psychologists would be able to continue their involvement in war-on-terror detention and interrogation operations. I examine the findings of the report, the firestorm they created, and the important and long-overdue reforms within the APA that followed.

Chapter 6, "The Empire Strikes Back," traces the emergence of reactionary and retaliatory responses from influential individuals and groups aligned with the military-intelligence establishment – within and outside of the APA – in their ongoing efforts to turn back the clock on these key ethics reforms. Many of those involved in these campaigns had been identified in the Hoffman Report as having facilitated the association's decade-plus deference to Department of Defense and CIA priorities. I describe and detail their campaign tactics, which have ranged from efforts to discredit the Hoffman Report, to proposed resolutions aimed at suppressing the report's findings, to ethics complaints and defamation lawsuits targeting dissidents, the law firm that conducted the independent review, and the APA itself.

In Chapter 7, "Operational Psychology: The Good, the Bad, and the Ugly," I turn my attention to a fuller discussion of a growing practice area in the national security arena that my colleagues and I call "adversarial operational psychology." This domain arguably represents an insidious threat to the foundation of psychological ethics because individuals are targeted for harm rather than care, voluntary informed consent is absent, and activities take place in classified settings beyond the ready reach of outside ethical oversight. Proponents of adversarial operational psychology argue that following lawful government directives aimed at protecting Americans is ethical for psychologists regardless of the tasks involved. This chapter explains why that's not necessarily so.

Finally, in Chapter 8, "Lessons Learned and the Road Ahead," I examine the causes and consequences of broader organizational and societal factors that have contributed significantly to what I see as the APA's fall, including institutional betrayal and the lure of militarism. These adverse influences are far from unique to professional psychology. They can and do regularly arise in a much wider range of civil society organizations. The chapter then concludes with recommendations for steps that the APA should take to enable it to move forward with the firm footing that an abiding commitment to ethics and human rights can provide.

I want to emphasize that I wrote *Doing Harm* from a perspective informed by certain values, most importantly the conviction that respect for human rights and human dignity should govern the choices we make and the actions we take. These values are not external to the academic discipline and profession of psychology, but deeply rooted within them. Indeed, they are values to which the APA has long claimed allegiance as well. At the same time, while far from a disinterested bystander, my aim here is not polemical. Faithful to the values and perspective I've described, my goal is to accurately document and explain the dynamics and decisions – both individual and institutional – that have created a years-long ethical crisis for the world's largest organization of psychologists.

Regarding those whose actions I criticize or deplore, I recognize that important decisions we make in our professional lives often reflect the complex interaction of psychological factors, situational demands, responsibilities to stakeholders, and human fallibility. Accountability is still essential, but I'm also cognizant that we're never fully understood by our worst choices alone. Ultimately, it is my hope that this case study of the APA illuminates recurring questions about leadership and dissent, and that it contributes more broadly to our understanding of the challenges that arise when expediency and ethics seem to recommend divergent paths.

1

Embracing the "War on Terror"

Befitting the organization's stature and ambitions, the headquarters of the American Psychological Association (APA) are located in the heart of Washington, DC, where the APA owns an eleven-story art deco building with penthouse towers and a lobby with marble floors and mahogany walls. One mile due south is the US Capitol; two miles west sits the White House; a four-mile trip southwest brings you to the Pentagon; and ten miles northwest is Langley, Virginia, home to the Central Intelligence Agency (CIA).

Founded in 1892, today the APA is the largest professional organization of psychologists in the world with approximately 100,000 members. Its yearly revenue exceeds $100 million from – in descending order – institutional licensing fees, journal subscriptions, real estate rental income, and membership dues. With a staff of over 500, the APA's top dozen executives are collectively paid more than five million dollars annually.[1] The association is governed by an elected Council of Representatives comprised of roughly 175 members and a much smaller, sixteen-person Board of Directors.

There are four directorates (Education, Practice, Public Interest, and Science) along with numerous standing committees – including ethics – and ad hoc task forces. Fifty-four divisions and societies within the APA represent sub-disciplines and substantive interest areas of professional psychology. Examples include clinical psychology, community psychology, educational psychology, industrial psychology, peace psychology, and military psychology.[2] This range reflects the fact that the field includes many activities quite different from psychotherapy, the arena that's often most familiar to members of the public. Among these non-clinical practice areas – all of which can serve important societal interests – are teaching, research, psychological testing, consulting on organizational effectiveness, conducting threat assessments, and recommending strategies for crime prevention.

The APA describes its mission as promoting "the advancement, communication, and application of psychological science and knowledge to benefit society and improve lives."[3] Principle A in the association's *Ethical Principles of Psychologists and Code of Conduct* is "Beneficence and Nonmaleficence." That principle states, in part, "Psychologists strive to benefit those with whom they work and take care to do no harm."[4] Principle B is "Fidelity and Responsibility," which states, in part, "Psychologists establish relationships of trust with those with whom they work. They are aware of their professional and scientific responsibilities to society and to the specific communities in which they work."[5] As will become clear, the relationship between these two principles isn't always entirely comfortable.

When hijacked airplanes gruesomely hit their targets on the morning of September 11, 2001, the APA sprang into action.[6] Within hours, its Disaster Response Network mobilized thousands of expert practitioners who worked with the American Red Cross to offer essential psychological support to rescue workers and to the families of the victims. The APA's Office of Public Affairs also acted quickly to assist families, children, and schools by developing and disseminating materials that provided guidance on coping with fear and trauma. Mental health professionals across the country embraced the unanticipated and urgent challenge of offering wise and compassionate care for the grieving and the panic-stricken.[7] These efforts undoubtedly helped a staggering nation begin the difficult process of healing and recovery.

But just as swiftly, the APA moved in an entirely different direction, working to ensure that the White House – having promised a "crusade" and the full wrath of the United States – would view the organization as a valued patriotic partner in the military and intelligence operations central to the new "war on terror."[8] Within days of 9/11, the APA's Science Directorate called upon research psychologists to identify how psychological science might contribute to burgeoning national security initiatives and APA senior staff began nurturing relationships with government agencies that could put this research to use in applied settings.[9]

In a column in the association's monthly magazine, *Monitor on Psychology*, the APA's then president Norine Johnson highlighted "the changing psychology agenda in the wake of the terrorist attacks and war."[10] That autumn the APA's Board of Directors also established the Subcommittee on Psychology's Response to Terrorism. It was chaired by Ronald Levant, a future president of the association. In part, the subcommittee directed its attention to "offering psychologists' expertise to decision-makers in the military, Central Intelligence Agency, Department of State and related agencies" and to "inventorying members' expertise and asking government psychologists how agencies could put that expertise to use."[11]

Beyond the call of patriotism, much of this strategizing and organizing was aimed at promoting the APA and the profession. Following the terrorist attacks, the nation's mood – a volatile combination of fear, anger, and urgency – had quickly opened floodgates to enormous new funding opportunities.[12] From the outset, the APA seemingly joined in the frenzy to win a share of the war-on-terror counterterrorism pie for psychology. As one member of Levant's subcommittee explained at the time, here was a chance to "define new roles for psychologists."[13]

Levant himself explained in an interview, "The most urgent task is to get the message out that psychological science has a lot to contribute to the effort to combat terrorism."[14] He also noted, "Terrorism is in many ways a psychological form of warfare … As one of the leading scientific groups in the country, we have a lot to offer in the fight against it."[15] The October 2001 report from his subcommittee identified a central goal: situating psychology "as a key national resource, perhaps as significant as the repositioning that occurred after WWII."[16]

That repositioning a half-century earlier had involved dramatic growth for the APA and US psychology. The APA had only a few thousand members in 1940. Over the next thirty years that figure grew tenfold, and then it more than doubled over the following quarter-century. The primary impetus came from the Department of Defense, the CIA, and other government agencies that turned increasingly to the profession to assist with the provision of psychological services to wounded soldiers and veterans and with military-intelligence-related research.[17]

Over the decades commencing with World War II, funding opportunities soared for psychologists involved in projects with military or intelligence applications, ranging from aptitude screening evaluations to leadership studies to mass persuasion techniques to investigations into sensory deprivation and other psychological methods for breaking prisoners of war. The profession's interest in such revenue streams has never really abated. Today the Defense Department remains a significant funder of behavioral science research, while the Department of Veterans Affairs has become the foremost provider of APA-accredited internships and postdoctoral training opportunities.[18] In his review of this history, dissident psychologist Frank Summers observed, "Psychology has provided the requested knowledge or service without questioning the ethics of the activity or the use to which the knowledge might be put."[19]

In that regard, amid the tumult and grief that characterized the earliest weeks after 9/11, questions were already being raised about whether harsh and abusive interrogation techniques might now be appropriate to protect the nation. Writing about prisoners suspected of al-Qaeda connections, *Newsweek* journalist Jonathan Alter asked, "Couldn't we at least subject them to psychological torture, like tapes of dying rabbits or high-decibel rap?"[20] Concurrently, human rights groups expressed serious concerns about growing threats to civil liberties, including increases in government secrecy, racial profiling, and the circumvention of personal privacy protections.[21] In testimony before the Senate Judiciary Committee, then attorney general John Ashcroft took a dim view of these concerns: "To those who scare peace-loving people with phantoms of lost liberty, my message is this: Your tactics only aid terrorists for they erode our national unity and diminish our resolve. They give ammunition to America's enemies."[22]

During this same period, not everyone within the psychology community was comfortable with the APA's seeming embrace of President George W. Bush's "either you are with us or you are with the terrorists" stance.[23] For example, responding to the Levant subcommittee's report, a group of Boston-area psychologists published a critical letter in the APA's *Monitor on Psychology*. They expressed dismay over the association's self-serving focus, and called instead for greater attention to ethics and to working "with others in our communities and institutions to find out what we have to offer that is useful to our collective struggle for a less violent and more just and humane world."[24] Regrettably, subsequent choices would show that this appeal arguably failed to win over the APA's leadership.

In December 2001, the APA Board of Directors employed its rarely used emergency powers to approve an official resolution on terrorism. In some ways, the text was well-considered and uncontroversial. It encouraged psychologists to offer their services to the victims of the attacks and help the public cope with feelings of fear and anxiety, and it condemned prejudice-based harassment and violence. More problematically, however, the same resolution advocated for "increased use of behavioral experts and behavioral knowledge in dealing with both the threat and impact of terrorism" and "increased support for behavioral research that will produce greater understanding of the roots of terrorism and the methods to defeat it, including earlier identification of terrorists."[25] Wittingly or not, it appears that these latter recommendations proved to be a prelude to the US government's placing of psychologists on the front lines in the development and implementation of brutal detention and interrogation operations.

That same month, former APA president Martin Seligman hosted a meeting at his home in the Philadelphia suburbs.[26] The attendees were a dozen university research psychologists, whom he dubbed the "Academics on Patrol," along with several members of the intelligence community. The main topic of discussion was how to counter Muslim extremism. Among the recommendations offered were taking steps to increase Americans' knowledge of Arab and Muslim cultures, finding ways to weaken the ties between terrorist extremists and their much larger base of sympathizers, and more closely monitoring the activities of mosques in the United States.

Among the intelligence professionals at the meeting were two psychologists working for the CIA: Kirk Hubbard and James Mitchell. Seligman has written that he did not invite them and doesn't know who did, but they apparently took a particular interest in his theory of "learned helplessness."[27] Earlier in his career, Seligman – the so-called father of "positive psychology" – had conducted research demonstrating that if dogs were first traumatized by inescapable electrical shocks, they later wouldn't move even when given an easy opportunity to escape the pain. That is, the dogs learned to be helpless. A few months after the meeting at his home, Seligman accepted an invitation to talk to a larger group of military and intelligence personnel about these ideas. As the next chapter will explain, it was shortly thereafter that Mitchell and his colleague John "Bruce" Jessen began subjecting war-on-terror prisoners to torturous "enhanced interrogation techniques" – reportedly based in part on Seligman's theory – at the CIA's overseas black sites.[28] Seligman has denied any awareness that his research might ever be used for such purposes.[29]

When January 2002 arrived, the new detention facility at Guantanamo Bay received its first prisoners, shackled and confined to open-air cages with concrete floors – and the APA's war-on-terror lobbying efforts intensified. In early March, APA senior scientist Susan Brandon, science policy director Geoff Mumford, and Heather Kelly of the APA's science policy staff joined several research psychologists for meetings with senior US Senate legislative staff. The avowed purpose of the Capitol Hill visit was to "raise awareness of how psychological research might be used to understand, prepare for and counter terrorism."[30]

Then in June, APA President Philip Zimbardo joined Brandon and Kelly for a meeting with senior staff from the National Security Council's Office of Combating Terrorism in a continuation of the effort to encourage federal agencies to recruit behavioral scientists.[31] In this instance, the APA team was asked to provide a list of researchers whose work was germane to counterterrorism efforts. Several months later, as the first year after 9/11 drew to a close, Brandon and Mumford arranged for Robert Sternberg, the APA's then president-elect, to give a presentation at the CIA to a group of psychologists from the intelligence community who were directly involved in counterterrorism operations.[32]

KEY PRINCIPLES OF INTERNATIONAL LAW

A close reading of the APA's own enthusiastic reports describing the high-level meetings that took place during this early post-9/11 period suggests that something important was seemingly missing. There was little expression of concern about whether psychologists would be expected to discard the profession's fundamental ethical principles in order to support activities geared toward safeguarding the nation's security. Moreover, the APA's embrace of the government's war-on-terror operations arguably required the willful or unknowing disregard of firmly established principles of international law, principles that share the common purpose of protecting human rights and human dignity. A brief review of several of the most relevant of these crucial documents is therefore in order here.

Nazi Germany's aggression under Adolf Hitler, including the extermination of six million European Jews and millions more from other marginalized groups, led to the Nuremberg Trials at the end of World War II.[33] The defendants in these trials were not only senior German military leaders and Nazi Party officials, but also doctors who had been involved in shocking medical experiments on concentration camp prisoners. Critically, these defendants found no escape from conviction for their crimes by insisting that they were just following the orders of their superiors. The trial of the Nazi doctors led to the formulation of the Nuremberg Code in 1947. The code, which philosopher and ethicist Evelyne Shuster has described as "the most important document in the history of the ethics of medical research," requires that voluntary informed consent be obtained from experimental research subjects and that these subjects be allowed to terminate their participation if they choose to do so.[34]

The following year, in 1948, the General Assembly of the newly formed United Nations (UN) proclaimed the Universal Declaration of Human Rights as "a common standard of achievement for all peoples and all nations."[35] Recognizing that "disregard and contempt for human rights have resulted in barbarous acts which have outraged the conscience of mankind," this benchmark document of thirty articles led to the adoption of dozens of other international treaties over the decades that followed.[36] Article 5 of the Declaration states that "no one shall be subjected to torture or to cruel, inhuman or degrading treatment or punishment." In a commentary on why the use of torture should matter to all of us, sociologist Lisa Hajjar has observed, "The right not to be tortured is the most important right of all because of the ways it speaks directly to the powers and limits of the modern state in its treatment of human beings."[37]

In 1949, the UN's Geneva Conventions were established as the core document of international humanitarian law regulating the conduct of armed conflict. These conventions are meant to ensure humane treatment for wounded soldiers, medical personnel, civilians, and prisoners of war. Geneva's Common Article 3 applies to conflicts of both an international and non-international character and prohibits torture and cruel, humiliating, and degrading treatment. Furthermore, the Third Geneva Convention states, "No physical or mental torture, nor any other form of coercion, may be inflicted on prisoners of war to secure from them information of any kind whatever. Prisoners of war who refuse to answer may not be threatened, insulted, or exposed to any unpleasant or disadvantageous treatment of any kind."[38]

Then, in 1950, a UN-authorized commission formulated the Principles of International Law Recognized in the Charter of the Nuremberg Tribunal.[39] Of particular note, Principle I states, "Any person who commits an act which constitutes a crime under international law is responsible therefore and liable to punishment," while Principle IV states, "The fact that a person acted pursuant to order of his Government or of a superior does not relieve him from responsibility under international law, provided a moral choice was in fact possible to him."[40]

Over thirty years later, in 1984, the UN adopted the Convention against Torture and Other Cruel, Inhuman or Degrading Treatment or Punishment.[41] The United States ratified the convention in 1994, but with various "reservations" and "understandings" that served to diminish the convention's full applicability. In Article 1 of the convention, torture is defined as follows:

> For the purposes of this Convention, the term "torture" means any act by which severe pain or suffering, whether physical or mental, is intentionally inflicted on a person for such purposes as obtaining from him or a third person information or a confession, punishing him for an act he or a third person has committed or is suspected of having committed, or intimidating or coercing him or a third person, or for any reason based on discrimination of any kind, when such pain or suffering is inflicted by or at the instigation of or with the consent or acquiescence of a public official or other person acting in an official capacity. It does not include pain or suffering arising only from, inherent in or incidental to lawful sanctions.[42]

The US understanding of this definition clarifies that "mental pain or suffering refers to prolonged mental harm." It also limits this form of torture to four specific circumstances, one of which involves the use or threatened use of "mind altering substances or other procedures calculated to disrupt profoundly the senses or the personality."[43] At the same time, a US reservation to Article 16 of the convention specifies that cruel, inhuman or degrading treatment or punishment will be interpreted as "the cruel, unusual and inhumane treatment or punishment prohibited by the Fifth, Eighth, and/or Fourteenth Amendments to the Constitution of the United States."[44]

Yet, even as it became increasingly clear that the Bush Administration had chosen to ignore the human rights protections provided by these and other international treaties, the APA's leadership seemed slow to express public concern. Professor George Annas, an expert in international law and bioethics, has written of the so-called war on terror, "The lawyers and physicians who counseled or cooperated in using torture, ignoring the Geneva Conventions, and disregarding the Nuremberg principles, can reasonably be labeled human rights outlaws."[45] Much the same could arguably be said about those psychologists who played similar facilitating roles.

The APA's accommodating stance during the post-9/11 period is all the more troubling given that the association had adopted its own Resolution Against Torture all the way back in 1986.[46] That document emphasized the protection of fundamental human rights. It highlighted the risk that psychological knowledge and techniques might be used to carry out torture. It acknowledged the long-lasting suffering experienced by victims of torture. And it expressed clear support for the UN Convention against Torture and Other Cruel, Inhuman, or Degrading Treatment or Punishment.[47] But this carefully plotted roadmap for ethical action was perhaps forgotten when the APA seemingly began its own journey to the dark side.

WEAPONIZING PSYCHOLOGICAL SCIENCE

In addition to its intensive networking with government agencies, the APA sought to advance its contributions to counterterrorism operations in another significant way. Multiple invitation-only conferences and workshops were designed to highlight what psychology and psychologists could offer the cause. Just a month after the 9/11 attacks, the APA's Brandon and Mumford began organizing meetings with members of the Federal Bureau of Investigation (FBI) Behavioral Science Unit for just this purpose. The first APA conference, co-sponsored by the FBI and the University of Pennsylvania, was titled, "Countering Terrorism: Integration of Practice and Theory." It was held at the FBI Academy in Quantico, Virginia, in February 2002.[48]

Promoted as a demonstration of the social science community's heightened awareness of the need for active engagement in national security, the event brought together dozens of academics and law enforcement personnel from various federal and lower-level agencies. Ethics Office director Stephen Behnke was among those who attended on behalf of the APA, while James Mitchell participated as a representative of the CIA. (As the executive director of the University of Pennsylvania's Solomon Asch Center at that time, I did not attend but was involved in assisting with some of the conference logistics.)

The participants broke into small groups to discuss scenarios that had been prepared in advance by the FBI. Examples included a local businessman reporting the suspicious activity of his Middle Eastern neighbor, an anonymous call to the police about a terrorism-related conversation at a local mosque, efforts by law enforcement to build effective ties to local Muslim communities, and a client telling her therapist that her son's friend might be planning a martyrdom mission. The last instance, the martyrdom scenario, conveys the extent to which even clinicians in their psychotherapy offices were viewed as resources for the war-on-terror effort.

There have long been "duty to warn" and "duty to protect" guidelines for psychologists. These guidelines either allow or require psychologists to breach patient confidentiality when necessary to protect an identified potential victim of harm.[49] Yet it's a very different – and highly fraught – question as to whether a psychologist should ethically be expected to violate confidentiality in order to operate as an informer by sharing terrorism suspicions with law enforcement. The provocative answer to that question, according to the final report on the conference, was that the APA should "develop an ethical code for practitioners for instances where a client may have information relevant to terrorism" and that psychologists should "be trained for what behaviors to look for."[50]

A second invitation-only workshop – "The Science of Deception: Integration of Theory and Practice" – was held in July 2003. Co-hosted by the APA and RAND Corporation with generous funding from the CIA, the meeting "provided an opportunity to bring together individuals with a need to understand and use deception in the service of national defense/security with those who investigate the phenomena and mechanisms of deception."[51] Participants included research psychologists and scholars in related areas along with representatives from the Department of Defense, CIA, FBI,

Department of Homeland Security, and the White House. Among those reportedly in attendance from the CIA were a familiar trio: James Mitchell, Bruce Jessen, and Kirk Hubbard.

Much like the 2002 conference on countering terrorism, this workshop – again organized in part by Susan Brandon and Geoff Mumford from the APA – relied on small-group discussions of thematic scenarios. The issues examined included "embassy walk-in informants, threat assessment, intelligence gathering, and law enforcement interrogation and debriefing."[52] Further details about the event were once available on the APA's website but, as dissident psychologist Jeffrey Kaye first discovered, that information was removed without explanation.[53] However, using the Internet Archive's "Wayback Machine" to retrieve the missing webpage reveals that three questions were among those that were used as a platform for discussion at the meeting: "What pharmacological agents are known to affect apparent truth-telling behavior?" "What are sensory overloads on the maintenance of deceptive behaviors?" "How might we overload the system or overwhelm the senses and see how it affects deceptive behaviors?"[54]

From an ethics perspective, it would seem that these three questions should reasonably have raised red flags for the APA representatives in attendance – even if not for the CIA and others – because the potential relevance of the questions to the psychological abuse of war-on-terror prisoners seems clear. In fact, when Mumford and Brandon later solicited feedback for the APA from the workshop attendees, the CIA's Kirk Hubbard apparently replied via email, "You won't get any feedback from Mitchell or Jessen. They are doing special things to special people in special places, and generally are not available."[55] I could find no public record indicating that this reply elicited worry within the APA. It may be true that hindsight is 20/20, but even at that time I believe it's rather hard to imagine how Hubbard's message could have been interpreted as anything other than a reference to some dark overseas activities by these two psychologists – activities which we now know involved torture.

A third meeting – this one titled "Interpersonal Deception: Integration of Theory and Practice" – took place in June 2004. The co-sponsors were again the APA, RAND Corporation, and the CIA. Brandon, who had now moved to the White House's Office of Science and Technology Policy, and the APA's Mumford continued to be key event organizers. Attendees came from various academic institutions, as well as the FBI, US Secret Service, CIA, Department of Defense, Department of Homeland Security, the United Kingdom Ministry of Defense and Home Office, and the New Scotland Yard. It shouldn't be a surprise that CIA contract psychologists Mitchell and Jessen were, once again, participants in this workshop.[56] According to the APA's *Science Policy Insider News*, the gathering was designed "to forge collaborations between operational staff working in the intelligence community and scientists conducting research on interpersonal deception."[57]

A key goal of the meeting was to better understand exactly what's involved in effectively deceiving other people – in other words, how to lie better.[58] It was hoped that insights from professionals who rely on cunning and trickery in their work would enable the group to create a compilation of best practices when it comes to successful deception. The APA's involvement could have raised questions, given that certain uses of deception run afoul of the association's Ethics Code for psychologists.[59] Years later, the release of government documents revealed that interrogators at times took deception to grisly extremes in order to heighten the psychological distress experienced by war-on-terror prisoners, including bringing a handgun and power drill into an interrogation room and staging a loud mock execution in a neighboring cell.[60]

The APA's sponsorship of these and other meetings accomplished much more than merely bringing psychologists closer to the center of the web of military-intelligence influence. Whether by accident or by design, by providing the patina of scientific scholarship and inquiry to these events and topics, the APA also may have protected and disguised the interests of individuals and groups with agendas that were far from noble, enlightened, or psychologically sound. For some of these parties, the end goal was as simple as it was ruthless: victory in a no-holds-barred "global war on terror" by whatever means were available. But despite this reality, cautionary warnings from the APA's leaders were seemingly hard to come by.

EXPEDIENCY TRUMPS ETHICS

The US government's forceful and often brutal response to the 9/11 attacks also brought into sharp relief another fateful decision by the APA. In August 2002, for the first time in a decade, the APA's full governing body – its elected Council of Representatives – voted to approve a revised version of the association's Ethics Code.[61] This code describes the enforceable standards that form the basis for sanctions when they're violated by APA members. In turn, these same standards are adopted by many state licensing boards and applied to licensed psychologists regardless of whether or not they are members of the APA.

Of greatest consequence were the revisions to Ethical Standard 1.02. Previously, this standard had stated: "If psychologists' ethical responsibilities conflict with law, psychologists make known their commitment to the Ethics Code and take steps to resolve the conflict in a responsible manner." The revision approved in 2002 instead stated: "If psychologists' ethical responsibilities conflict with law, regulations, or other governing legal authority, psychologists make known their commitment to the Ethics Code and take steps to resolve the conflict in a responsible manner. *If the conflict is unresolvable via such means, psychologists may adhere to the requirements of the law, regulations, or other governing legal authority*" (emphasis added).[62] It appears that the phrase "in keeping with basic principles of human rights" had been included in an earlier draft version of the revision to 1.02, but was removed prior to the council's vote.[63]

To be sure, the Ethics Code Task Force charged with developing these and other changes to the Ethics Code began its work long *before* September 11, 2001, at a time when few might have imagined hijacked planes becoming deadly weapons and causing mass casualties on American soil. Defenders of the revision to 1.02 have explained that the change was designed to address issues of confidentiality, such as when a court issues a subpoena for a psychologist's records in the context of a parental custody dispute.[64] That type of situation could place the psychologist in a difficult position in regard to the otherwise conflicting requirements of the court on the one hand and the Ethics Code on the other. But there's also no disputing the fact that the task force members themselves, and then the APA's Council of Representatives, had ample opportunity to reconsider the proposed revision with their eyes open to the starkly different reality that faced everyone – including psychologists – in August 2002, nearly a full year *after* the so-called war on terror had begun.

Within broad limits, the permissive nature of the revised Ethical Standard 1.02 gave military-intelligence psychologists the option to ignore the profession's longstanding ethical principles if authorities instructed them to do so. Presumably, this was welcome news to the officials running detention and interrogation operations for the Pentagon and the CIA. With this change, when called to account for ethically suspect actions, APA members and other psychologists serving in military and intelligence positions could turn to the long-condemned Nuremberg defense and argue that they were following orders, and that these orders superseded all other considerations. Ken Pope, a former chair of the APA's Ethics Committee and a one-time recipient of the association's award for distinguished contributions to public service, summarized the profound implications of the change to 1.02 this way: "APA's vote to reject the Nuremberg Ethic ... clearly communicated to the profession, policy makers, and the public its shift in values."[65]

But the revision of 1.02 wasn't the only significant change that the APA made to its Ethics Code in 2002. Revisions to two standards focused on research practices, also drafted prior to 9/11, can be seen as highly problematic as well. Standard 8.05 specifies the conditions under which informed consent need *not* be obtained from a research participant. Because of the profession's commitments to doing no harm and to respecting human dignity, along with the recognition that the abuse of vulnerable populations for research purposes has a very ugly history, the APA's 1992 ethics code required that "psychologists consider applicable regulations and institutional review board requirements, and they consult with colleagues as appropriate" before dispensing with informed consent – even in cases where the research would only involve anonymous questionnaires.[66] However, with the 2002 revision, psychologists were given permission to dispense with informed consent under previously unauthorized circumstances: namely, "where otherwise permitted by law or federal or institutional regulations."[67]

Years later, in 2011, my research led me to discover that medical ethicist Evelyne Shuster had resigned in 2002 as the sole public member of the APA's Ethics Committee. We met in person a few weeks later and she shared some recollections of her brief time on the committee.[68] Shuster recalled thinking that her views didn't seem to matter much, and that committee members largely followed the lead of Ethics Office director Stephen Behnke. Her clearest memory seemed to be how distressed she felt when the proposed revision to 8.05 was presented on a large display screen during a committee meeting. She immediately raised strong objections based on her perspective as a research ethicist, but she recalled that others didn't seem as concerned.

Meanwhile, the 2002 revision to Standard 8.07 expanded the conditions under which psychologists could employ deception in pursuing their research. Previously, the 1992 Ethics Code had stated that psychologists "never deceive research participants about significant aspects that would affect their willingness to participate, such as physical risks, discomfort, or unpleasant emotional experiences."[69] The 2002 change substantially changed this threshold, instead stating that psychologists "do not deceive prospective participants about research that is reasonably expected to cause physical pain or severe emotional distress."[70] As it turned out, the loosening of both research standards would mesh well with the Bush Administration's growing penchant for unethical experimentation on war-on-terror detainees.[71]

The APA leadership's growing prioritization of expediency also seemed evident in its treatment of a task force that the association's Council of Representatives created in 2003 to assess the psychological effects of the US government's efforts to prevent terrorism.[72] Viewing their work as a serious science-based project, the task force members offered nuanced analyses on a variety of different topics. For example, their reports included warnings about conformity-driven thinking, about communicating with the American public in ways that could encourage unwarranted stereotyping, and about the dangers of relying on oversimplified images of "The Enemy."

Several members of the task force expressed concerns about Bush Administration rhetoric that promoted black-and-white ideas about "us versus them," that emphasized the importance of loyalty to a central authority, and that fostered the view that US cultural norms were universal truths. One task force member – social psychologist Clark McCauley, a recognized expert on terrorism and the "jujitsu politics" involved in effectively confronting it – wrote that the government's response to the terror attacks, if mishandled, could ultimately prove more dangerous than the terrorists themselves.[73]

According to task force chair Paul Kimmel, these task force findings and critiques were troubling to some of the APA's senior staff who worried about friction with the White House.[74] In an email to APA CEO Norman Anderson, Rhea Farberman – then the association's executive director for public and member communications – warned, "This report, if it gets any attention, will do real harm to APA's public image."[75] In the end, through a series of procedural maneuvers, the final report was quashed by the APA's leadership and never made public.[76] A few years later, most of the task force studies and recommendations were elaborated upon and published as a book – *Collateral Damage: The Psychological Consequences of America's War on Terrorism* – edited by Kimmel and Chris Stout, without APA endorsement.[77]

DISTURBING MEDIA REPORTS

As we'll see in the chapters that follow, once revelations about US psychologists' involvement in abuse and torture began to proliferate, APA leaders turned to arguably suspect and self-serving defenses for the association's apparent failure to adequately oppose the cruelty, inhumanity, and degradation inflicted upon those who were designated the country's enemies. Often, the defenses from the APA revolved around claims that so little was really known and that hard evidence of wrongdoing was lacking. But these and other rationalizations fail to explain the APA's choice to push ahead full-bore with its counterterrorism collaboration during the early post-9/11 years. For any organization committed to human dignity and the fundamental precept of do no harm, one might have expected warning lights to be flashing from the very outset.

After all, throughout the immediate post-9/11 years, the public – and certainly the leaders of the APA – had access to credible published reports leaving little doubt as to whether extreme measures were being used to prosecute the new "war on terror." As far back as February 2002, Molly Moore reported for the *Washington Post* that Afghan villagers misidentified by US forces as Taliban and al-Qaeda fighters had been detained, beaten, and imprisoned in wooden cages.[78] A month later, in March 2002, an article by Rajiv Chanrasekaran and Peter Finn in the same publication described how dozens of terror suspects around the world were being transported by the US government to Egypt and Jordan where torturous interrogations were known to routinely take place.[79]

Later that year, *Washington Post* Pulitzer Prize–winning journalists Dana Priest and Barton Gellman published an investigative piece that summarized the treatment of CIA prisoners in Afghanistan as "a brass-knuckled quest for information, often in concert with allies of dubious human rights reputation, in which the traditional lines between right and wrong, legal and inhumane, are evolving and blurred."[80] The physical and psychological abuse they identified included beatings, confinement to tiny rooms, stress positions in which the prisoner's own weight is used against him to create extreme pain, disorienting loud noises, and sleep deprivation. According to the article, an official involved in the capture and transfer of prisoners said, "If you don't violate someone's human rights some of the time, you probably aren't doing your job."[81]

The disturbing news reports continued in 2003. In March, for example, a story by Jesse Bravin and Gary Fields in the *Wall Street Journal* recounted the capture of alleged terrorist mastermind Khalid Sheikh Mohammed. It noted that government interrogators were free to prey upon his phobias, deprive him of food, water, and sleep, subject him to painful stress positions, and use the capture of his two young children as further inducement to cooperate.[82] The same month, Carlotta Gall of the *New York Times* reported that the death of a prisoner in US custody in Afghanistan had been ruled a homicide, and that the autopsy performed listed blunt force trauma as a contributing cause.[83] In June 2003, the *Washington Post's* April Witt reported that another Afghan man had died in US custody; it was subsequently learned that he had been repeatedly beaten and kicked by a CIA contractor while chained to a cell floor.[84]

The following year, in April 2004, the world was flooded with unauthorized photos from the US-controlled Abu Ghraib prison in Iraq.[85] The images were horrifying and obscene: a pyramid of naked Iraqi inmates piled on top of each other; a hooded prisoner standing on a box with electrical wires attached to his hands; a prisoner being dragged around by a dog leash; and many, many more. Around the same time, a leaked report from the International Committee of the Red Cross (ICRC) described a broader pattern of abuses at Department of Defense detention facilities – a pattern that extended well beyond Abu Ghraib and the soldiers stationed there.[86]

Two months later, in June 2004, the Bush Administration responded to growing pressure from human rights groups, the media, and members of Congress by declassifying and releasing various documents about its interrogation policies.[87] Among other starkly disturbing revelations, these official memos argued that torture was not off-limits because the commander-in-chief could do whatever he considered necessary to protect the country, that inflicting severe pain during an interrogation didn't constitute torture if causing such harm wasn't the intent or objective, and that war-on-terror prisoners were not entitled to prisoner-of-war status and the protections against mistreatment provided by the Geneva Conventions.[88] Outrage from certain quarters was swift. The chief advocate for Human Rights Watch told the *Washington Post*, "It appears that what they were contemplating was the commission of war crimes and looking for ways to avoid legal accountability."[89] I could find no similar statement of concern from the APA.

As 2004 drew to a close, in two articles for the *New York Times* Neil Lewis reported on the complicity of psychologists in abusive operations at Guantanamo Bay. The first revealed that the ICRC had described the treatment of Guantanamo prisoners as "tantamount to torture."[90] The ICRC report also specifically identified psychologists as participants in these operations. The second article, based on interviews with former intelligence officers and interrogators, revealed that prisoners were subjected to sleep deprivation, "shackled for hours and left to soil themselves," and sometimes given forced enemas – and that the role of psychologists was to help "break them down."[91]

UNHEEDED WARNINGS FROM
PSYCHOLOGICAL RESEARCH

Nevertheless, despite this drumbeat of disturbing revelations, the APA – and US psychology more broadly – seemingly embraced and clung to precisely the kind of black-and-white, good-versus-evil, all-hands-on-deck narrative that psychologists themselves have long recognized as defining characteristics of potentially dangerous demagoguery. In fact, psychological science cautions that, especially during periods of crisis, self-serving authorities may use fear-driven propaganda to short-circuit the public's critical thinking skills and propel them toward action before the evidence has been carefully examined or the consequences have been fully considered.[92] Yet, rather than standing as a bulwark against this kind of onslaught, at this momentous turning point the APA instead became part of the tragic chorus.

Furthermore, APA leaders likely had some familiarity with decades of research by fellow psychologists that should have served as a wake-up call and warning siren. For example, among the most famous of all social psychology experiments are the conformity studies conducted by Solomon

Asch at Swarthmore College in the early 1950s.[93] Volunteers were instructed to look at a line drawn on a card and then find its match among three other lines of varying lengths drawn on a different card. The correct choice was always obvious, but each research participant was part of a small group seated around a table.

Everyone else at the table was a confederate secretly working for the experimenter, and these group members offered their own answers first. One by one, as instructed, they spoke aloud and gave the same *wrong* answer. In repeated trials, when their own turn came a substantial majority of the naïve participants also gave that wrong answer at least some of the time. Rather than asserting the obvious truth, they instead concurred with the confederates' incorrect choices, either doubting their own judgments or simply not wanting to stand out as different. Asch himself was troubled by these results, noting, "We have found the tendency to conformity in our society so strong that reasonably intelligent and well-meaning young people are willing to call white black is a matter of concern. It raises questions about our ways of education and about the values that guide our conduct."[94]

In related research in the 1960s, social psychologist Stanley Milgram conducted a series of controversial experiments at Yale University examining obedience to authority.[95] His naïve volunteers were assigned the role of "teacher" and were instructed to give an electric shock to a "learner" whenever a mistake was made on a memory test. For this purpose, the teachers were given a dial with interval markings that ranged from "Slight Shock" to "Danger: Severe Shock." The learner was a confederate of the researcher and never actually received any shocks at all.

But not knowing that the cries of pain and pleas for mercy were staged, many of the participants – themselves distraught over the situation – nevertheless obeyed the experimenter's insistent prodding that they continue. Nearly two-thirds administered what they believed were the highest levels of electric shock. Not surprisingly, Milgram was disturbed by his findings, writing that they "raise the possibility that human nature, or – more specifically – the kind of character produced in American democratic society, cannot be counted on to insulate its citizens from brutality and inhumane treatment at the direction of malevolent authority."[96]

During the decade or so immediately preceding the "war on terror," noteworthy research and writing by psychologists further illuminated the conditions under which people are likely to accept and even participate in the immoral infliction of harm. For example, Morton Deutsch, Susan Opotow, Ervin Staub, and others have studied various aspects of "moral exclusion."[97] The term describes the tendency to construct psychological boundaries that exclude some individuals or groups as fully deserving of our fair and moral treatment. Those placed beyond this "scope of justice" are deemed expendable and as legitimate targets for deprivation or exploitation. The adverse consequences for the outsiders include an increased likelihood of becoming victims of human rights violations – especially when such mistreatment is socially condoned or encouraged by influential figures or the public at large.

Adopting a similar focus during this pre-9/11 period, psychologist Albert Bandura developed a widely recognized model of "moral disengagement" in which he identified several of the psychological mechanisms we use to rationalize our own immoral actions.[98] These cognitive maneuvers include: justifying our wrongful behavior as serving a greater good (e.g. torture is necessary to protect US citizens); using euphemistic labels to disguise our brutality (e.g. torture becomes "enhanced interrogation techniques"); favorably comparing our actions to even worse ones by others (e.g. waterboarding isn't as bad as beheading); insisting that mistreatment was required by higher authorities (e.g. "I was just following orders"); blaming the victims for the abuse they've received (e.g. we had no choice but to defend ourselves); and dehumanizing those who we've treated cruelly (e.g. designating prisoners by numbers rather than names). Bandura concluded that societal safeguards are needed to make moral disengagement less commonplace and less effective.

All of these research findings, and more, were available to help the APA's leadership in formulating a cautionary and forceful public challenge to the Bush Administration's dark side, gloves-off "war on terror." But instead of turning to these resources for guidance and conviction, APA leaders apparently directed their attention to foregrounding psychology and psychologists as essential contributors to the military-intelligence establishment's forceful – and often brutal – response to the 9/11 attacks. With this priority, the APA's focus was almost always on what psychologists were capable of doing – and hardly ever on what they *shouldn't* do. As a result, the insights of psychological science and the constraints of professional ethics, developed over decades, were seemingly jettisoned like so much excess baggage to ensure a rapid ascent into the rarefied air of Washington's corridors of power and prestige. And shortly thereafter, what I perceive as the APA's downward spiral into a moral abyss began.

2

The Perversion of a Profession

THE TORTURE MACHINE LIFTS OFF

US combat operations in Afghanistan commenced less than a month after the 9/11 attacks and quickly led to the detention of thousands of prisoners. Some were undoubtedly connected to terrorism. But others, including many rounded up by local forces and sold to the United States for bounty payments, were merely in the wrong place at the wrong time.[1] Either way, they all soon found themselves imprisoned – at Bagram Air Base in Afghanistan, or the Defense Department's detention facility at Guantanamo Bay, or various Central Intelligence Agency (CIA) clandestine overseas black sites. It wasn't long before the abusive and sometimes torturous interrogations began – even though US government-funded research decades earlier had raised strong doubts about the effectiveness of harsh interrogation methods for obtaining reliable information.

Beginning in the 1950s, the CIA had started conducting a series of extensive, covert, and frequently unethical research programs – often utilizing psychologists, psychiatrists, and other scientists at distinguished universities and hospitals – in an effort to uncover the secrets of human consciousness and mind control.[2] During the early Cold War era, the MK-ULTRA project investigated the effects of hallucinogenic drugs, hypnosis, electroshock treatments, and sensory deprivation on both witting and unwitting individuals. Later, in the 1960s, the CIA's KUBARK manual cautioned that coercive interrogations were likely to produce false confessions.[3] In the 1980s, the agency's *Human Resource Exploitation Manual* warned that "use of force is a poor technique, yields unreliable results, may damage subsequent collection efforts, and can induce the source to say what he thinks the interrogator wants to hear."[4] And in 1989, over thirty years ago, the CIA reported to Congress that "inhumane physical or psychological techniques are counterproductive because they do not produce intelligence and will probably result in false answers."[5]

Nevertheless, after the 9/11 terrorist attacks, the push for actionable intelligence seemingly overwhelmed all other considerations, including the constraints imposed by the well-established standards of international and US law. The gloves-off White House dismissed these legal obstacles through sleight of hand. Much as Lewis Carroll's Humpty Dumpty once explained to Alice that words meant whatever he wanted them to mean, government lawyers decided they could simply interpret the laws prohibiting torture however they chose – and differently from almost everyone else.[6]

A now-infamous August 2002 memo from the Department of Justice's Office of Legal Counsel did just that.[7] As described earlier, according to the United Nations (UN) Convention against Torture and Other Cruel, Inhuman, or Degrading Treatment or Punishment, the term torture refers to "any act by which severe pain or suffering, whether physical or mental, is intentionally inflicted on a person for such purposes as obtaining ... information or a confession."[8] But the memo drafted by Deputy Assistant Attorney General John Yoo and Assistant Attorney General Jay Bybee to Alberto Gonzales, counsel to the president, redefined physical torture much more narrowly, as "physical pain ... equivalent in intensity to the pain accompanying serious physical injury, such as organ failure, impairment of bodily function, or even death." Mental or psychological torture was redefined this way: "For purely mental pain or suffering to amount to torture ... it must result in significant psychological harm of significant duration, e.g., lasting for months or even years." And the memo also argued that torture under US law occurs only when there is the "specific intent" or "express purpose" to inflict severe pain or suffering. These interpretations paved the way for all kinds of abusive and torturous "enhanced interrogation techniques" that previously had been off-limits – and should have remained so.[9] Consider the following abbreviated list.

Authorization was given for detainees to be kept awake without sleep for days at a time. This sleep deprivation was often accomplished by forcing prisoners to stand upright or by bombarding them with loud noise or bright lights.

Isolation and sensory deprivation became standard techniques. Small, windowless detention cells were commonplace. For weeks at a time, all human contact was kept to a minimum, and direct access to fellow prisoners was prevented or severely limited.

Detainees were placed in "stress positions" that produced increasing pain and discomfort as the hours passed. These positions included forced sitting on the floor with legs extended in front and arms raised above the head, forced kneeling on the floor while leaning back at a 45-degree angle, and forced standing with arms raised and shackled to the ceiling.

With the "walling" technique, a collar or towel was wrapped around the prisoner's neck to reduce the likelihood of whiplash. He was then pulled forward, and then slammed backward into a flexible wall directly behind him, so that his shoulder blades hit the wall. This was often done repeatedly in rapid succession.

The "cramped confinement" technique involved restricting the prisoner's ability to move by placing him in a small or large box, in total darkness, for hours at a time. It was also permissible to add insects to the box to heighten the detainee's distress.

Waterboarding involved strapping the prisoner to an inclined board and immobilizing him, with his head lower than his feet. A cloth was placed over his face, covering his nose and mouth, and water was then poured through the towel, preventing him from breathing and creating the experience of controlled, slow-motion drowning.

Forced nudity, facial slaps, and hooding were also frequently employed. Unsurprisingly, the methods actually used at CIA and Defense Department detention sites sometimes strayed beyond the already gruesome authorized techniques described above. Examples include threatening a prisoner with a power drill and handgun, threats that family members would be captured and then tortured or murdered, staged mock executions in which prisoners were led to believe that they were being shown the bodies of other dead detainees, and various forms of sexual and cultural humiliation.[10]

In its effort to ensure that this brutal treatment could be defended as somehow reasonable and appropriate, the Bush White House specifically turned to psychologists to assist with the charade. Emphasizing the profession's do-no-harm ethics, the psychologists involved were character-ized as so-called safety officers.[11] In short, the inhumane psychological abuse inflicted upon war-on-terror prisoners was disguised by a simple yet fraudu-lent argument: the health professionals on hand would never let an interro-gation go so far as to cause severe and prolonged mental pain and suffering.

Indeed, numerous subsequent memos during this period from the Department of Justice's Office of Legal Counsel – some written for the CIA and others for the Department of Defense – all asserted that psychologists and other health professionals serving as consultants and monitors as-sured that interrogations were neither dangerous nor torturous, and that they were therefore legal. For example, one memo specified that a partic-ular technique was lawful if it was combined with "an assessment of the prisoner's psychological health."[12] Another memo asserted that abusive techniques, including waterboarding, were acceptable because consulting psychologists had concluded that their use would not result in "prolonged mental harm."[13] And a third memo claimed that specific techniques were prohibited only if "medical and psychological evaluations or ongoing mon-itoring suggest that the detainee is likely to suffer serious harm."[14]

But on the whole, it appears that psychologists did *not* play the prisoner-protecting roles that they were supposedly assigned. Rather, the public record tells us that, over a period of years, they were routinely present at CIA and Defense Department detention facilities when detainees in US custody were cruelly confined and ruthlessly interrogated.[15] The involvement of psychologists arguably contributed to the grievous harm suffered by these prisoners and left an indelible stain on the profession – all while the American Psychological Association (APA) seemingly failed to take effective steps to diminish these consequences. The following descriptions of how specific psychologists allegedly strayed from the profession's do-no-harm foundations serve to provide valuable context here.

WATERBOARDING FOR THE CIA

Within weeks after the 9/11 attacks, the CIA turned to the two former mil-itary psychologists mentioned earlier – James Mitchell and Bruce Jessen – to develop the abusive and torturous interrogation methods that were euphemistically called "enhanced interrogation techniques."[16] As handsomely paid contractors, Mitchell (an APA member at the time) and Jessen recommended the reverse-engineering of SERE training techniques. An acronym for Survival, Evasion, Resistance, and Escape, SERE school is designed to prepare US soldiers for the extreme physical and psychological pressures they might experience if captured by forces that don't observe the Geneva Conventions, the core of international humanitarian law.[17] In the military, "captured" SERE trainees are placed in a mock prison where they are subjected to various extreme physical and psychological stressors to teach them how to resist such abuses.[18]

But even at the time of Mitchell and Jessen's earliest experimental use of these harsh techniques on war-on-terror prisoners, I believe the dangers should have been clear. Based on research studies, it was already recognized within the scientific community that SERE-type stressors could cause significant psychological harm, including psychiatric illnesses such as post-traumatic stress disorder (PTSD).[19] And these adverse and unwanted outcomes occurred even though soldiers subjected to SERE techniques knew that they had the option to discontinue the training whenever they chose.

The SERE-based techniques that were approved for the CIA's use by the Office of Legal Counsel were described earlier; they included walling, stress positions, sleep deprivation, confinement in a box with insects placed inside, isolation, sensory deprivation and overload, and waterboarding, among others.[20] The CIA's Office of Medical Services highlighted that the techniques had a psychological purpose, explaining that they were designed "to psychologically 'dislocate' the detainee, maximize his feeling of vulnerability and helplessness, and reduce or eliminate his will to resist our efforts to obtain critical intelligence."[21] The agency also noted that "in all instances the general goal of these techniques is a psychological impact, and not some physical effect."[22]

In short order, Mitchell and Jessen, lacking significant real-world interrogation experience, went to work implementing their brutal and unproven methods. The first victim of their experimental techniques was Abu Zubaydah, a Palestinian born and raised in Saudi Arabia, who was misidentified as a member of al-Qaeda.[23] He had been shot and captured in Pakistan in March 2002 and was then brought to the CIA's secret black site in Thailand. After weeks of isolation, Zubaydah was subjected to nearly a month of continuous, twenty-four-hours-a-day torture that included forced nakedness, sleep deprivation, intermittent confinement in a coffin-sized box, and multiple daily waterboarding sessions. During at least one of these sessions, he "became completely unresponsive, with bubbles rising through his open, full mouth."[24]

Eventually, the conclusion was reached that Zubaydah had never been withholding any useful intelligence. But as investigative journalist Katherine Eban reported in her 2007 *Vanity Fair* article "Rorschach and Awe," the CIA "would go on to claim credit for breaking Zubaydah, and celebrate Mitchell as a psychological wizard who held the key to getting hardened terrorists to talk."[25] Responding to questions from Eban, the two psychologists reportedly released a statement: "We resolutely oppose torture. Under no circumstances have we ever endorsed, nor would we endorse, the use of interrogation methods designed to do physical or psychological harm."[26]

It's now well-documented from other sources that Mitchell and Jessen were misrepresenting the truth – even though, despite a court order that the evidence be preserved, the videotapes of these torture sessions were shredded by the CIA.[27] In his memoir, Mitchell acknowledges that he wanted the tapes destroyed.[28] It seems not everyone who worked for the agency subscribed to the biblical verse etched on the wall at CIA headquarters: "And ye shall know the truth, and the truth shall make you free." Today, to prevent embarrassment over further public revelations about the torture he suffered, the US government holds Zubaydah as a "forever prisoner" at Guantanamo Bay.[29]

Mitchell and Jessen were also involved in the similarly gruesome interrogations of the following prisoners: Khalid Sheikh Mohammed, the alleged 9/11 al-Qaeda mastermind who was waterboarded nearly two hundred times; Abd al-Rahim al-Nashiri, alleged to have plotted the 2000 suicide bombing of the USS *Cole*, who was threatened with a hand drill and the rape of his family members by other CIA interrogators; and Gul Rahman, suspected to be an Islamist extremist, who was found frozen to death in his cell in a black site in Afghanistan.[30] In total, well over 100 prisoners suffered in the CIA's dungeons; many more were rendered to partner countries – Egypt, Jordan, Libya, Morocco, and Syria – where they were subjected to torture.[31]

Meanwhile, in 2004 Mitchell and Jessen formed a consulting firm that received over $81 million to continue overseeing the CIA's torture program (the contract was canceled in 2009).[32] It was at an APA annual convention around that time that they reportedly recruited some of their first employees; total employment at the firm grew to sixty within a couple of years.[33] The CIA also provided the two psychologists with a $5 million indemnity promise to cover legal expenses that might arise if they were ever sued for their roles in the program.[34] In 2017, Mitchell and Jessen did face – and settle – a lawsuit filed by the American Civil Liberties Union (ACLU) on behalf of three former CIA prisoners.[35] They were accused of designing, implementing, and supervising the agency's experimental program of abuse and torture.

The evidence against the two psychologists included a detailed Senate report, multiple depositions, newly declassified documents, and even Mitchell's own self-congratulatory memoir.[36] Remarkably, in defending their clients, the attorneys for Mitchell and Jessen apparently compared the psychologists' role to that of a low-level technician whose employer provided the lethal gas for Hitler's extermination camps.[37] A British military tribunal had acquitted that technician, while the owner was executed.

Although the full terms of the settlement agreement are confidential, the plaintiffs and defendants did issue a joint statement. While acknowledging both that "they worked with the CIA to develop a program ... that contemplated the use of specific coercive methods to interrogate certain detainees" and that the plaintiffs were subjected to techniques that caused them pain and suffering, Mitchell and Jessen also stated that they were not responsible for any abuse of these prisoners.[38]

GUANTANAMO: WHERE DECENCY GOES TO DIE

The authorization of the CIA's reverse-engineered SERE tactics supported the Pentagon's creation of its own Behavioral Science Consultation Team (BSCT) at Guantanamo. These teams were initially comprised of psychologists, psychiatrists, and technicians. According to government reports, the teams reviewed the files of prisoners, constructed personality profiles, figured out what their "buttons" were, and identified their "vulnerabilities."[39] They also observed interrogations and provided strategy recommendations, including when to push harder for intelligence information. Few of these responsibilities and activities appear to fit well with the safety officer role purportedly assigned to psychologists – or with the do-no-harm foundations of the profession.

One Guantanamo BSCT, which included APA member John Leso and psychiatrist Paul Burney, was created in 2002. In September of that year, psychologist Morgan Banks – then the director of Psychological Applications for the US Army Special Operations Command – reportedly urged them to fly up to Fort Bragg in North Carolina to attend SERE-based interrogation training sessions designed by Bruce Jessen and hosted by Banks.[40] In an interview years later, Banks explained to investigative reporter Jason Leopold that he warned the BSCT members not to use "physical pressures" and told them that "you can't torture people, and … there's a US definition."[41] As described in the preceding chapter, that definition had been significantly altered by the Bush Administration, and in a much more permissive direction.

After returning to Guantanamo, Leso and Burney reportedly wrote a "Counter-Resistance Strategies Memorandum."[42] This memo recommended a set of increasingly severe detention and interrogation tactics. The mildest category included incentives and warnings, such as telling a prisoner that if he failed to cooperate, he'd spend the rest of his life at Guantanamo. A second category included harsher techniques: stress positions, a month's isolation, back-to-back twenty-hour interrogations, food deprivation, hooding, and the removal of all religious and other comfort items. The BSCT's recommendations in the third and most extreme category included daily twenty-hour interrogations, strict extended isolation, removal of clothing, exposure to shivering temperatures, and scenarios designed to make the detainee believe he could die.

Leso and Burney did in fact caution against the use of *physical* pressures, but the memo concluded that all aspects of the detention environment should "enhance capture shock, dislocate expectations, foster dependence, and support exploitation to the fullest extent possible."[43] Leonard Rubenstein, the former executive director of Physicians for Human Rights, has written that the participation of BSCT psychologists in the design of interrogation techniques quite possibly led to a significant expansion in "the use of torture and cruel, inhuman, and degrading treatment in the interrogation of terror suspects – and in the infliction of severe or serious mental harm."[44]

Leso's BSCT role wasn't limited to writing memos. Credible reports indicate that, along with Burney, he observed and consulted on interrogation operations at Guantanamo. Among these was the "special interrogation program" designed for Mohammed al-Qahtani, the so-called twentieth 9/11 hijacker. Over objections from members of the Criminal Investigation Task Force and some other experienced intelligence personnel assigned to Guantanamo, for weeks in late 2002 al-Qahtani endured abusive and torturous treatment that few would have imagined could ever become part of authorized US policy.

From a leaked interrogation log and subsequent government reports, we know that al-Qahtani was subjected to almost daily twenty-hour interrogations, during which he was kept awake by loud noise and other noxious means; he was held in isolation without contact with other detainees; he was forcibly injected with excessive fluids until his limbs swelled; he was frequently hooded; he was repeatedly strip-searched and forced to stand naked with female interrogators present; he was told that his mother and sister were prostitutes and whores; he was held down while a female interrogator straddled him; he was forced to wear a woman's bra and had a woman's thong placed on his head; he was terrorized by growling military dogs; and he was led around by a leash and forced to perform dog tricks. During this period, al-Qahtani also required hospitalization when his body temperature and heart rate dropped to dangerously low levels.[45]

Additional disturbing information is available from the partially redacted sworn statement of an unidentified BSCT member involved in al-Qahtani's interrogation.[46] The statement asserts that "at least one of the members of the BSCT was always present and witnessed his interrogation" and that the BSCT "logged hundreds of hours of observations of the interrogation practices and procedures." It notes that afterward, Guantanamo's commanding general presented awards to individuals involved in the interrogation. And the same sworn statement includes this acknowledgment: "It is possible for some of the detainees to have some kind of long term or unintended difficulties because of the interrogation practices, but I did not see detainees being subjected to pointless cruelty." That this BSCT member didn't consider the cruelty "pointless" would seem to speak volumes about the inhumanity that has characterized Guantanamo.[47]

Seven years later, in 2009, Susan Crawford was the Bush-appointed judge overseeing the military commission proceedings against Guantanamo detainees. These "show trials," which continue to this day, allow the prosecution's use of evidence that has been obtained through torture and deny war-on-terror defendants a range of other fundamental due process protections.[48] As law professor David Luban has described it, "At Guantanamo, it seems, evidence about torture is out; statements obtained by torture are in."[49] But Crawford, recognizing al-Qahtani's treatment as torture, declined to approve charges against him.[50] It still took another thirteen years – into early 2022 – before the mentally ill prisoner who had been diagnosed as suffering from schizophrenia and PTSD was finally repatriated, to a custodial program in his home country of Saudi Arabia.[51]

John Leso wasn't the only APA member involved in Guantanamo's harsh detention and interrogation operations. After Leso departed, Larry James became the chief BSCT psychologist at Guantanamo in 2003. James has written that he was expected "to oversee ... the interrogation process at Gitmo and to fix what had gone so wrong in the past."[52] But his tenure on the island corresponded to a period during which abusive treatment reportedly persisted, including the requirement that all newly arrived detainees be subjected to four weeks of absolute isolation in order to enhance and exploit their disorientation and disorganization.[53] James has denied any responsibility for abuses at Guantanamo.

In 2004, James accepted a Presidential Citation award from the APA "for his exemplary balance of professional psychology and military leadership."[54] Several years later, describing his time at Guantanamo, James endorsed a seemingly worrisome see-no-evil, hear-no-evil, speak-no-evil approach, explaining, "I learned a long, long time ago, if I'm going to be successful in the intel community, I'm meticulously ... going to stay in my lane ... If I don't have a specific need to know about something, I don't want to know about it. I don't ask about it."[55] This self-protective philosophy appears inconsistent with any claim that psychologists were expected to vigilantly protect the welfare of detainees and report abuses to higher authorities.

James has acknowledged responsibility for the twenty-hour transport and subsequent handling of three Afghan juveniles – none older than fifteen – who were flown to Guantanamo from Bagram Air Base in Afghanistan.[56] They were bound and blindfolded for the lengthy trip. Other adult detainees transferred that same day were chained around the waist, wrists, back, and ankles and were unable to speak, see, hear, move, or even breathe properly. James wrote that these adult prisoners "looked and smelled repulsive. They smelled like shit or a foul stench of body odor – it was hard to tell the difference."[57]

James has described these boys as "flat-out dumber than a bag of rocks."[58] As months passed, the US government apparently never notified the parents of the whereabouts of their missing sons. According to the UN, enforced disappearance represents "a grave and flagrant violation of ... human rights and fundamental freedoms."[59] But in James's view, the three juveniles were returned home a year later "better than we found them."[60] For a contrasting perspective, consider journalist David Rose's account of Guantanamo during this period: "This is Gitmo's first meaning: the shattering of innocents' lives, and for detainees' families, an indeterminate sentence of uncertainty and loss."[61]

According to published reports, another military psychologist and former APA member – Diane Zierhoffer – was consulted during the 2003 abusive interrogation of Guantanamo detainee Mohammed Jawad. The teenager, accused on questionable evidence of throwing a grenade at US troops in Afghanistan, was subjected to prolonged isolation, sleep deprivation, excessive heat, constant lighting, loud noise, and other psychologically destructive conditions of confinement.[62] Zierhoffer was apparently called upon to evaluate Jawad after he was observed crying, calling for his mother, and talking to a poster on a wall. She allegedly advised the interrogators to take additional steps to break Jawad, recommending that they isolate him even further, tell him that he had been forgotten by his family, and "make him as uncomfortable as possible."[63]

Jawad subsequently attempted suicide in his cell. At a 2008 military commissions hearing held on a motion to dismiss the charges against Jawad due to misconduct by the government, Zierhoffer reportedly refused to testify, invoking the military's equivalent of her Fifth Amendment right against self-incrimination.[64] The lead prosecutor, Lieutenant Colonel Darrel Vandeveld, quit the case, citing a lack of due process, doubts about Jawad's guilt, and grave concerns with the fairness of the military commissions. In his declaration, Vandeveld also wrote that, in his view, the BSCT psychologist involved – not identified by name in the declaration – had employed "his or her" training and expertise in a manner that was "particularly despicable" and "profoundly unethical."[65] In 2009, seven years after his incarceration began, Jawad was released by a federal judge and repatriated to Afghanistan;

three years later, the Society for Military Psychology (APA's Division 19) ostensibly welcomed Zierhoffer as a new member.[66]

Reports indicate that Zierhoffer was also consulted when detainee Mohamedou Ould Slahi began experiencing auditory hallucinations during the torturous "special interrogation plan" devised for him in 2003.[67] Slahi, suspected of terrorism despite the lack of hard evidence, was brutally beaten, exposed to extreme temperatures, subjected to sensory and sleep deprivation, and told that his mother might be brought to Guantanamo and incarcerated there. When his interrogator contacted Zierhoffer for guidance about the hallucinations, she allegedly explained that "sensory deprivation can cause hallucinations, usually visual rather than auditory, but you never know ... In the dark you create things out of what little you have."[68]

It appears unclear from the public record what steps, if any, Zierhoffer then took to address Slahi's mental breakdown. Slahi was never charged with a crime. Lieutenant Colonel V. Stuart Couch refused to prosecute him because his incriminating statements had been obtained through torture; the Pentagon later prohibited Couch from testifying about the matter before Congress.[69] In 2016, at the age of forty-five, Slahi was transferred home to Mauritania, fourteen years after being brought to Guantanamo.[70]

There's an important distinction to be made here, one that will be relevant throughout the chapters that follow. Despite their training as clinicians, the BSCT psychologists involved in detainee interrogations were engaged in an area of specialization that's called *operational psychology*. Different from the traditional work of health professionals, operational psychologists apply "behavioral science principles to enable key decision makers to more effectively understand, develop, target, and/or influence an individual, group or organization to accomplish tactical, operational, or strategic objectives within the domain of national security or national defense."[71] In short, their goal is to improve the effectiveness of military and intelligence operations – not to provide care for those who are experiencing psychological distress. As will become increasingly clear, aspects of this specialization raise serious ethical questions for the profession of psychology.

Because so much information about these operations is still classified and shrouded in secrecy, the total number and the identities of the psychologists who were involved in war-on-terror abuses – as either active participants or knowing bystanders – will likely never be known. It should also be emphasized that the prisoners I've identified by name are far from the only ones to have suffered at the hands of US military-intelligence personnel. They represent a small fraction of the much larger number of abused war-on-terror detainees, many of whom were innocent of any wrongdoing.[72]

In regard to accountability, thus far what we know is that not a single psychologist has been sanctioned by the APA for his or her involvement. State licensing boards have also failed to take action. Complaints have been filed against James Mitchell in Texas, John Leso in New York, Larry James in Louisiana and Ohio, and Diane Zierhoffer in Alabama. None of these psychologists has acknowledged any wrongdoing, and each case has been dismissed – reportedly *not* after a thorough investigation that concluded the allegations were false, but rather on assertions relating to lack of jurisdiction or lack of standing.[73] Meanwhile, public records suggest that the psychologists I've mentioned have successfully transitioned into private practice, university appointments, lucrative consulting work, or comfortable retirements.

PSYCHOLOGICAL TORTURE

Before we turn to examining the APA's arguably wholly inadequate response to these and other violations of human rights and basic decency, it's important to emphasize the extent to which many forms of abuse and torture authorized by the Bush Administration were explicitly *psychological* in nature. So, more than anyone else, psychologists, along with other health professionals, should have recognized how devastating and debilitating these torture techniques – euphemistically referred to as "hands-off" or "torture-lite" methods – would be in their long-term and often permanent effects.[74] Indeed, physician Steven Miles, who has comprehensively documented government-sanctioned torture around the world, has described health professionals as "'privileged witnesses' to torture in that their training and position puts them in a unique position to see and authoritatively assess and report torture."[75] Of course, *seeing* and *reporting* are two very different things.

Across multiple theaters of operation in Afghanistan, Iraq, Guantanamo Bay, and various CIA black sites, a range of psychologically abusive practices by US forces – all designed to break detainees – were commonplace.

This has been confirmed by government documents, reports from the ICRC, interviews with prisoners, and other sources.[76] And even if we ignore for the moment the stronger strictures of the Geneva Conventions and other instruments of international law, the detention conditions and interrogation techniques used against prisoners in US custody still fit a key element that defines psychological torture under US law: severe mental pain or suffering resulting from "procedures calculated to disrupt profoundly the senses or the personality."[77]

In a 2020 report, UN Special Rapporteur on Torture Nils Melzer described seven primary sub-categories of psychological torture, noting that each of them targets a psychosocial need of the victim.[78] Melzer's list includes: *security* (targeted by inducing fear, anxiety, and phobia); *self-determination* (targeted through domination and subjugation); *dignity and identity* (targeted via humiliation and the breach of privacy and sexual integrity); *environmental orientation* (targeted through sensory manipulation); *social and emotional rapport* (targeted by isolation, exclusion, and betrayal); *communal trust* (targeted via institutional arbitrariness and persecution); and *torturous environments* (targeted through the accumulation of stressors).

All of the psychological techniques used against US war-on-terror prisoners served to demonstrate to these detainees that they had lost control over their lives, that their daily circumstances were uncertain and were determined entirely by the choices of nameless interrogators and those who directed them behind the scenes. As described decades ago in a CIA exploitation training manual, such methods aimed to "induce psychological regression in the subject" by creating debility, dependency, and dread.[79] In his detailed account of decades of US torture, historian Alfred McCoy has described techniques like these as "a hammer-blow to the fundamentals of personal identity."[80]

In recent years, chilling first-person accounts from former war-on-terror prisoners have added to our understanding of the abuse they endured. In *Guantanamo Diary*, for example, Mohamedou Ould Slahi – Detainee #760, whose torture was described earlier – recounts his experiences during his first few years in the detention camp.[81] The book chronicles the period during which he was transferred to "the secret place" away from all the other prisoners. It was here that "the physical and psychological suffering must be at their highest extremes." He was kept in "crazy darkness," unable to tell whether it was night or day. He was deprived of food, and then given food but not given enough time to eat it. He wasn't allowed to sleep, which the guards accomplished, in part, by forcing him to drink large quantities of water every hour or two. Eventually he began to hallucinate and hear voices.[82]

In *Don't Forget Us Here: Lost and Found at Guantanamo*, Mansoor Adayfi from Yemen – Detainee #441, also imprisoned for fourteen years without charge – paints a similarly disturbing picture.[83] His book describes how in solitary confinement his life narrowed "to the sight of green walls, the smell of pine cleaner and bleach, and the sound of the machinery." He explains how his interrogators controlled everything: "food, air, clothing, water, light, sun, talking, sleep, rest, knowing the time, news from the outside, where we lived and our health care." He identifies sleep deprivation as one of the "worst tortures"; he'd be kept awake by recurrent beatings and by being moved repeatedly from one cell block to another as soon as he fell asleep. And about the psychologists at the Behavioral Health Unit, he writes, "They restrained you to metal beds and paralyzed you with shots. It's where your worst nightmares came true."[84] In 2016, Adayfi was released to Serbia, a country completely unfamiliar to him, where he now lives alone without a passport.[85]

The adverse consequences from being broken in these ways are anything but short-term, and psychologists are among the leading experts – as researchers and clinicians – when it comes to understanding the lasting impact of such extreme abuse. They know that deep psychic wounds can persist without end.[86] Describing what she learned from her decades of work with torture survivors, psychologist Mary Fabri has written that survivors describe the experience of torture "as dismantling their personalities and that even though they may physically survive, the person they were before being tortured died at the hands of the torturers."[87]

Psychologists also know that survivors of psychological torture experience overwhelming feelings of helplessness, shame, and disconnection from other people, the direct result of having been subjected to agonizing mistreatment and humiliation at the hands of another human being.[88] They know that trauma survivors are haunted by PTSD, anxiety, and depression, by flashbacks and nightmares, and by a lasting sense that safety and solace are impossible to achieve.[89] And psychologists know that torture, regardless of the form it takes, is an assault on human dignity and is therefore inherently and profoundly psychological – and immoral.[90]

Nevertheless, evidence suggests that even those psychologists and other military health professionals responsible for detainee healthcare didn't always adequately acknowledge the effects of abuse in the medical records that were kept. Consider, for example, that the possibility of prisoner mistreatment went unmentioned in a 2009 article published in the APA journal *Psychological Services* by members of the behavioral health services team at Guantanamo.[91] Moreover, these authors wrote that a large percentage of the detainees involved in treatment there were suffering from a *pre-existing* personality disorder – a diagnosis that failed to acknowledge the psychological harm caused by any trauma these prisoners suffered *after* their incarceration.[92]

It's worth contrasting that report with an article published two years later in *PLoS Medicine* by two independent doctors, Vincent Iacopino of Physicians for Human Rights and retired Brigadier General Stephen Xenakis. After reviewing the medical records and case files of nine Guantanamo detainees involved in legal proceedings, they found that *all* of them showed signs of physical and psychological torture or ill-treatment – but *none* of the health professionals assigned to their care had inquired into or documented the causes of these severe symptoms. The authors concluded that "medical doctors and mental health personnel … neglected and/or concealed medical evidence of intentional harm."[93]

Sadly, perpetrators and their government sponsors find fertile ground persuading themselves and the public that psychological torture via "enhanced interrogation techniques" should be acceptable in national security contexts. Recall, for example, President Bush's stance regarding the restrictions imposed by Common Article 3 of the Geneva Conventions, which prohibits "outrages upon personal dignity, in particular humiliating and degrading treatment." During a Rose Garden press conference in 2006, he commented, "It's very vague. What does that mean, 'outrages upon human dignity'? That's a statement that is wide open to interpretation."[94]

As philosophy professor Jessica Wolfendale has explained, compared to physical torture, psychological techniques "encourage torturers to feel less responsible for their actions, promote the belief … that what is being done to the victim is not really torture, make victims feel responsible for their suffering, and undermine the credibility of victims in the eyes of their community."[95] Wolfendale has further noted that distinctions between physical and psychological torture also encourage a misguided rationalization: "Torturers who use such methods as beatings and mutilations are clearly brutal and sadistic, whereas those who use torture lite techniques can be portrayed as professionals motivated by the need to gain intelligence essential for saving lives."[96]

In this context, ever since the 9/11 attacks, polling has shown that many Americans support the use of torture against suspected terrorists, more so than citizens of most other countries.[97] To a troubling degree, it seems that large segments of the country misjudge the effectiveness of torture and have grown comfortable with a worldview that defends and excuses the brutal mistreatment of other human beings – even though our use of torture has badly damaged the moral authority of the United States around the world.[98] The rationales offered run the gamut of psychologically appealing justifications: we torture because our country is in grave danger; the people we torture are monstrous wrongdoers; we torture for the greater good; only torture can keep us safe; and those who criticize our stance on torture cannot be trusted.[99] Journalist and sociologist Eyal Press has also noted that there are important and often overlooked parallels between terrorism and torture: "Proponents of each practice maintain that the ends justify the means. They explain away violence by framing it as a necessary 'last resort.' And they obscure the human impact of that violence by refusing to register the humanity of their victims."[100]

Regrettably, government propaganda touting this dark perspective often succeeds despite compelling evidence that torture is ineffective in improving the collection of actionable intelligence.[101] In 2006, during debate over the Military Commissions Act, twenty former Army interrogators sent a letter to the Senate Armed Services Committee. It read, in part, "Prisoner/ detainee abuse and torture are to be avoided at all costs, in part because they can degrade the intelligence collection effort by interfering with a skilled interrogator's efforts to establish rapport with the subject."[102] More recently, psychologist and neuroscientist Shane O'Mara has also explained that torture techniques impair the very brain circuits necessary for the production of reliable information. As he has emphasized, "The practice of torture is self-defeating ... The veridical intelligence yield from torture through the ages shows that it has been paltry and subject to an astonishingly low signal-to-noise ratio, with many false positives occurring."[103]

Although not my focus here, it's important to acknowledge the serious and lasting harm that torture, abuse, and other acts of violence can also bring to perpetrators and bystanders. Especially in the context of the so-called war on terror, the phenomenon of "moral injury" has received increasing and well-deserved attention.[104] Definitions vary, but in simple terms moral injury can result from "perpetrating, failing to prevent, or bearing witness to acts that threaten to transgress deeply held moral beliefs and expectations."[105] A range of negative emotions – guilt, shame, anger, and alienation – can dominate an individual's life after such experiences, in some cases leading to drug use, addiction, and suicide. In his detailed account of US soldiers traumatized by their own involvement in torture, journalist Joshua Phillips quotes one who told him, "None of us were like this before … No one thought about dragging people through concertina wire or beating them or sandbagging them or strangling them or anything like that … before this."[106]

THE ROAD NOT TRAVELED

This chapter has provided only a brief glimpse into an ugly history. But there should be no confusion about one key point. As philosophy professor Rebecca Gordon has emphasized, the torture of war-on-terror prisoners is best understood as an institutionalized, socially embedded *practice* rather than the discrete, occasional acts perpetrated by a "few bad apples."[107] In a similar vein, Richard Matthews, also a professor of philosophy, has warned that any intelligence operation undertaken with the repugnant view that torture can be an effective intervention would inevitably require a broad range of disturbing governmental supports. These would include: an established program for the selection and training of torturers; extensive funding for the scientific research necessary to assess the desirability of alternative torture techniques; a system of legal protections so that proficient torturers are willing to ply their trade; and the participation of health personnel to ensure that the minds and bodies of those subjected to torture remain sufficiently unimpaired to permit their continuing violation by government agents.[108]

After the 9/11 attacks, the Bush White House instituted a government-wide system of lawlessness and brutality. Those calling the shots were among the most powerful individuals in the country, and their game plan gave crucial roles to psychologists.[109] Against that backdrop, opposition was neither easy nor cheap. Yet when credible reports from human rights organizations and respected media outlets began to emerge, highlighting the involvement of health professionals in detainee mistreatment, the APA's leadership could have prioritized professional ethics over political expediency. Instead, they seemingly ignored or rejected the growing calls to remove psychologists from participation in the government's dark-side operations around the world.

It's also important to recognize here that, from the earliest months after 9/11, there was in fact meaningful opposition within the government – and within the military-intelligence community itself – to the abusive war-on-terror operations of the CIA and Pentagon. Historian and national security expert Karen Greenberg has summarized some of the concerns raised by these insiders, including some of the military's top attorneys, this way: "The possible illegality of such acts under domestic law; the importance of maintaining the high moral ground as a mark of American national identity; the protection of human rights worldwide; the potentially dangerous repercussions that might come from alienating our allies; and the endangerment of our citizens and our troops in a world in which reciprocity in the decent treatment of prisoners might no longer be honored."[110]

From this perspective, then, the APA would not have been alone and without allies if it had chosen a different path. Moreover, vocal opposition from the APA could have threatened the White House's flimsy legal foundation for its harsh operations since psychologists were designated and promoted as guarantors against prisoner torture and mistreatment. Put simply, it appears that the Bush Administration benefited from support from the APA in legitimizing the ongoing involvement of psychologists in detainee interrogations and related roles – involvement that was seemingly essential for these operations to continue. And for the APA, preserving the association's hard-earned "seat at the table" within the national security establishment was apparently quite important as well.

In the next chapter we'll see how, when given opportunities to change course, the APA clung to arguments at odds with traditional do-no-harm

principles of professional ethics and made decisions that arguably contributed to years more abuse for war-on-terror prisoners. APA leaders opted for
policy choices that served to support, rather than oppose, the government's
interrogation and detention operations, all while insisting that psychologists helped to protect the welfare of the detainees. In so doing, I believe the
world's largest organization of psychologists allowed crucial determina-
tions about psychological ethics in national security settings to be guided
by the preferences of a White House that had already embraced torture as
part of its war strategy.

The Pretense of Deliberation

CONTROVERSY BUILDS, BUSINESS AS USUAL PREVAILS

Despite the many credible reports that prisoners in US custody were being subjected to grave abuses, firm denials from government officials mostly succeeded in keeping widespread public disapproval at bay. But the ghastly photos from Abu Ghraib in the spring of 2004 changed that.[1] Although psychologists reportedly played no direct role there, the documented horrors in Iraq seemingly provided sufficient reason for leaders of the American Psychological Association (APA) to do two things: first, reflect on the depravity with which the US military was treating some of its prisoners, and second, reconsider the APA's own ongoing efforts to expand the involvement of psychologists in these war-on-terror operations.

Such steps might have averted much of the harm and public embarrassment that eventually came to the association in the years that followed. But the APA failed to acknowledge important connections between Abu Ghraib and abusive US detention and interrogation operations elsewhere around the globe – operations where psychologists and other health professionals were indisputably present. Instead, the APA opted to promote psychology as a tool for understanding and addressing what had gone awry at Abu Ghraib, all while largely ignoring other reports of detainee abuse that ought to have posed much the same concerns.

At a June 2004 congressional briefing on "Psychological Science and Abu Ghraib," Steven Breckler, then the director of the association's Science Directorate and currently a program director at the National

Science Foundation, offered attendees "the wisdom and insight ... of behavioral science."[2] He described how "people underestimate the power of the situation to influence and shape their behavior," highlighting obedience to authority as a key example. He also used the occasion to make what seems like a not-so-subtle fundraising appeal, emphasizing that "decades of research, much of it funded by US federal agencies, can help us to understand what happened and to prevent similar incidents in the future."[3]

Of course, that unwanted future of similar incidents had already arrived – and it wouldn't go away anytime soon. As Breckler held forth in the nation's capital about psychology's role in the *prevention* of abuse, some US psychologists – including APA members – had become cogs in elaborate systems of prisoner maltreatment and torture at other locales. But accountability didn't appear to be a top priority on Breckler's agenda. As he explained, "We are not here to point fingers, to assign blame, or to assess guilt."[4] This mantra would characterize the APA's standard operating procedures for years to come.

In fact, the same message was conveyed the following month, when the APA's Ethics Office director Stephen Behnke hosted a private meeting to discuss issues facing psychologists in national security work. Along with senior APA staff, the invited guests comprised a small group of Central Intelligence Agency (CIA) and Defense Department psychologists.[5] Behnke assured the attendees that they would "neither assess nor investigate the behavior of any specific individual or group."[6] He went even further, promising that their names and the substance of their discussions would remain confidential and that the APA wanted to express its appreciation for the important work they were all doing. Among the participants was Kirk Hubbard, the CIA behavioral scientist who first introduced James Mitchell and Bruce Jessen to the agency.[7] When Hubbard left the CIA the following year, he joined Mitchell Jessen & Associates, the company that had received $81 million from the CIA to manage its brutal black site interrogations.[8]

A few months after Breckler's testimony and Behnke's meeting, the APA was still pushing forward on outreach efforts to war-on-terror powerbrokers while singing its own praises. By the APA's account, these ventures were bearing fruit. In October 2004, for example, Geoff Mumford and Heather Kelly from the Science Directorate met with high-ranking psychologists within the Department of Defense's Counterintelligence

Field Activity (CIFA) office to discuss possible areas of collaboration. The APA's *Science Policy Insider News* boasted of the close connections sought and obtained: "APA members are remarkably well-positioned within CIFA to bring operational and research expertise to bear on counterintelligence activities."[9] The following year, CIFA briefly made headlines for its reported involvement in domestic spying, including data collection targeting anti-war protest groups; the secretive unit was closed a few years later.[10] Still, the association's leadership remained unabashed in touting the role that psychologists could play in tackling national security challenges. As the APA described it, the strategy was simple: "leverage demonstrable success stories" and "continue elevating the profile of psychology."[11]

But the APA's public relations campaign on the national security front – consistently highlighting the contributions of behavioral scientists – took a serious hit as 2004 came to a close. As noted earlier, two articles by *New York Times* reporter Neil Lewis provided disturbing details about a leaked confidential investigation of the Guantanamo detention facility by the International Committee of the Red Cross (ICRC). The distinguished humanitarian group had found clear evidence that – in a "flagrant violation of medical ethics" – psychologists were involved in detention and interrogation operations that were "tantamount to torture."[12] Prisoners were subjected to humiliating acts, solitary confinement, temperature extremes, and the use of stress positions. The account uncomfortably echoed the shocking abuses at Abu Ghraib.

As the first half of 2005 unfolded, reports recounting the mistreatment suffered by war-on-terror prisoners in US custody continued to appear in the news. In a February article in the *Washington Post*, Carol Leonnig and Dana Priest described how Guantanamo's female interrogators engaged in behaviors designed to sexually humiliate devout Muslim detainees.[13] In May, Tim Golden of the *New York Times* revealed shocking details about abuses that had occurred at the Army's Bagram Air Base in Afghanistan, including the 2002 torture and death of a twenty-two-year-old taxi driver named Dilawar. His body had been so badly beaten that a coroner's report described Dilawar's legs as having been "pulpified."[14]

Then in late June, three separate reports directly implicated health professionals in the abuses at Guantanamo. First, *Time* correspondents Adam Zagorin and Michael Duffy published a leaked log from the interrogation of detainee Mohammed al-Qahtani.[15] The involvement of Behavioral Science Consultation Team (BSCT) members in al-Qahtani's torturous mistreatment was described in Chapter 2. Two days later, in an article published online in the *New England Journal of Medicine*, physician and law professor M. Gregg Bloche and bioethics professor Jonathan Marks revealed that health professionals at Guantanamo had "prepared psychological profiles for use by interrogators; they also sat in on some interrogations, observed others from behind one-way mirrors, and offered feedback to interrogators."[16]

These scholars also noted their concern about the "wholesale disregard for clinical confidentiality" regarding detainees' medical files, and they described abusive tactics at Guantanamo as "a matter of national shame."[17] And then later that week, based on interviews with former Guantanamo interrogators, Neil Lewis of the *New York Times* disclosed that military doctors "aided interrogators in conducting and refining coercive interrogations of detainees, including providing advice on how to increase stress levels and exploit fears."[18]

STACKING THE DECK?

In late June of 2005, as this onslaught of revelations ignited growing concern and outrage from psychologists and non-psychologists alike, the APA held a three-day meeting of its newly formed ad hoc Presidential Task Force on Psychological Ethics and National Security (PENS) in Washington, DC. The primary charge given to the PENS group by the APA's Board of Directors was to assess whether the association's current Ethics Code adequately addressed the issues faced by psychologists working in national security settings.

To pursue that agenda effectively would seemingly have required input from participants who not only had expertise in psychological ethics and related domains, but were also unencumbered by professional commitments that might color their objectivity or curtail their freedom of expression. Toward these ends, M. Gregg Bloche has noted that the APA could have opted for "high-profile fora with prominent speakers; special issues of professional journals; an interdisciplinary panel of ethicists, legal scholars, and others to draft guidance; and a call for a public investigation with subpoena power to clarify the facts."[19] That approach would have made a lot of sense – but the APA went in a very different direction.

The membership of the PENS Task Force was selected by a committee that included Ethics Office director Stephen Behnke, President Ronald Levant, and President-elect Gerald Koocher. Six of the nine voting members were operational or forensic psychologists, involved in, or consulting to, military-intelligence interrogation operations or research. Four had links to the chains of command at Guantanamo, Bagram, and CIA black sites where detainee abuses were alleged to have taken place.[20] Their support for the ongoing participation of psychologists in national security detention and interrogation operations – as well as their accommodation to the Bush Administration's permissive stance toward prisoner abuse – may have been a foregone conclusion. Some further background, including public statements made before and after the PENS meeting, sheds light on whether these particular individuals – regardless of other credentials and accomplishments – were desirable choices for a task force focused on protecting and prioritizing well-established principles of psychological ethics.

As described earlier, Larry James, selected for the PENS Task Force, had been the chief BSCT operational psychologist at Guantanamo during a period in which the abusive treatment of detainees took place (he denies any involvement). In his memoir, published a few years after the PENS meeting, James outrageously dismissed monitors from the ICRC as "a bunch of radical left do-gooders, mostly from Europe, who were as interested in giving America a black eye as they were in truly helping the innocent."[21] He also recounted an episode at Guantanamo in which, after pouring himself a cup of coffee, he sat back behind a one-way mirror and watched for several minutes as an interrogator and three guards struggled to force a pink nightgown onto a prisoner who was already unwillingly outfitted in pink panties, a wig, and lipstick. In his account, James doesn't indicate that he reported this abuse to his superiors.[22]

A second PENS member was Army psychologist Morgan Banks, reportedly a close friend of James Mitchell.[23] After 9/11 he served at the Bagram prison in Afghanistan before becoming the director of psychological applications for the Army's Special Operations Command. As noted earlier, in the latter role Banks apparently assisted with arrangements to teach some of Guantanamo's interrogation personnel about Survival, Evasion, Resistance, and Escape (SERE) techniques.[24] Some of these psychologically coercive methods were subsequently adapted for use on prisoners at the detention facility. Several years after the PENS meeting, Banks appeared to downplay the harm suffered by detainees, writing with a colleague that "performing a 15-second simulated drowning upon an individual ... should not be equated to the wanton burning, flailing, breaking of limbs, and decapitations that jihadists routinely impose upon their captives."[25]

Navy captain and special forces operational psychologist Bryce Lefever was also a member of the PENS Task Force. He too had previously been stationed at the Bagram prison in Afghanistan. In his own words, he "coached interrogations of Taliban and al Qaida prisoners" and "provided a series of lectures on methods pertaining to difficult resistors."[26] In a National Public Radio interview almost four years after the PENS meeting, Lefever indicated that abuse could be an effective way to obtain information. As he explained in the context of SERE training, "The tough nut to crack, if you keep him awake for a week, you torture him, you tie his arms behind him, you have him on the ground – anyone can be brought beyond their ability to resist." In the same interview, Lefever also appeared to defend abuses such as locking a phobic prisoner in a small box with insects, insisting that "the things that are called ... torture or exploitative are also therapy techniques."[27]

PENS member Scott Shumate had worked for both the CIA and the Defense Department. Before becoming chief psychologist for CIFA, a Pentagon counterintelligence unit mentioned earlier, he served in a similar operational position for the CIA's Counterterrorist Center. In the latter role, he was present for the early part of the black site interrogation of Abu Zubaydah by fellow psychologist James Mitchell. Shumate reportedly left the facility in disgust when his two-week assignment ended.[28] Whether he took further steps in an effort to prevent the continued use of so-called enhanced interrogation techniques is unclear from the public record. It's also noteworthy that at the time Shumate was selected for the PENS Task Force, he was a direct target of APA efforts to promote further collaborative opportunities with Defense Department counterintelligence agencies.[29]

A fifth military-intelligence member of the PENS Task Force was Michael Gelles, formerly the chief psychologist for the Naval Criminal Investigative Service. He has appropriately received positive recognition for both objecting to certain abusive SERE-based techniques that were being used at Guantanamo shortly after 9/11 *and* reporting his concerns to his superiors.[30] But in 2003 Gelles also published an article with colleague Charles Ewing examining the non-traditional roles and ethical challenges that often characterize the work of psychologists in national security settings. They seemingly concluded that these operational psychologists should have a different code of ethics, writing, "We cannot continue to place them in situations where the ethics of their conduct will be judged, *post hoc*, either by rules that have little if any relevance to their vital governmental functions or by professional organizations or licensing authorities."[31] Having expressed opposition in this way to ethical oversight by the APA, Gelles seems at best an incongruous choice for a task force charged with offering guidance concerning APA's own ethics policies in this arena.

The other voting members of the task force were Robert Fein, a national security and forensic psychologist with a long history of working closely with law enforcement and intelligence agencies, and three civilians without any military intelligence connections: Jean Maria Arrigo, Nina Thomas, and Michael Wessells. The non-voting task force chair was Olivia Moorehead-Slaughter. I find it hard to imagine that the APA's leadership didn't realize that heavy reliance on military-intelligence operational psychologists in the composition of the PENS Task Force would significantly influence the conclusions reached by the group. And while people with first-hand knowledge of national security operations may have been uniquely qualified to provide information relevant to the deliberations, the task force could have called upon these individuals as expert consultants, without making them participating members of the task force itself. Instead, in effect the APA empaneled a jury where a majority of the jurors might have their livelihoods affected by the verdict they rendered.

PERMITTING THE NUREMBERG DEFENSE

Given the group's composition, it's unsurprising that the PENS Task Force issued a report – written primarily by the APA's Ethics Office director Stephen Behnke – asserting that psychologists play a critical role in keeping detainee interrogations "safe, legal, ethical, and effective."[32] Despite the allegations regarding psychologists' involvement in prisoner abuse – allegations that were deemed entirely off-limits for the weekend's discussions – the task force adopted this wording from the Pentagon's own BSCT guidelines. These guidelines had already been drafted before the task force even met – in part by PENS member Morgan Banks and Debra Dunivin, another BSCT psychologist stationed at Guantanamo.[33] In this way, by arguably abandoning meaningful independence from the avowed preferences of government officials, the APA became the sole major professional health-related organization to affirmatively support practices contrary to the international human rights standards that many believe are the benchmark against which professional codes of ethics should be judged.

Particularly significant in this context was the APA's Ethical Standard 1.02. As described earlier, a revision was adopted by the association's Council of Representatives in 2002. The change allowed psychologists to "adhere to the requirements of the law, regulations, or other governing legal authority" when faced with an ethical conflict. The revision was developed prior to the 9/11 attacks, so it wasn't specifically designed to establish a more permissive ethical environment for psychologists working in post-9/11 national security settings. But this variation of the Nuremberg defense – absent from earlier versions of the Ethics Code – may have had that disquieting effect nonetheless. For some, this 1.02 loophole could serve to justify involving psychologists in war-on-terror practices that diverged from the fundamental do-no-harm principles of the profession's ethics.[34]

From this perspective, then, the PENS Task Force meeting in 2005 provided an ideal opportunity for the APA to revisit 1.02 and carefully consider whether the standard's just-following-orders rationale posed a problem in light of the government's alleged reliance on psychologists in its abusive detention and interrogation operations. It seems the answer should have been obvious: given the wording of 1.02, which prioritized US law and military regulations over ethics, the APA's current Ethics Code was clearly inadequate in a world where well-recognized forms of torture and other illtreatment were deemed acceptable by the White House.

But despite the mounting evidence and the growing alarm from the human rights community, the PENS Task Force – dominated by the members with military-intelligence ties and heavily influenced by APA senior staff and other insiders who wanted psychologists to remain in these war-onterror roles – concluded that the association's Ethics Code was "fundamentally sound" when applied to national security-related work.[35] In this way, the PENS Report became a gift-wrapped package to the CIA and Defense Department, permitting psychologists to continue their participation in abusive operations with little worry of professional sanctions.

At the same time, the language of the PENS Report made it impossible for military psychologists to tell their commanding officers that the APA's Ethics Code *required* that they not participate in these harm-inducing operations. The report stated that "psychologists do not engage in behaviors that violate the laws of the United States, although psychologists *may* refuse for ethical reasons to follow laws or orders that are unjust or that violate basic principles of human rights" (emphasis added).[36] Furthermore, acknowledging that the "war on terror" had led to significant developments in rules and regulations, the report also stated that "psychologists have an ethical responsibility to be informed of, familiar with, and follow the most recent applicable regulations and rules."[37] One of those developments, only three months prior to the PENS meeting, was updated doctrine from the Department of Defense. It specified that detainees categorized as "enemy combatants" did *not* fall under the provisions of the Geneva Conventions; they were only "entitled to be treated humanely, *subject to military necessity*" (emphasis added).[38]

In sum, the PENS Report concluded that it was ethically permissible for psychologists to be involved in detention and interrogation operations that the Bush White House deemed lawful, even when those tactics strayed far from long-established international understandings of what constituted prisoner abuse. This position by the APA likely added further pressure on psychologists to participate in these operations, if so ordered.[39] In an email addressing disagreements among task force members over this key issue, Olivia Moorehead-Slaughter – the PENS Task Force chair – wrote this about international human rights standards: "Our colleagues from the military were clear that including such standards in the document would likely (perhaps definitely) put the document at odds with United States law and military regulations."[40] That deal-breaking assessment is troubling in its own right. But just as disturbing is what may have been a failure to even solicit opinions from legal experts on this important point of contention.

The PENS Report's stance on psychological research was also reason for significant concern.[41] Consider that just months before the task force met, in responding to media reports about Guantanamo, the executive director of Physicians for Human Rights raised the possibility that health professionals – including psychologists – were involved in "calibrating levels of pain inflicted on detainees."[42] Such activities, which certainly ring of experimentation, would constitute a clear violation of international ethical standards. Yet the PENS Report was silent in regard to any research prohibitions of this sort. In fact, the report specifically *encouraged* psychologists to engage in investigations aimed at uncovering "cultural differences in the psychological impact of particular information-gathering methods and what constitutes cruel, inhuman, or degrading treatment."[43]

Whether intended or not, this recommendation seems to suggest that psychological research should be pursued with the aim of determining when various forms of coercion and abuse go too far. Several years later, a Physicians for Human Rights white paper, *Experiments in Torture*, provided compelling evidence that psychologists and other health professionals at CIA black sites had conducted research and experimentation as part of the agency's so-called enhanced interrogation program – without the informed consent of these prisoners, obviously.[44]

INCONSISTENCIES AND IRREGULARITIES

Ultimately, the task force vote in favor of the PENS Report and its suspect conclusions was unanimous. But two of the three civilian voting members without connections to the military-intelligence establishment – Jean Maria Arrigo and Michael Wessells – expressed reservations prior to the meeting, during the meeting, and after the report was published.[45] Their strongest concerns revolved around the stark unwillingness of the other task force members to prioritize international standards and documents, such as the Geneva Conventions, over Bush-era US laws when assessing the ethics of psychologists' behaviors.[46]

Perhaps emblematic of this dismissiveness was a task force listserv message from then APA president-elect Gerald Koocher – a key task force participant-observer – in which he wrote, "I have zero interest in entangling APA with the nebulous, toothless, contradictory, and obfuscatory treaties that comprise 'international law.'"[47] Along with the White House, it seems he may have had limited regard for the consideration that, according to the US Constitution, treaties like the Geneva Conventions constitute the "supreme Law of the Land."[48] At an earlier point in this same listserv discussion, Koocher had also noted that he was "addicted" to the television show 24, in which the protagonist – government agent Jack Bauer – routinely tortured suspected adversaries to obtain information from them.[49]

Arrigo and Wessells were reportedly given assurances that the PENS Report would be only the first step in the APA's plan to fully address these thorny issues, and that a nuanced and comprehensive interrogation ethics casebook would soon be developed to remedy any shortcomings in the PENS Report. A casebook with those qualities never materialized. Six months after the PENS Report was issued, Wessells resigned from the task force over the APA's inadequate engagement with these matters, citing "the wider silence and inaction of the APA on the crucial issues at hand."[50]

Beyond the worrisome conclusions of the PENS Report, the entire process was seemingly tainted by significant procedural irregularities, including a failure to honor various governance checks and balances. For example, within days of the PENS meeting, the APA's Board of Directors invoked its rarely used emergency powers and endorsed the report as APA policy. The association's president at that time, Ronald Levant, described the emergency as a reputational one: "APA and psychology are getting pretty well trashed in the media, damaging our public image."[51] By adopting the PENS Report on an emergency basis, the board eliminated a comment period for APA members to provide feedback on the report and preempted a standard review and vote by the APA's governing Council of Representatives. That vote would have taken place just over a month later.

Also, senior APA staff member Russ Newman – a lawyer and psychologist who was then the executive director of the association's Practice Directorate – was present for the meeting. According to task force member Jean Maria Arrigo, from the outset Newman took on a directive role and urged the task force to quickly "put out the fires of controversy" and affirm the ethics of psychologists' involvement in interrogations and other national security operations.[52] But Newman was married to Debra Dunivin, who, as noted earlier, was a BSCT psychologist; she had also played a behind-the-scenes role in the selection of some PENS Task Force members.[53] The personal relationship between Newman and Dunivin arguably constituted a significant conflict of interest. And yet, although the marriage was known to military members of the task force and to some APA leaders, the information apparently was never shared at the PENS meeting with the civilian members who lacked military-intelligence ties.

In addition, in a highly unusual move, the identities of the PENS Task Force members were not included in the final report, they weren't posted directly on the APA's website, and in specific cases they weren't revealed to members of the APA or the press who requested them.[54] Via email, Michael Gelles even applauded Stephen Behnke for successfully "insur[ing] the confidentiality of the panel, despite pressure to reveal the identities of the task force members" during the APA's annual convention in August 2005.[55] The names were finally broadly publicized by investigative journalist Mark Benjamin – a full year after the PENS Report was published.[56]

Further still, an agreement apparently pushed by the military-intelligence participants prohibited task force members from taking notes during the meeting and bound them from discussing the process or the report public-ly. These arrangements served to conceal the composition of the task force and the reasoning behind its decisions, limiting informed review by APA members and other interested stakeholders. The APA has never meaning-fully explained why such secrecy was needed or how it served the needs of professional psychology or the public.

Given the seeming irregularities she had witnessed, Jean Maria Arrigo left for home after the PENS meeting convinced that something was very wrong and that she'd been played as an easy mark. Still, in her view, the task force confidentiality agreement, by a majority vote, left her no recourse but to remain silent. That changed a year later when Arrigo happened to learn, for the first time, that Newman and Dunivin were married. On the basis of this perceived betrayal of transparency and collegiality, she considered the task force's confidentiality agreement nullified and finally felt free to seek outside consultation.

Arrigo turned first to David DeBatto and Lawrence Rockwood, two former Army counterintelligence officers she knew. According to her, as though it were "just a simple arithmetic problem," without hesitation they independently researched the task force's so-called observers and, in DeBatto's words, identified PENS as "a typical legitimization process for a decision made at a higher level in the Department of Defense."[57] When she then sought guidance about how to proceed in light of what she felt was a disturbing analysis, three eminent psychologists warned her that speaking out could have adverse professional consequences.

But Arrigo's mentor Ray McGovern, a former CIA analyst, offered a different and simpler perspective about publicly sharing what she knew: "It's your duty." Soon thereafter, she did just that, and also arranged for the archived listserv discussions among the PENS participants, which covered the period from April 2005 to June 2006, to be made available online via *ProPublica*.[58] Arrigo later became a key member of the Coalition for an Ethical Psychology. In more than one subsequent conversation with me, she denied that there was anything valiant in her actions, telling me that it was what anyone should have done – and she insisted that I not use the word "courageous" in describing her.

Taken as a whole, the full array of choices and decisions made by the APA's leadership in regard to the PENS process may potentially be explained as a well-planned and carefully orchestrated effort to assist the national security establishment in securing the ongoing participation of psychologists in detention and interrogation operations. With all that is now known, it is painfully ironic that a seemingly hidden agenda of this sort was repeatedly couched in terms of protecting war-on-terror detainees by supposedly keeping these operations safe, legal, ethical, and effective.[59]

With the PENS Report, the APA had an opportunity to reassess the role of psychologists in the light of a fuller awareness of reported abuses and at a greater distance from the shock of 9/11. But any substantive policy changes would have compromised the association's standing with the military and intelligence agencies, and would have obstructed operations that the highest-ranking government officials deemed justified. In fact, only a month after the PENS Report was released, Dunivin and task force members Banks and James met with Army Surgeon General Kevin Kiley to develop further BSCT guidance based on the report – just one indication of how much the Pentagon welcomed the outcome of the PENS meeting.[60]

ADMIT NOTHING, DENY EVERYTHING, MAKE COUNTERACCUSATIONS

The brief and hurried meeting of the ill-conceived PENS Task Force was likely intended to calm growing apprehensions about prisoner abuse and the APA's policies among members and the public. Faced with a choice between a focus on organizational reputation management or an earnest reckoning with the concerns underlying that reputational threat, it seems that APA leaders opted for the former. But the report's permissive and even encouraging stance toward psychologists' active participation in the coercive interrogation of war-on-terror detainees had an unintended and unanticipated effect, setting off a firestorm of disapproval from psychologists and non-psychologists concerned about the apparent disregard for psychological ethics and human rights.

This uproar intensified when, just days after the PENS meeting, *New Yorker* investigative journalist Jane Mayer published an essay – "The Experiment" – with revelations that cast further doubt on any claim that psychologists and other health professionals were steady beacons of morality or decency at US war-on-terror detention facilities.[61] For example, when Mayer interviewed Baher Azmy, an attorney representing a Guantanamo detainee, he told her that psychologically abusive techniques were "prevalent and systematic. They're tried, measured, and charted. These are ways to humiliate and disorient the detainees. The whole place appears to be one giant human experiment." Another defense attorney, Rob Kirsch, told Mayer that medical care was sometimes withheld if a prisoner failed to provide the information that his interrogators wanted. Mayer also reported that, according to a former Guantanamo interrogator, psychologists would "control the most minute details of interrogations, to the point of decreeing, in the case of one detainee, that he would be given seven squares of toilet paper per day."[62]

Morgan Banks, one of the PENS Task Force members, was among the interviewees for Mayer's story. He acknowledged that he provided assistance at Guantanamo and told her that he supports the involvement of psychologists in the interrogations there, "as long as they don't break the law." Whether professional ethics were also a topic of discussion isn't clear. Mayer's article also identified then APA member James Mitchell as a contract psychologist who had been involved in the CIA's black site interrogations of an al-Qaeda suspect in 2002. According to a counter-terrorism expert interviewed by Mayer, Mitchell pushed for rougher methods and argued that the prisoner should be treated like the dogs in a classic psychology experiment, a reference to the learned helplessness studies of former APA president Martin Seligman. The magnitude of Mitchell's essential role in the CIA's torture program only became evident later.[63]

The predominant reaction among APA leaders to the waves of negative publicity that followed the release of the PENS Report seemed to be a combination of defensiveness and self-righteousness. Perhaps the CIA's informal motto – "Admit nothing, deny everything, make counteraccusations" – summed up the APA's public relations strategy rather well. Variations of the following message from Ethics Office director Stephen Behnke became a recurrent theme: "For over 20 years, the American Psychological Association's position has been clear and unwavering: It is unethical for a psychologist to participate in torture or other cruel, inhuman, or degrading treatment, under any circumstances, at any time, for any reason."[64] This unequivocal claim of rectitude was likely welcomed and accepted as the final word by many APA members eager for reassurance. Behind the scenes, however, the maintenance of close ties with the military-intelligence establishment – which insisted that no torture or abuse was taking place – seemed to remain an ongoing priority for the APA.

Behnke appeared to take the lead on the APA's reputation-salvaging campaign during the immediate post-PENS years. He was frequently assisted by Gerald Koocher, who had been involved in selecting PENS members and later criticized concerns raised by the non-military members of the task force. A month after the PENS Report was approved by the APA Board of Directors, Behnke appeared on the independent news show *Democracy Now!* hosted by broadcast journalist and investigative reporter Amy Goodman. He criticized press reports alleging abuses by psychologists as "long on hearsay and innuendo, short on facts." He insisted that the APA "wants the facts." And he promised that "if individuals who are members of our association have acted inappropriately, the APA will address those very directly and very clearly."[65]

But when Behnke made this statement in August 2005, he likely should have known that James Mitchell and John Leso – both mentioned in press reports – were APA members at that time. And as director of the association's Ethics Office, he certainly could have strenuously urged that the Ethics Committee investigate the allegations against them. Yet, despite the reports of alleged ethical breaches by psychologists, it appears that he may not have done so. Although one can only speculate about the reasons, some of Behnke's public comments, like the PENS Report itself, are suggestive of a primary focus on legality rather than traditional standards for ethical conduct. "Psychologists have an absolute ethical obligation," he said, "never to violate any United States law."[66] Those laws, of course, had been reinterpreted by the Bush Administration to make even some forms of torture "legal."

Meanwhile, upon becoming the APA's president in 2006, Koocher immediately used his column in the association's monthly magazine to defend the PENS Report and the process that produced it. This wasn't surprising. In an email to task force members a month prior to the PENS meeting, Koocher had written of the role psychologists could play in "the incarceration, debilitation, or even death" of suspected perpetrators.[67] In the February 2006 issue of the APA's *Monitor on Psychology*, he criticized those who raised concerns about reports of psychologists' involvement in torture and abuse, describing them as "opportunistic commentators masquerading as scholars."[68] In the same piece, he claimed that "no APA members have been linked to unprofessional behaviors" – even though allegations had been made involving both Mitchell and Leso by this time.

A few months later, in his July 2006 column, Koocher adopted a different but similarly defensive stance. He wrote that war-on-terror-era psychologists couldn't legitimately be held responsible for *creating* techniques such as "sleep deprivation, social isolation, extreme temperature changes or degrading and embarrassing interventions" because these methods of abuse had existed many years before.[69] Critics, of course, had never disputed that history. What they had charged – and what Koocher did not address – was that prisoners were tortured at Guantanamo and CIA black sites and that psychologists apparently helped to design the specific programs that were used there.

Behnke also pressed forward with the APA's public relations campaign. In mid-2006 both the American Psychiatric Association and the American Medical Association issued statements declaring that, for ethical reasons, their members should *not* assist with interrogations.[70] The former group stated, in part, "No psychiatrist should participate directly in the interrogation of persons held in custody by military or civilian investigative or law enforcement authorities."[71] The latter stated, in part, "Physicians must not conduct, directly participate in, or monitor an interrogation with an intent to intervene, because this undermines the physician's role as healer."[72]

In response, the Department of Defense announced that psychologists alone would continue in BSCT roles.[73] This news led dissident psychologist Stephen Soldz to create an online petition, directed to Koocher, opposing the participation of psychologists in these operations. The petition read, in part, "As a profession aimed at improving the human condition built upon a respect for human dignity, we believe that our shared base of psychological knowledge should not be used to further what is, at minimum, abusive treatment and, at worst, torture."[74] It quickly garnered hundreds of signatures from APA members and other psychologists.

Seemingly dismissing such concerns, Behnke reportedly offered assurances that "psychologists knew not to participate in activities that harmed detainees."[75] In his July/August 2006 *Monitor on Psychology* ethics column, he also emphasized that psychologists differed from physicians in that they alone had the "unique competencies" necessary to prevent abusive "behavioral drift" on the part of interrogators.[76] Behnke offered no substantive evidence to support his claim that psychologists are trained in observing and intervening to protect detainees from harm, and he gave no explanation for why the BSCT psychologists themselves would not also drift toward abuse.[77] Even more, Behnke's claims arguably ignored what had become an obvious reality to others. As sociologists Gregory Hooks and Clayton Mosher emphasized, many of the abuses were *not* aberrations and chain-of-command failures at all. Rather, they reflected a "systemic commitment to callous cruelty" and a "highly rationalized system of interrogation" that simply valued the extraction of information over the protection of human rights.[78]

Years later dissident psychologist Jeffrey Kaye discovered that at this time Behnke had begun serving as a consultant to the Department of Defense, participating in a training program for Guantanamo BSCT psychologists at Fort Huachuca in Arizona.[79] Email correspondence from June 2006 reveals that Behnke discussed with Morgan Banks and Debra Dunivin whether he should alert the APA's Board of Directors to his participation in these trainings. He apparently opted not to do so, explaining to Banks and Dunivin, "Given how hot things are at the moment discretion may be the better part of valor for the time being, at least in terms of the broader APA community."[80] Although the APA received payments from the Defense Department for Behnke's services, it appears that for almost a decade relatively few within the association were aware of the exact nature of his participation.

In August 2006, the APA held its annual convention in New Orleans, and Koocher invited Army surgeon general Kevin Kiley to speak to the association's Council of Representatives. A few weeks prior to the meeting, in an email to Koocher, Levant, APA general counsel Nathalie Gilfoyle, and Rhea Farberman from the association's Public Affairs Office, Behnke described his own view of the ongoing interrogation controversy this way: "It has become clear that there is, for lack of a better term, a 'left wing conspiracy' against APA on this issue, something I've suspected for a long while but have become entirely convinced of now."[81]

Having received the PENS Report with much appreciation just over a year earlier, Kiley accepted the invitation to speak. Behnke followed up by providing Kiley's office with an advance list of recommended talking points.[82] But in addition to his prepared remarks, the surgeon general went off-script when he offered a provocative and what I believe was an ethically misguided take on exactly what the profession offered the military: "Psychology is an important weapons system," he told the attendees.[83]

Koocher reportedly rejected a proposal to invite Leonard Rubenstein, then the executive director of Physicians for Human Rights, to provide a countervailing perspective.[84] Instead, dissident APA member Steven Reisner was given the opportunity to speak to council members about his opposition to Kiley's message. He argued that the PENS Report should be suspended, that a moratorium should be declared on psychologists' participation in military-intelligence interrogations, and that the APA should consult with ethicists from the United Nations, human rights groups, and other health professions regarding appropriate roles for psychologists in national security settings.[85] Other psychologists at the convention expressed similar views. Brinton Lykes, a founder of the Martín-Baró Fund for Mental Health and Human Rights, emphasized, "Failure to speak out now to end current interrogation processes and to end our involvement in interrogation is not only a failure of conscience, but a failure of our own practices as psychologists and as citizens committed to human rights and international justice."[86]

Behind the scenes during this period, APA senior staff created public relations communications seemingly designed to obscure the APA's activities and stymie any press coverage that might lead to further unwelcome revelations. In late 2006, for example, journalist Katherine Eban had begun working on a *Vanity Fair* article – mentioned in Chapter 2 – which focused on CIA contract psychologists Mitchell and Jessen.[87] She approached APA staff members Geoff Mumford and Rhea Farberman with a few questions about prior meetings between APA staff and military-intelligence personnel, and about the role of psychologists in the "war on terror."

Mumford and Farberman recruited Behnke and fellow APA staffer Heather Kelly to assist with formulating answers. Perhaps cautious and fearful of what Eban might know or might learn, Mumford suggested in their email exchange that he could reach out to Kirk Hubbard, the former CIA official who was then working for Mitchell Jessen & Associates. Farberman warned that one of Eban's questions – about the APA's 2003 invitation-only workshop on deception, where interrogation techniques were discussed – "is the one we really have to be careful about!!" Kelly cautioned Mumford, "You probably don't want to say something specific about the military that might contradict whatever I said." Behnke drafted a diverting response to Eban and reassuringly told his colleagues, "By this point she should be asleep."[88]

The following year, Behnke and Koocher teamed up to co-author a 2007 commentary in which they returned to the familiar refrain that "any psychologist found to have any involvement in torture or cruel, inhuman, or degrading treatment or punishment will face sanction by the APA Ethics Committee."[89] But they also expressed skepticism that sufficient evidence would ever be available for this purpose, thereby making their assurances of limited value. As this era unfolded further, it appears that the full Ethics Committee was not given the opportunity to evaluate the evidence in any investigation of CIA or military psychologists following complaints filed with the Ethics Office.[90] In contrast, as will become clear shortly, the APA's leadership took multiple steps to preserve the association's deference to the military-intelligence establishment and the roles it assigned to psychologists.

Koocher was also involved in what was arguably one of the lowest points in the APA leadership's stubborn defense of its position. In the fall of 2007, he wrote an open letter to Amy Goodman of *Democracy Now!* expressing his displeasure over Jean Maria Arrigo's account of her distressing experience as a PENS Task Force member. Koocher's letter included this: "Until now, I had remained respectfully silent in public regarding Dr Arrigo's biases, history of personal trauma, and lack of boundaries, but will no longer do so. Her behavior during the portions of the meeting I attended, and in subsequent public forums, has underscored the sad emotional aftermath of a troubled upbringing complicated by the suicide of a parent who engaged behaviors she now abhors."[91] This ad hominem attack wasn't only mean-spirited, it was also counterfactual: Arrigo's parents were still very much alive at that time. Dismissing the letter's outrageous content, Arrigo later noted that she was bothered less by Koocher's "idiotic" personal onslaught than by the fact that, by and large, the APA did nothing in response.[92]

THE END OF THE BEGINNING

There's no circumstance or time in which crucial judgments about psychological ethics should be guided principally by the views and agenda of the White House, or the Pentagon, or the CIA. But I believe that captures reasonably well what happened with the PENS Task Force. As psychologists themselves, the organizers were presumably aware of the potent psychological influences of power differentials on group dynamics, of authority structures and conformity pressures on independent decision-making, and of self-interest on objective, unbiased analysis. Rather than working to mitigate these problematic and often unwelcome dynamics, they were instead seemingly harnessed to advance a preordained agenda.

The APA's leadership quickly embraced the suspect thesis that psychologists have a critical role to play in preventing the mistreatment of war-on-terror detainees. In so doing, the association became the only organization of its kind to officially support their members' involvement in detention and interrogation operations that were condemned as inhumane around the world. The PENS Report immediately became an influential and authoritative policy document on multiple fronts. Within the military, the report was used by the Department of Defense as guidance to preserve roles for BSCT psychologists. Within the APA, the report was promoted as clear evidence that fraught ethical issues had been appropriately resolved – claims that were welcomed by those eager to further expand the role of operational psychologists in counterintelligence and counterterrorism activities.

Despite growing evidence over the next several years that psychologists acted as planners, consultants, researchers, and overseers to abusive and torturous detainee interrogations, key APA leaders chose not to reconsider the PENS process or the report's conclusions. Nor did they publicly express regret for any of the decisions that had been made. But as we'll see in the next chapter, the PENS Report and the APA's efforts to defend it failed to stem the rising tide of outrage. Indeed, the leadership's stonewalling served to make the voices of dissent that much louder and more numerous.

4

Revelations and Resistance

DISSIDENT PSYCHOLOGISTS CONFRONT THE APA

With the Psychological Ethics and National Security (PENS) Report, the American Psychological Association (APA) arguably molded its ethics policies around the avowed preferences of the military-intelligence establishment. Key leaders of the association decided it was very important to ensure that psychologists could continue to participate in detention and interrogation operations, notwithstanding the steady drumbeat of disturbing news reports about detainee mistreatment and the apparent conflict with the profession's do-no-harm ethical foundations.

Although the motivations of the APA's decision-makers during this period may never be fully known, the record I've described casts substantial light. The APA had devoted considerable time, effort, and resources during the post-9/11 years to nurturing stronger ties with the US military and national security agencies. For some, relinquishing those hard-earned connections – and any future opportunities they might bring – would likely have been an unwelcome prospect. Moreover, even beyond any motive for institutional aggrandizement, the APA's leaders consistently adopted a deferential posture toward the government's war-on-terror choices – reasoning, perhaps, that whatever practices were deemed necessary and legal by the country's elected leaders and national-security apparatus ought to be good enough for psychological ethics, too.

That posture may have come naturally in light of the profession's extensive history of overt collaboration with the military, dating back decades before 9/11, and the stock of trust and networks that it had yielded. But even if this attitude of deference might have been understandable at first, I think it grew less so as the gulf between the Bush Administration's policies and human rights norms became more obvious. Other leading medical associations responded to the same facts by bringing their own independent ethical standards to bear, rather than aligning those standards with the administration's legal rationalizations for abuse and torture. In contrast, the APA seemed to dutifully follow the White House's war-on-terror game plan, despite the increased likelihood that its members would thereby be called upon to engage in activities much more familiar to medieval dungeons than to hospital wards or university classrooms.

Over the decade that followed the PENS Report, key APA leaders rarely wavered. Rather than reversing their endorsement of psychologists' involvement in frequently abusive operations, they only grudgingly gave ground amid calls for reform – all the while working to minimize the consequences of any concessions. Forced to choose between facing the shamefulness of an ugly reality or hiding behind falsehoods and distortions, I believe those with the most influence within the APA regularly opted for the latter. And when pressed to reconsider, they often turned to military-intelligence psychologists, including those involved in the very operations that were the target of condemnation, to help craft their strategies for resisting change – just as the association had called upon the same interests to produce the PENS Report itself.

Some psychologists reacted with concern and anti-torture advocacy when the earliest reports emerged revealing that health professionals were involved in the prisoner abuses that characterized the US "war on terror." But the outrage intensified when the PENS Report demonstrated that the APA had opted to take what appeared to be an accommodative stance in support of Defense Department and Central Intelligence Agency (CIA) detention and interrogation operations. It was during this period, then, that organized dissident opposition to the association's policies took hold as numerous groups of psychologists became increasingly outspoken critics of the APA's failure to adequately defend the profession's do-no-harm principles.

My own involvement in this work has been primarily as a member of the Coalition for an Ethical Psychology (hereafter the Coalition). The group, originally comprised of psychologists Stephen Soldz, Steven Reisner,

Brad Olson, and Jean Maria Arrigo, was formed in 2006 when the Nobel Prize–winning organization Physicians for Human Rights mobilized health professionals to oppose cooperation with abusive war-on-terror interrogations. Bryant Welch, Trudy Bond, Yosef Brody, and I later joined the Coalition. Because of their critical roles in the struggles that followed, some additional information about my Coalition colleagues should be helpful here.

Stephen Soldz is a faculty member at the Boston Graduate School of Psychoanalysis, where his teaching has included a focus on social justice and human rights. He is also an expert in research methodology. Stephen's ethical compass, careful objectivity, and exhaustive knowledge of relevant facts have served an essential gatekeeping role for the Coalition, consistently ensuring the accuracy and thorough documentation of our provocative – and often unwelcome – statements.

Steven Reisner is a trauma expert and a practicing psychoanalyst in New York City. Motivated in part by stories from his parents who had survived the Holocaust, Steven has been an impassioned and charismatic spokesperson for the Coalition. On multiple occasions, he ran for APA president on an anti-torture platform. While his campaigns as an outsider did not ultimately succeed, they helped to elevate awareness of our concerns among the APA's broad membership.

Brad Olson is a community psychologist and a professor at National Louis University in Chicago. Brad's extensive experience and expertise in activism and organizing – along with his affable and energetic nature – were crucial in building bridges with other psychologists who shared the Coalition's priorities. His investigatory skills were also a valuable asset in uncovering connections that clarified our understanding of key issues.

Jean Maria Arrigo, a social psychologist and oral historian from California, has specialized in the study of military-intelligence professionals and the ethical challenges they face. As described earlier, Jean Maria became an unexpected and unassuming whistleblower after she concluded that the purported independence of the PENS Task Force was a sham. Her selfless determination served as a touchstone for the Coalition's pursuits.

Bryant Welch is a clinical psychologist and attorney, now living in California. For over a decade, he was a senior staff member at the APA, including a lengthy period as the first leader of the association's Practice Directorate. Bryant's first-hand knowledge and insights into the APA's history, policies, and politics – and his familiarity with a wide range of past and current leaders of the association – have been indispensable.

Trudy Bond is a psychologist with a solo psychotherapy practice in Ohio. Driven by a keen and longstanding no-nonsense approach to social justice activism, she didn't hesitate to file ethics complaints with the APA and with state licensing boards when she became aware of the reports of suspect activities involving psychologists at Guantanamo Bay. Although more accustomed to working independently, when Trudy joined the Coalition she brought an intensity and fearlessness that served our group very well.

Yosef Brody became a member of the Coalition in more recent years. A resident of Brooklyn, New York, after spending the better part of a decade living in Paris, France, Yosef is a staff psychologist at the United Nations Secretariat where he provides various clinical services for the organization and its staff members around the world. He has brought to the Coalition a heightened awareness of international issues related to our work.

Finally, throughout much of the Coalition's history, human rights investigator Nathaniel Raymond – a former director of the anti-torture campaign at Physicians for Human Rights – also provided close, expert guidance and inspiration. Later, Sarah Dougherty, a senior anti-torture fellow at Physicians for Human Rights with a background in law and public health, also became a dedicated contributor.

As for me, I joined the Coalition after serving as president of Psychologists for Social Responsibility. Before establishing an independent consulting practice, for much of the prior decade I was the executive director of the Solomon Asch Center for Study of Ethnopolitical Conflict at the University of Pennsylvania. As a Coalition member, my responsibilities have included conducting research, taking a lead role in drafting statements, and maintaining our website, which includes numerous resources related to the Coalition's work and to other issues of human rights and psychological ethics.

Despite our name, the Coalition has always been a small, tight-knit, invitation-only group of activists. Although from the outset we've been a very low-budget operation, the combination of dedication to a shared cause, intensive and extensive research, unflinching, carefully documented writing, and the refusal to be silenced in publicly confronting what we saw as the APA's failures made the Coalition a surprisingly significant and effective force.[1] Our thorn-in-the-side efforts became all the more uncomfortable for the APA's leadership as we found support from like-minded, resolute dissident psychologists, human rights organizations, and partner groups like Psychologists for Social Responsibility and Psychologists for an Ethical APA.

Psychologists for an Ethical APA, with a substantially larger and more loosely defined membership than the Coalition, was an especially important allied group that formed during this post-PENS period. Dan Aalbers, Ghislaine Boulanger, Martha Davis, Diane Ehrensaft, Ruth Fallenbaum, Ryan Hunt, Brad Olson, and Frank Summers comprised the original steering committee.[2] Some of the organization's crucial campaigns are described in this and later chapters. In addition, it should be emphasized that the writing and advocacy work of many other psychologists and human rights advocates were also an essential part of this broader network's successes. I regret that a list of names would be impractical here.

Collectively, our volunteer efforts, spanning years, involved daily engagement on the pressing issues at hand. Dozens of official statements were issued by the Coalition. Concerned psychologists and allies published hundreds of articles and reports online and in print. There were countless email exchanges and phone calls to develop and move collaborative projects forward. Less frequently, face-to-face strategy meetings were held at the APA's annual conventions, where public protests were sometimes planned and executed. And over the years, several dedicated activists were elected to the APA's Council of Representatives, which enabled them to push for change from the inside. Although I am hardly a disinterested observer on this point, I believe there's little indication that the APA would have faced or corrected what were arguably egregious failures but for the activism and organizing promoted by those who've come to be known as "the dissidents."

In this context, a recent qualitative analysis by Susan Opotow, who has held numerous leadership positions within the APA over her distinguished career, identifies "(a) abuse of power, (b) promulgation of misinformation, (c) covert collaborations, (d) insufficient oversight by APA officials, and (e) silencing/ignoring members' ethical concerns and complaints" as key organizational processes that contributed to the subversion of the APA's ethical commitments.[3] She considers the last of these five to be the most important, observing that, "had members' concerns been heard respectfully and taken seriously rather than rebuffed in the early 2000s, the ethical and human rights tragedies that unfolded at micro-, meso-, and macro-levels over the next decade could have been avoided."[4]

Indeed, there were many confrontations during this period between dissidents and the APA's leadership. In this chapter, I describe six examples in greater detail. In each case, dissident demands for stronger do-no-harm policies and for investigations into psychologists' wrongdoing and into the APA itself were met with stubborn resistance. I'll look closely at the defeat of a moratorium resolution, the adoption of a loophole-filled anti-torture resolution, the apparent failure to enforce a membership referendum vote that required removal of psychologists from Guantanamo, the Ethics Committee's delay in modifying Ethical Standard 1.02, the Coalition-led campaign to annul the PENS Report, and the APA's decision not to pursue sanctions against Guantanamo psychologist John Leso (who has denied all wrongdoing). Taken together, they capture the lengths to which the association's leadership was willing to go in order to preserve a seemingly ethically deficient status quo.

THE MORATORIUM DEFEAT

With anti-torture protesters wearing orange jumpsuits outside the Moscone Center, the APA's 2007 annual meeting in San Francisco demonstrated just how hard some of the association's leaders would fight for the policy preferences of the military-intelligence establishment. Sometimes that support seemed deceptively disguised, while at other times this top priority was visible for all to see. The most consequential measure considered by the APA's Council of Representatives that weekend was a proposal calling for a moratorium on psychologist involvement in interrogations at US detention centers for foreign detainees. It represented a direct threat to the APA's ongoing support for the Bush Administration's war-on-terror operations.

The moratorium initiative was spearheaded by Neil Altman of the APA's Division 39 (Psychoanalysis), with support from dissident psychologists, the Society for the Psychological Study of Social Issues (Division 9), the Society for the Study of Peace, Conflict, and Violence (Division 48), and other groups within the association.[5] With the passage of the Military

Commissions Act of 2006, the US government had created a broad definition of "unlawful enemy combatants" – a category of prisoners for whom
the fundamental human rights protections of the Geneva Conventions did
not necessarily apply. The same act also provided retroactive immunity for
government officials involved in prisoner torture and abuse, while authorizing the president to determine whether specific detention conditions and
interrogation techniques – including those which transgressed both international standards and the APA's own anti-torture stance – could lawfully
be used.[6]

The core argument in favor of the moratorium, then, was that there were
disturbing discrepancies between the profession's fundamental ethical
obligations and what US law permitted. The divergences simultaneously
endangered detainees and placed psychologists in the untenable position
of being expected to participate in activities that violated their professional
ethics and the APA's avowed commitment – as an accredited non-
governmental organization at the United Nations – to the lofty principles
of the Universal Declaration of Human Rights.[7]

Nevertheless, after a tightly controlled period of debate, council members voted overwhelmingly *against* the moratorium proposal, siding
with the Ethics Committee, other APA governance groups, and the military psychologists who opposed it. This was seemingly the outcome that
Ethics Office director Stephen Behnke and other APA insiders had hoped
to achieve. For months prior to the vote, via email Behnke had consulted
with former PENS Task Force member Morgan Banks and other military
operational psychologists in an apparent effort to strategize about how to
discourage support for the proposal. On one occasion, Banks made it clear
that any APA stance restricting psychologists from working at Guantanamo
would "be more than a killer" and "have very negative repercussions."[8]
Meanwhile, during this period Behnke also offered and wrote drafts of letters for others to sign and disseminate as their own, expressing concerns
about the proposed moratorium and related dissident initiatives.[9]

APA leaders had also made arrangements for former PENS Task Force
member Larry James to travel from Guantanamo to speak to council members on the day of the vote. They likely knew what they'd be getting. Six
months earlier, as a representative of the APA's Divisions for Social Justice,
Coalition member Brad Olson was among the invited attendees at the

February 2007 association meetings in Washington, DC.[10] According to Olson, at one session then past president Gerald Koocher claimed that no psychologist alleged to have been involved in detainee abuse had ever been identified by name. Olson responded matter-of-factly: "We *have* given a name: John Leso." At that point, James rose from his chair and, in his own words, "threatened to shut his mouth for him if he didn't do it himself." James apparently felt good about what he'd done, later writing, "I'm told it was the most excitement at an APA meeting in about twenty years."[11]

So, arriving from Guantanamo and dressed in his military uniform for the August council meeting, it probably wasn't a surprise when James assured the assembled representatives that no military psychologist would ever support "inhumane treatment." He concluded his brief speech with a more provocative claim: "When you don't have psychologists involved in policy decision-makings, when you don't have psychologists involved in the day-to-day activities, bad things are going to happen. Innocent people are going to die."[12] Responding to this claim, council member Laurie Wagner observed, "If psychologists have to be there in order to keep detainees from being killed … those conditions are so horrendous that the only moral and ethical thing to do is to protest it by leaving it."[13] As one indication that this dispute was much more than merely an internecine battle among psychologists, the editorial staff of the *Houston Chronicle* wrote, "Any interrogation system that teeters so close to atrocities needs more than a psychologist."[14]

Unbeknownst to most who heard James's dire forecast, he would retire shortly after the convention and soon publish a self-congratulatory memoir.[15] His book revealed that he likely was rather prone to exaggeration and outrageous statements. As noted in the preceding chapter, he described the International Committee of the Red Cross (ICRC) as "a bunch of radical left do-gooders" and three captured Afghan juveniles as "flat-out dumber than a bag of rocks."[16] He also described a female soldier in Iraq as a "short, fat, seriously ugly young lady" and psychologists whose views differed from his own as "clowns [who] have never sat in a room and looked in the whites of a terrorist's eyes."[17] Several years later, Mark Fallon, a former director of the Pentagon's Criminal Investigation Task Force at Guantanamo, wrote that in his opinion James "viewed Gitmo as a career opportunity to psychologically exploit detained prisoners" and "became personally involved in the spread of, and medical justification for, torture."[18]

A LOOPHOLE-FILLED RESOLUTION

At the same 2007 convention, the APA's Council of Representatives did approve a much weaker resolution that reaffirmed the association's opposition to torture and other cruel, inhuman, or degrading treatment or punishment.[19] The resolution was a modest step forward because, unlike the 2005 PENS Report, it identified specific techniques that were deemed out-of-bounds for psychologists. But the text apparently had been primarily crafted by Behnke – in covert consultation with military operational psychologists.[20] The resolution wasn't as restrictive as it likely appeared to council members, who were given little opportunity to thoroughly weigh its merits and drawbacks before the vote. In fact, as the Coalition and others noted, the resolution suffered from some serious shortcomings.[21]

Foremost, prohibiting the worst abuses didn't come close to outlawing *all* abuses. By focusing on condemnation of torture or cruel, inhuman, or degrading treatment, the resolution seemingly left the door open for psychologists to participate in a wide range of coercive tactics that fell short of this extreme threshold. In other words, "do no grievous harm" was substituted for the profession's fundamental do-no-harm principle. Additionally, because the APA's Ethics Code still included Standard 1.02's just-following-orders defense, psychologists remained potentially unaccountable for their wrongdoing. None of these worrisome realities was addressed by the tepid resolution.

There were other loopholes as well. For example, the resolution called for an "absolute prohibition" against psychologist involvement in certain abuses such as waterboarding. But other abusive techniques – "hooding, forced nakedness, stress positions, the use of dogs to threaten or intimidate, physical isolation, sensory deprivation and over-stimulation and/or sleep deprivation" – were only banned *conditionally*. On the positive side, they were prohibited "for the purposes of eliciting information in an interrogation process" and "in a manner that represents significant pain or suffering or in a manner that a reasonable person would judge to cause lasting harm."[22]

But on the negative side, the text as written meant that psychologists were permitted to use these techniques to "soften up" or "break" a detainee *before* his interrogation session began – they just couldn't employ them as part of the interrogation itself. This distinction was important, and it aligned with how abuses like sleep deprivation had already been employed at Guantanamo. The infamous "frequent flyer program" at the detention facility, for instance, involved repeatedly transferring a prisoner from one cell to another throughout the night in order to disrupt his sleep and reduce his resistance to questioning by interrogators the next day.[23] In sum, then, this anti-torture resolution arguably ensured that psychologists could continue to be involved in abusive practices. In response to sustained objections from the Coalition and other dissidents, the resolution text was amended the following year to address some of these issues.[24]

Later that day, after the two council votes, hundreds of convention attendees gathered for a contentious town hall meeting.[25] Many were outraged by the APA's ongoing failure to take more forceful action. Among the dissident psychologists who took to the microphone, Dan Aalbers warned that "the moral issue of our time has landed at our doorstep," and with the rejection of the moratorium resolution, "we will find that we have secured the best cabin on the Titanic." Coalition member Steven Reisner questioned whether it made ethical sense to remain a member of the APA. Ruth Fallenbaum called for "some house-cleaning" at the APA and said she was appalled by the Ethics Committee that had "given such poor consultation to this organization and then led us into this abyss of shame."[26]

Michael Wessells, who had resigned from the 2005 PENS Task Force after the report was issued, reminded everyone that "tyrants of the world get their warrant to torture ... by saying national law trumps international and human rights standards." He then asked, "What is the Association going to actively do to stop fiddling around with relatively minor resolutions when it's not even on the path of actively supporting international and human rights standards in everything that it does?" Nathaniel Raymond, from Physicians for Human Rights, echoed these concerns, emphasizing, "We're not talking about bad apples ... We're talking about a government which since after September 11th has created a systematic regime of psychological torture with the assistance of mental health professionals and mental health expertise."[27]

Shortly after the town hall meeting began, a representative from the APA's Public Affairs Office – citing a ten-minute-maximum filming rule of unknown origin – threatened to call security if Amy Goodman and her team from *Democracy Now!* failed to turn off their cameras. The crowd's incensed reaction led to a quick policy change that allowed the press coverage to continue. Predictably, before the gathering concluded, APA insiders presented the council meeting as an underappreciated success story. One of the few members of the board who attended the town hall emphasized that diverse constituencies had contributed to the approved resolution. Stephen Behnke told those assembled, "I can say on behalf of the Association we can all agree it is a step in the right direction." But it also could have been described as protecting the status quo while deceptively appearing to support urgently needed change.[28]

Dissident psychologists and other human rights advocates were not fooled. Renowned psychologist Mary Pipher, bestselling author of *Reviving Ophelia*, responded to the convention's events by returning the APA Presidential Citation award she had received a year earlier. In an open letter she wrote, "I do not want an award from an organization that sanctions its members' participation in the enhanced interrogations at CIA black sites and at Guantanamo ... The presence of psychologists has both educated the interrogation teams in more skillful methods of breaking people down and legitimized the process of torture in defiance of the Geneva Conventions."[29] Quoted in the widely circulated *Chronicle on Higher Education*, Michael Wessells summed it up this way: "I think psychology has allowed itself to be manipulated as a political tool for purposes that are really quite evil."[30]

THE 2008 MEMBER-INITIATED REFERENDUM

While the moratorium resolution's defeat in 2007 was a painful setback for dissidents, it was presumably satisfying to APA leaders and military psychologists who had gone to considerable lengths to ensure its failure. Despite the moral depravity that characterized US war-on-terror detention and interrogation operations, a policy change that would remove psychologists from these activities was apparently a bridge too far for those who ran the APA. But the dissidents hadn't given up and they hadn't run out of ideas. The following year, Dan Aalbers, Ruth Fallenbaum, Brad Olson, and Ghislaine Boulanger of Psychologists for an Ethical APA hit upon a novel strategy: reaching out directly to the APA's general membership with a petition resolution that would bypass a council vote and thereby make leadership support unnecessary.

The core text of this resolution was simple: "Psychologists may not work in settings where persons are held outside of, or in violation of, either International Law ... or the US Constitution (where appropriate), unless they are working directly for the persons being detained or for an independent third party working to protect human rights."[31] And the petition's rationale was well-founded: torture and other forms of detainee mistreatment are abhorrent; the United Nations (UN) and human rights organizations have determined that these abuses are taking place at Guantanamo Bay; and psychologists have been involved in their design and implementation.

Behnke and other APA officials may have been caught off-guard by the unique membership-wide petition but they moved quickly in constructing obstacles to its success. They started by disseminating statements suggesting that the resolution would have consequences extending well beyond national security detention sites and would threaten the livelihoods of psychologists working in domestic settings. Even though the petition made it clear that such concerns were unwarranted, Behnke warned that it had "a hugely broad scope – it could be applied to state or federal jails and prisons, psychiatric hospitals, juvenile detention centers, potentially even therapeutic camps for troubled children and adolescents."[32] Similarly, he drafted listserv posts for other APA leaders. One written for board member Melba Vasquez, a future president of the association, stated in part, "This petition would seriously impede psychologists' efforts to ensure that interrogations are conducted in a safe and ethical manner ... It seems to me that the way to ensure bad things will happen is to remove good people."[33]

The APA's leadership also decided that "pro" and "con" statements would be included with the ballots mailed to the membership. Based on past history in similar situations, they had good reason to think that this ploy would sink the petition because the "con" statement would likely raise concerns in members' minds and encourage them to maintain the status quo.[34] Behnke made a point of downplaying his own role in crafting the "con" text, telling those who were identified as its authors, "It's Ethics Office policy to provide feedback on ethics-related matters to anyone who asks, as you have done, and we are happy to be a resource for APA members. Of course, the statement is entirely yours and *should be presented as such*" (emphasis added).[35]

APA senior staff who opposed the resolution took further steps to secure a soft landing if the vote somehow went against them. They made the determination that any prohibitions emerging from a successful referendum would *not* be tied to the APA's Ethics Code – which would make it unenforceable and toothless. In an email to the Board of Directors, Nathalie Gilfoyle, the association's general counsel, wrote that "the proposed new policy does not mention the word 'ethics' and does not suggest that there are any consequences of not following the policy."[36] It's important to recognize that, even if this was a legitimate interpretation, the Ethics Office could have planned to respond to passage of the referendum by moving to amend the Ethics Code to reflect the significant change in APA policy. That's what one might reasonably expect the organization to do if it took the will of the membership seriously and intended that its ethics rules align with its policies.

Ironically, in light of their efforts to address all possible contingencies, APA leaders couldn't control what transpired in a Guantanamo court-room in August 2008, only a month before the referendum voting period was scheduled to end. Behavioral Science Consultation Team (BSCT) op-erational psychologist Diane Zierhoffer refused to testify about her pur-ported role in the abusive treatment of young detainee Mohammed Jawad – on the grounds that she might incriminate herself.[37] As described earlier, Zierhoffer had allegedly advised interrogators on how to break Jawad, and he later attempted suicide in his cell.[38]

Disconcerted and perhaps embarrassed by these unanticipated develop-ments at the military hearing, the APA's Public Affairs Office quickly issued a press release. It stated, in part, that "no psychologist – APA member or not – should be directly or indirectly involved in any form of detention or interrogation that could lead to psychological or physical harm to a detainee."[39] That message is readily seen as a perhaps cynical attempt at face-saving, given that prisoners at Guantanamo were being harmed *every day* by the facility's oppressive standard operating procedures – and the APA's leaders presumably knew this.

The APA leadership's growing worry about the dissident community and the referendum vote became visible in an entirely different way that same month at the association's annual convention in Boston. At one point during the weekend, several Coalition members had gathered around a table at the convention center, quietly discussing psychologists' involve-ment in national security interrogations with French documentarian

Marie-Monique Robin and her film crew. Shortly after the private interview began, a woman reportedly drew up a chair nearby.

As the discussion unfolded, Bryant Welch noticed that the woman had a miniature black digital recorder on her lap, barely distinguishable against her black slacks. According to his recollection, when he confronted her, she told him that it was her job "to listen to what APA members were saying." Her name tag revealed that she was Kim Mills, the APA's associate executive director of public and member communications at that time (she is now a communications senior advisor for the association). Mills remained for the entire interview, apparently asserting her right to record conversations in public spaces at the APA convention. Later that day, she could be seen wandering, with her mini-recorder in hand, among the hundreds who were attending a dissident protest outside the convention hall. In an email exchange with Jean Maria Arrigo a couple of weeks later, filmmaker Marie-Monique Robin commented that the experience was reminiscent of her time as a journalist in the former Soviet Union. Coalition complaints to the APA's CEO were never satisfactorily answered.[40]

A month later, the APA leadership's concerns proved to be well-founded, and the unenforceability loophole built into the membership-wide referendum became a crucial escape hatch for them. Following weeks of outreach and advocacy by the informal network of dissident psychologists, the referendum confounded expectations and was overwhelmingly approved in September 2008 by 59 percent of the members who cast votes.[41] But when an advisory group, comprised of more opponents than supporters, was brought together in November to decide exactly how the referendum would be implemented, APA leaders still had one more card to play.

The new policy was given the name "Psychologists and Unlawful Detention Settings with a Focus on National Security."[42] The word "unlawful" was the key. As Behnke explained in an email to Ellen Garrison, the APA's senior policy advisor, military psychologists would be able to dismiss the resolution as inapplicable to their situation. Pentagon officials could simply assure them that Guantanamo – or wherever else they were stationed – was in compliance with the Geneva Conventions and the UN Convention Against Torture, and therefore wasn't an "unlawful" setting.[43] The *actual* circumstances at these facilities wouldn't matter.

If any military operational psychologists were still worried, Garrison reassured them in a February 2009 email to the director of Guantanamo's BSCT psychologists. She wrote, "What is also significant here is that the petition resolution itself does not amend the Ethics Code, nor is it enforceable in any other way ... I hope the information that I have provided here helps to allay your concerns. Please feel free to circulate this note to others who might be interested in its contents as well."[44] The message was simple: they'd be able to continue their engagement in detention and interrogation operations with little fear of sanction from the APA.

Thereafter, the new referendum policy was seemingly ignored by both the APA and the Defense Department. The association did send letters to President Obama and other government officials alerting them to the policy change, as was mandated by the referendum. But Department of Defense documents make it clear that they knew not to care. For instance, a Pentagon directive issued in 2012 – three years later – continued to assign specific roles to BSCT operational psychologists, including making "psychological assessments of the character, personality, social interactions, and other behavioral characteristics of interrogation subjects."[45] Similarly, a May 2014 online posting from the military's Joint Task Force at Guantanamo described how psychologists working there "provide consultative services to support authorized law detention and intelligence activities."[46] I could find no evidence that APA leaders objected to these apparent violations of the membership referendum resolution.

In short, having failed to block the referendum policy's official adoption, the APA arguably accomplished the same result by acting as though it didn't really matter. Indeed, in 2011 – two years *after* the policy went into effect – the APA published a book titled *Ethical Practice in Operational Psychology: Military and National Intelligence Applications*. A chapter by several operational psychologists, including Debra Dunivin and Morgan Banks, explicitly described the roles of BSCT psychologists – roles that were seemingly prohibited by the referendum vote. Psychologists were even able to obtain continuing education credits from the APA – in ethics, no less – for reading the book.[47] In my view, nothing better sums up the lack of seriousness with which APA leaders regarded the membership-wide referendum vote.

ADDING HUMAN RIGHTS TO THE
ENFORCEABLE ETHICS CODE

The unwillingness of APA leaders to cross the military-intelligence establishment appeared to be a consistent pattern throughout these years. Time and again, it seemed that the senior leadership would trumpet the association's commitment to psychology's do-no-harm ethics but then retreat when those principled words required actions that ran counter to the government's own detention and interrogation preferences. Yet another example was what looked to be foot-dragging following the council's call in August 2005 for the Ethics Committee to "move forward as expeditiously as reasonably possible" in considering the addition of the words "in keeping with basic principles of human rights" to Ethical Standard 1.02.[48]

Recall that it was only one month earlier, in July 2005, that the APA's Board of Directors resorted to an emergency vote in order to approve the PENS Report – without any input from council members. In fact, despite representations to the contrary, the Council of Representatives never officially accepted, endorsed, or approved that report.[49] And as it turned out, whereas the PENS Task Force concluded that "the Ethics Code is fundamentally sound in addressing the ethical dilemmas that arise in the context of national security-related work," council members weren't so sure – especially in light of the credible reports linking psychologists to the ill-treatment of detainees. The language change that the council sought to Ethical Standard 1.02 would serve to eliminate the Nuremberg defense loophole and make it unethical for psychologists to obey orders that involved disregard for the human rights of detainees, thereby offering greater protection to war-on-terror prisoners who might otherwise be subjected to harsh detention and interrogation tactics.[50]

But it seems that, over many years, the APA had moved increasingly toward a self-protective guild orientation in which the welfare of psychologists became more important than the well-being of clients or those who were the targets of the psychologists' interventions.[51] This troubling prioritization appeared most evident in matters that involved the Department of Defense and related national security agencies. So, it was hardly surprising that some senior leaders at the APA were slow to add this human rights language to the Ethics Code. For over three years, the Ethics

Committee failed to respond substantively to the council's 2005 charge. The ongoing intransigence prompted Ken Pope, a former chair of the APA's Ethics Committee, to resign from the APA. In his letter to the Council of Representatives, Pope wrote that the APA had moved "so far away from its ethical foundation, historic traditions, and basic values, and from my own personal and professional view of our responsibilities, that I cannot support them with my membership."[52]

During this period, Psychologists for an Ethical APA continued to be a significant force in efforts to reform the association. One 2006 initiative of the dissident group encouraged APA members to withhold their membership dues until the association took stronger action to oppose psychologist involvement in detainee abuse and torture.[53] At that time, the APA's bylaws allowed members to postpone dues payments for two years (during which time they would not receive certain membership benefits) before they'd be deemed to have resigned from the organization. Although the number of APA members who followed this course of action is uncertain, hundreds of psychologists joined the group's "Withhold APA Dues" listserv. Other members, like Ken Pope, resigned their memberships outright (I did so in 2010).

When the Ethics Committee finally sought online comments in late 2008 regarding the desirability of adding "in keeping with basic principles of human rights" to Ethical Standard 1.02, some military operational psychologists presented a united opposition. Behnke had sent an email specifically requesting that they contribute in this way.[54] Morgan Banks wrote that military personnel were already required to "uphold human rights, as defined by the US Constitution," and that "we, as psychologists and military officers, must maintain the ability to do the right thing, legally, ethically, and morally, without fear of sanction by our professional organization." Debra Dunivin warned that "the proposed change would create an impermissibly vague ethical standard that would require psychologists in certain circumstances to violate law." Larry James expressed the view that the ethics code already provided sufficient guidance to the membership. Carroll Greene wrote, "Providing an ambiguous and frequently debated set of international guidelines – as the base by which American psychologists could be censured or prosecuted is an unwise move." And Pennie Hoofman expressed the concern that "subjectively enforcing a standard that is not well defined could lead to accusations based on self-serving interests."[55]

While the phrase "in keeping with basic principles of human rights" may have lacked some precision or specification, it is perhaps telling that the proposed language was seen as such a threat to and by psychologists involved in detention and interrogation operations at Guantanamo and elsewhere. Seeming to share this worry, the Ethics Committee finally brought forward a recommendation in 2009, one that was presumably welcomed by the Pentagon and CIA: namely, "in keeping with basic principles of human rights" should *not* be added to Ethical Standard 1.02 of the Ethics Code.[56]

But in a perhaps rare rebuke and display of independence, the APA's Council of Representatives insisted that this do-nothing option was unacceptable. The Ethics Committee therefore returned a few months later with revised language for 1.02. The revision removed one key sentence – "If the conflict is unresolvable via such means, psychologists may adhere to the requirements of the law, regulations, or other governing legal authority" – and added another instead: "Under no circumstances may this standard be used to justify or defend violating human rights."[57] These changes eliminated the possibility of future Nuremberg defense arguments. Council members overwhelmingly approved the revision in February 2010, *five years* after first calling upon the Ethics Committee to revisit 1.02 – and a full year after Barack Obama had become US president. During his first week in office, the new commander-in-chief had issued executive orders to ban "enhanced interrogation techniques" and to shut down Guantanamo. (The latter still hasn't happened.)

THE COALITION'S PENS ANNULMENT CAMPAIGN

The following year, in September 2011, on behalf of the Coalition for an Ethical Psychology, I spearheaded a petition effort calling for annulment of the PENS Report.[58] Since 2005, the report had continued to be an influential policy document for the APA and for the national security establishment – despite the many serious problems associated with it. As described in detail in the preceding chapter, the report seemingly gave primacy to US law and military regulations over international law and professional ethics. Of equal concern, in my judgment, the report was produced through processes that were inconsistent with APA's own standard practices, failing to meet norms for transparency, independence, and deliberation.

From the perspective of the Coalition and other dissidents, annulment was a crucial step. It was essential not only to repair some of the damage the PENS Report had caused, but also to demonstrate that the APA was willing to acknowledge responsibility for the misguided actions involved in its development and implementation. Annulment was also necessary to set the stage for a long-overdue open, broad-based, and independent examination – by psychologists, by human rights advocates, by national security experts, and by ethicists – of whether or not it is actually ethical for psychologists to participate in harsh detention and interrogation operations and other similar activities in national security settings. Even in the absence of torture or cruel, inhuman, or degrading treatment, do these roles violate fundamental do-no-harm principles when they involve coercion, deception, manipulation, humiliation, or other non-beneficent actions? This fundamental question had never really been addressed by the APA because the PENS Report, in offering the appearance of meaningful discussion and debate, gave the impression that the matter had been legitimately and decisively resolved.

The Coalition's petition calling for PENS annulment received considerable and diverse support. Over just a few months, it garnered endorsements from dozens of national organizations – the American Civil Liberties Union, Physicians for Human Rights, the Center for Constitutional Rights, the National Lawyers Guild, the National Religious Campaign Against Torture, and Veterans for Peace, among others – as well as several divisions within the APA itself.[59] Moreover, nearly 2,500 individuals signed the petition. These signers included two civilian members of the PENS Task Force, then current and past presidents of APA divisions, psychologists who worked with torture survivors, and psychologists who had spent their careers working with veterans at VA hospitals. Recognition of the need for PENS annulment also extended well beyond the profession of psychology alone. Among the petition signers were psychiatrists such as Robert Jay Lifton (author of *The Nazi Doctors*) and Stephen Xenakis (retired brigadier general, US Army), scholar-activists such as Daniel Ellsberg and Noam Chomsky, attorneys who had represented Guantanamo detainees, former members of the military and intelligence community, and members of the general public.

Of course, not everyone welcomed our call for annulment. The most common response from the leaders of most APA divisions was no response at all – they simply never replied to the endorsement requests that they received from me via email. But with Division 42 – Psychologists in Independent Practice – it was an entirely different matter. On behalf of the division's board, President Jeffrey Younggren responded with an open letter in which he emphasized that Division 42 would "vehemently oppose" any effort to annul the PENS Report. And he went considerably further, accusing us of "giving false and biased information," of harming the independent practices of his division's members, and of "damaging the entire field of psychology." Although his letter refuted none of our core claims about the PENS process, it concluded with a call for the APA "to maintain a vigorous response" to any future public criticisms from the Coalition.[60] Undeterred, we thanked the Division 42 Board of Directors for their engagement and assured them that the Coalition would "continue its efforts to bring wider recognition among fellow psychologists, national leaders, and the general public to the urgent need to examine psychological ethics in national security settings."[61]

As with previous reform efforts, the APA's leadership stepped in once it became clear that the Coalition's annulment campaign was gaining momentum. In February 2012, six months after the petition was launched, the association's board assisted five APA members in creating a "task force" that described its purpose this way: "To replace the PENS report and related Council resolutions focused on torture, ethics, detainee welfare, and interrogation with a unified, comprehensive APA policy document to offer clear guidance for psychologists in national security settings."[62] The group identified itself as a "grassroots" and "member-initiated" effort, but revealingly one of the listed contacts was the APA's own senior policy advisor, Ellen Garrison.

At least three of the five "task force" members had expressed reservations about the 2008 membership referendum prohibiting psychologists from working at Guantanamo and other unlawful sites. One of them, William Strickland, was the president of Human Resources Research Organization (HumRRO), a company that had apparently received millions of dollars in military contracts over the preceding decade. In 2010, former Guantanamo psychologist and PENS Task Force member Larry James had thanked Strickland for his "hard fight on the floor of the Council of Representatives over the petition resolution and changes to the APA Ethics code."[63]

Of particular note, in announcing its formation this "task force" credited the Coalition's annulment petition, thereby giving the appearance of sharing a common cause. But when it came to the PENS Report, this was far from true. The Coalition and other dissidents sought the repudiation of PENS. In sharp contrast, this group, with support from the APA's board, asserted that "the PENS report offers unique contributions to APA policy" and emphasized that its own work – unlike PENS annulment – would *not* involve any changes to current APA policy.[64] Their intention was simply to reproduce key elements of the PENS Report – including the controversial presumption that psychologists could ethically participate in national security detention and interrogation operations – in a larger, "unified" policy document. In this way, "replacing" the report seemingly meant enshrining several of its core tenets within a different document under a different name. At the time, I compared this to the way the Patagonian toothfish was renamed Chilean sea bass in an effort to improve sales.[65]

For all of these reasons, the Coalition continued collecting organizational and individual signatures for its annulment petition. Other related Coalition actions during this period included rejecting an invitation to consult with the "task force," sending an open letter to APA leaders with a draft PENS annulment resolution for their consideration, and raising concerns about the February 2013 draft "comprehensive document" in an open letter to board and council members.[66] When the Council of Representatives met in August 2013, they approved a revised version of a report titled "Policy Related to Psychologists' Work in National Security Settings and Reaffirmation of the APA Position Against Torture and Other Cruel, Inhuman, or Degrading Treatment or Punishment."[67]

At the same meeting, council members also voted to rescind – but not to repudiate – the PENS Report. This was only a partial victory for dissidents because there was no acknowledgment that the report was deeply flawed and that the process that led to it needed careful re-examination to prevent any reoccurrence in the future. Instead, giving no hint that anything had ever been amiss, the only explanation offered for the rescission was that "these policies had become outdated or rendered inaccurate with the passage of subsequent policies."[68]

THE ETHICS COMPLAINTS AGAINST JOHN LESO

All of the examples I've offered thus far in this chapter have highlighted the APA's stubborn resistance to holding psychologists accountable for involvement in war-on-terror abuses. This reality becomes even more obvious when we consider how the Ethics Office handled complaints filed by Alice Shaw in 2006 and by Trudy Bond in 2007 against Guantanamo military psychologist John Leso for his alleged unethical actions (which he has denied). These complaints were likely very unwelcome, given that APA leaders had repeatedly insisted that there was no evidence any member had ever been involved in prisoner mistreatment. Rather, their recurrent claim was that psychologists helped to prevent harm to the detainees. With Behnke at the helm, for over six years the Ethics Office failed to take decisive action on the allegations against Leso. Then, in 2013, the complaint was dismissed outright – apparently without a full Ethics Committee review having ever been conducted. The saga is instructive.[69]

As described earlier, according to the US Senate Armed Services Committee's 2008 report on detainee treatment, Leso and fellow BSCT team member psychiatrist Paul Burney were co-authors of a "Counter-Resistance Strategies Memorandum" in October 2002.[70] The memo recommended physically and psychologically abusive detention and interrogation tactics. The most extreme included daily twenty-hour interrogations, isolation without visitation from doctors or the ICRC, the use of scenarios designed to convince the detainee he might die, forced nudity, and exposure to shivering temperatures.

The same memo also offered recommendations for how detainees should be treated in their cells. It proposed that "resistant detainees might be limited to four hours of sleep a day; that they be deprived of comfort items such as sheets, blankets, mattresses, washcloths; and that interrogators control access to all detainees' Korans." It described "using fans and generators to create white noise as a form of psychological pressure" and suggested that "all aspects of the [detention] environment should enhance capture shock, dislocate expectations, foster dependence, and support exploitation to the fullest extent possible."[71]

Some of the proposed techniques – including those that were subsequently used in the torturous interrogation of Mohammed al-Qahtani while a BSCT member was present – appear to constitute, at the very least, cruel, inhuman, and degrading treatment.[72] As a reminder, the intentional infliction of severe psychological pain and suffering is a grave breach of the Geneva Conventions, the United Nations Convention against Torture, and other norms of customary international law.[73] Leso's alleged conduct while at Guantanamo also bears upon four other enforceable ethical standards that apply to psychologists' work more broadly: not harming those with whom they work; not exploiting people over whom they have authority; not harassing or demeaning people with whom they interact; and not providing services beyond the boundaries of their competence.

A "preponderance of the evidence" is the standard that the APA's Ethics Office uses when adjudicating a complaint. That's a relatively low threshold, requiring only that it be more likely than not that *at least one* ethical violation has occurred. By comparison, "clear and convincing evidence" and "beyond a reasonable doubt" are substantially higher thresholds. If this preponderance standard is deemed to have been met by the Ethics Office director and by the Ethics Committee chair, then a formal case is opened for investigation and for review by the full Ethics Committee. And yet a formal case was never opened against Leso.

In late 2012, in a lengthy letter to the committee's chair, Lindsay Childress-Beatty – then the director of adjudication within the APA's Ethics Office – explained that she favored closing the complaint. Referencing some of the techniques that had been proposed by Leso (and Burney), Childress-Beatty wrote that sleep deprivation, withholding of food, and isolation "may not be cruel, unusual, inhuman, degrading treatment or torture depending upon factors such as the situational context, length of time used, and intensity."[74] But she did not explain how it might be ethical for a psychologist to support abusive treatment as long as it fell short of this extreme threshold. A year later, in a December 2013 letter, the Ethics Office notified Trudy Bond that, "on the basis of a careful and thorough review of the record ... we have determined that we cannot proceed with formal charges in this matter. Consequently, the complaint against Leso has been closed."[75]

After the fact, attempts by the APA leadership to justify this decision appeared to be a hodgepodge of illogic, misdirection, and obfuscation. For example, one argument the Ethics Office offered in Leso's defense was that he was "an early career psychologist."[76] But this is arguably irrelevant. According to the APA's Ethics Code, behaviors deemed unethical for a senior psychologist are similarly impermissible for a junior member of the profession. Likewise, the code doesn't advise that ethical breaches should be disregarded if a psychologist finds himself in a role that he neither trained for nor wanted. So, despite the Ethics Office's suggestion otherwise, it doesn't seem to matter that Leso was "trained as a health care provider" and "did not request to become involved with detainee interrogations."[77]

Another seemingly flawed justification used to close the case was that "the military lacked a standard operating procedure" for the BSCT role when Leso arrived at Guantanamo, and "APA did not issue its first policy on interrogations until three years later."[78] But this purported lack of clarity appears to be illusory. The profession's enforceable standards regarding torture, abuse, exploitation, and other forms of misconduct were long-established, as APA leaders have often emphasized when it has served their purposes to do so.[79] Indeed, as noted earlier, the APA's 2005 PENS Report asserted that "the Ethics Code is fundamentally sound in addressing the ethical dilemmas that arise in the context of national security-related work."[80]

The Ethics Office also noted that Leso faced "pressure from the highest levels of the Bush Administration which strongly supported 'enhanced' interrogation tactics" and that he sought consultation.[81] This is undoubtedly true. But pressures to engage in misconduct don't free a psychologist from following the profession's ethical standards, and prior consultation doesn't relieve a psychologist from ultimate responsibility for his conduct. Potentially mitigating factors only come into play when the full Ethics Committee chooses among various sanctions. There's a world of difference between imposing a lesser sanction on the one hand and simply refusing to find that the conduct in question violated the Ethics Code on the other.

Even when these and other arguments in Leso's defense are stacked one on top of the other, they're rather unconvincing as the basis for the decision not to even open a full case review. Meanwhile, it would seem that there are some troubling possibilities as to why the Ethics Office might have acted as it did. Would sanctioning Leso for ethical misconduct have threatened the APA's carefully cultivated ties with the Department of Defense and the intelligence community? After all, in 2008 then Army surgeon general Eric Schoomaker had sent a letter to the APA's Ethics Office in which he wrote, in part, "On behalf of Dr. Leso, and other Army psychologists similarly situated, I respectfully request that the American Psychological Association determine that the ethical allegations against him are not credible."[82] Or would future career opportunities and research funding for psychologists have been put at risk? Or would the credibility of the APA's key narrative that psychologists were essential in keeping interrogations "safe, legal, ethical, and effective" have been undermined? Considerations like these, of course, shouldn't have mattered in the Leso case. But is it unreasonable to wonder whether they did?

The APA's refusal to sanction John Leso – after six years of delays – wasn't the only unsuccessful outcome that Trudy Bond encountered in pursuing ethics complaints against Guantanamo military psychologists alleged to have been involved in prisoner abuse. Driven by a strong sense of responsibility to these detainees and to her profession, between 2007 and 2010 Bond also filed detailed complaints with the APA Ethics Office against Larry James and with state licensing boards against Leso in New York, James in Louisiana and Ohio, and Diane Zierhoffer in Alabama. The APA Ethics Office closed the complaint against James six months after receiving it – without taking action.[83] In the state cases, the relevant licensing authorities similarly declined to pursue charges. They did so *not* on the basis of conclusions linked to careful scrutiny of the evidence, but rather on procedural grounds such as lack of jurisdiction or lack of standing.[84]

Human rights attorney Deborah Popowski and students from the International Human Rights Clinic at Harvard Law School had provided pro bono assistance to Bond, Colin Bossen, Michael Reese, and Josephine Setzler in their Ohio complaint against James.[85] Popowski later wrote, "The licensing boards, like the APA, stonewalled and refused to bring formal charges, offering opaque, implausible, or seemingly pretextual justifications for their decisions."[86] This intransigence was perhaps captured well by a scheduled face-to-face meeting between the Ohio Board of Psychology and the complainants and their attorneys. Given the opportunity, members of the board reportedly chose not to ask even a single question about the fifty-page complaint.[87] Not long after, a three-sentence letter from the board notified the complainants that "it has been determined that we are unable to proceed to formal action in this matter," adding the assurance that "this matter was carefully considered."[88]

Reflecting back on what she'd initially expected, after learning of the allegations against these psychologists, Bond admitted, "I was so naïve. It seemed obvious to me that there were clear ethical violations and that the APA and state licensing boards would be compelled to take action."[89] But her dedicated efforts weren't for naught. They brought greater awareness to the issue of detainee abuse, they galvanized other dissidents, including her fellow Coalition members, and they helped to make plain an apparent distressing truth: overly sensitive to the winds of political fortune, no governing body responsible for ethical oversight had the courage to go up against the Pentagon and the CIA. In fact, in 2011 the Texas state licensing board dismissed an ethics complaint against psychologist James Mitchell, citing insufficient evidence – even though it was widely reported by that time that he had helped design and implement the CIA's torture program.[90]

THE DISSIDENTS' CHALLENGE

Just weeks after the 9/11 attacks, Norine Johnson, the APA president at that time, had highlighted "the changing psychology agenda in the wake of the terrorist attacks and war."[91] Thereafter, throughout the decade and more that followed, the association's leadership arguably clung to three face-saving claims. First, psychologists had an indispensable and ethical role to play in war-on-terror operations. Second, psychologists were not involved in detainee abuse. Third, criticisms from APA dissidents were unfounded and unfair. In regard to that last claim, in January 2010 the incoming APA president, Carol Goodheart, used her first column in the association's *Monitor on Psychology* to chastise critics of APA's policies on interrogation, among others. Advising that it was time to "turn down the temperature on outrage," she compared those who "strain the collegiality within APA" to the Dementors of Harry Potter fame – frightening cloaked figures who feed on human happiness.[92]

But as the examples in this chapter demonstrate, deference to the military-intelligence establishment had become the APA's calling card. That's why so many key decisions during this period fit the same obstructionist pattern: staunch opposition to the moratorium; formal resolutions with Pentagon-friendly loopholes; tactics that made the membership referendum toothless; prolonged delays in revising the Ethics Code; the refusal to repudiate the PENS Report; and the failure to sanction John Leso or any other psychologist allegedly linked to detainee mistreatment. All of these choices may have reflected the same worry from APA headquarters – that a heightened focus on human rights could imperil carefully nurtured relationships with the US government's national security establishment.

Meanwhile, for those of us who were members of the community of dissident psychologists, the setbacks we faced were always disappointing and difficult to accept. We recognized how high the stakes were, for detainees in US custody and for our profession. But we also knew that the odds of victory were consistently tilted in the APA's favor. We were all volunteers with very limited resources compared to the deep pockets and staffing available to the APA and its mammoth allies, the Department of Defense and the intelligence community. We also lacked the enormous megaphone available to the association's leaders. They had email lists that numbered in the tens of thousands, they could contact the entire APA membership at the touch of a button, and they could generate press releases that would quickly draw the attention of news outlets. By contrast, we struggled to garner the profession's and the public's attention and engagement in our efforts to move the needle when it came to changing what we felt were the APA's ethically bankrupt policies.

At the same time, we realized that our only chance to eventually bring reform and accountability to the APA was to constantly maintain the pressure for change, as best we could. Though it stung and required some emotional regrouping whenever one of our initiatives seemed to prove fruitless, there were often less recognizable benefits. Even when we lost, we learned more about the adversaries arrayed against us, the interrelationships among them, and their standard operating procedures.

It was also our belief that we could fall short of our immediate goals yet still change some minds and open some eyes, and that some people – including some members of the APA's Council of Representatives – could someday become crucial allies. Over time, the stubborn resistance we faced from the APA's leadership, along with their apparent efforts to undermine our credibility, served to strengthen our collective conviction that something significant was truly amiss – and that we might be seeing only the tip of an iceberg that threatened to sink the ethical foundations of our profession.

We believed that the APA's seeming prioritization of expediency over ethics was horribly misguided – and immoral. Given the crucial responsibilities bestowed upon psychologists by the Bush Administration, the government's brutal war-on-terror detention and interrogation operations might never have gained traction if the APA had demonstrated a firmer and more vocal commitment to human rights from the very outset. But rather than upholding the profession's do-no-harm principles, it appeared to us that whenever necessary the association's leaders instead relied on strategic public relations campaigns to deny wrongdoing, malign dissidents, and elevate the work of military psychologists. As for the victims of torture and abuse at Guantanamo, CIA black sites, and elsewhere, the APA had much less to say.

For years after the PENS Report, key leaders of the APA seemed confident that they could withstand whatever evidence suggestive of deception or deceit might arise. In 2014, they finally began to find out that they were wrong.

The Reckoning

PAY ANY PRICE

In the fall of 2014, it appeared that the decade following the 2005 meeting of the Psychological Ethics and National Security (PENS) Task Force would draw to a close without the Coalition for an Ethical Psychology and other dissidents successfully turning the tide within the American Psychological Association (APA). As the preceding chapter has shown, the association's entrenched leadership seemed to grudgingly give ground in some areas while generally holding firm against truly prioritizing do-no-harm principles over the preferences of the military-intelligence establishment. But things changed dramatically that October when Pulitzer Prize–winning investigative reporter James Risen published *Pay Any Price: Greed, Power, and Endless War.*[1]

Risen's book provided a wide-ranging account of moral outrages linked to the US "war on terror." Only a single section of one chapter was about the APA. It was largely a reprise of past allegations about the improper influence of national security interests on the association's ethics policies. But unlike others who had made these claims before him, Risen had a proverbial smoking gun.

Nathaniel Raymond – a Physicians for Human Rights investigator who at times also assisted the Coalition – had apparently alerted Risen to the possibility that there might be illuminating emails on the computer of recently deceased Central Intelligence Agency (CIA) contractor Scott Gerwehr.[2] Risen contacted the family and obtained a cache of hundreds of emails primarily involving Gerwehr and three fellow psychologists:

APA senior staff member Geoffrey Mumford; Kirk Hubbard, who for years worked for the CIA; and Susan Brandon, who had moved to a position at the White House after leaving the APA. The APA never anticipated that these communications would become public.

One particularly revealing email exchange involved Mumford and Hubbard. As described earlier, Hubbard had introduced psychologists Mitchell and Jessen to the CIA as potential contractors for the "enhanced interrogation program." Hubbard had also met multiple times with former APA president Martin Seligman, whose theory of learned helplessness was reportedly a key element in the brutal techniques subsequently employed by these psychologists at CIA black sites.[3] Hubbard himself has written that psychologists who were engaged in national security interrogations "should not be bound by the doctor/patient relationship code of ethics."[4]

In an email to Hubbard and other CIA-linked recipients shortly after the June 2005 meeting of the PENS Task Force, Mumford wrote, "I also wanted to semi-publicly acknowledge your personal contribution … in getting this effort off the ground … Your views were well represented by very carefully selected task force members."[5] At the time he received the message from Mumford, Hubbard had moved on from the CIA and had started a new job – with Mitchell Jessen & Associates. The email's key acknowledgment – that some members of the PENS Task Force presumably had been selected with the preferences of the military-intelligence community in mind – appeared to be a heavy blow to the APA's repeated insistence that everything about the PENS meeting was above board, and that criticism from dissidents was unjustified.

The APA quickly issued a press release in response to the publication of *Pay Any Price*.[6] The organization's leadership accused Risen of "innuendo and one-sided reporting," but they offered no persuasive defense against his most significant claims and the evidence behind them. They insisted that it was "absurd" to suggest that financial considerations played any role in their decisions. They used the label "invitation-only" to justify secret meetings where the names of the national security participants and the topics discussed were never publicly revealed. And they argued that nobody had reason to doubt the association's "long-standing efforts to safeguard against the use of torture." The Coalition responded with a press release of our own. We posed several specific questions for the APA Board of Directors to answer regarding key claims in Risen's book (they never did), and we called for an independent investigation of the APA.[7] In an interview a few days after the APA's press release, Risen described the association's objections as a "non-denial denial."[8]

More accustomed to being challenged by dissidents who lacked Risen's public reach, APA leaders were seemingly caught off guard when outrage over the book's revelations didn't rapidly subside. The executive director of Physicians for Human Rights went so far as to call for the Department of Justice to investigate the allegations.[9] A month later, in November 2014, while still asserting that Risen's claims had been refuted, the APA's Board of Directors hired attorney David Hoffman and his legal team from the Sidley Austin law firm to conduct an independent review.[10] The purpose was to determine whether there was evidence that the APA colluded with the Bush Administration, the CIA, or the Department of Defense in promoting, supporting, or facilitating the abuse and torture of war-on-terror detainees.

The combination of Risen's book and Hoffman's investigation ushered in a new era for the APA. To be sure, not everyone was happy about it. But dissidents realized that this was probably our best chance at bringing to light some disturbing truths and winning over some stubborn opponents of reform.

Adding fuel to the fire before Hoffman's team had hardly even started their work, in early December of 2014 the Senate Intelligence Committee released the 600-page executive summary of its long-awaited report on CIA torture.[11] Based on the review of millions of pages of agency memoranda and other documents, the Senate report reached several damning conclusions. First, the CIA grossly misrepresented its lack of success in obtaining actionable intelligence to prevent future attacks. Second, dozens of prisoners in CIA custody were subjected to torturous and ineffective techniques, including waterboarding and "rectal hydration."[12] Third, former military psychologists James Mitchell and Bruce Jessen – identified by the pseudonyms Grayson Swigert and Hammond Dunbar respectively – designed the CIA's "enhanced interrogation program," were actively involved in the torture of detainees, and owned the firm that was paid tens of millions of dollars for contract work on behalf of the CIA. And fourth, some personnel in the CIA's Office of Medical Services had raised concerns about the effectiveness and safety of these procedures, but those concerns were "regularly overridden by CIA management."[13]

In its own analysis of the Senate report, Physicians for Human Rights emphasized that Mitchell, Jessen, and other health professionals working for the CIA were also involved in "calibrating levels of pain," "evaluating and treating detainees for purposes of torture," "conditioning medical care on cooperation with interrogators," and "failing to document physical and/or psychological evidence of torture."[14] The following year, the American Civil Liberties Union (ACLU) filed a lawsuit against Mitchell and Jessen on behalf of three former tortured prisoners – Suleiman Abdullah Salim, Mohamed Ahmed Ben Soud, and Gul Rahman. As noted earlier, a confidential settlement was reached in the case in 2017, without an acknowledgment of responsibility from the two psychologists.[15]

Relatively little in the Senate report was surprising. But the details of gruesome treatment were stunning nonetheless. With yet another searing indictment of the role played by psychologists now in public view, the APA issued another press release, describing the CIA techniques as "sickening and morally reprehensible," and distancing the association from Mitchell and Jessen. It emphasized that neither psychologist was a member of the APA, and that they were therefore beyond the reach of sanctioning by the APA's Ethics Office.[16] Unmentioned, however, was that Mitchell had been an APA member at the time he began working for the CIA. In fact, an ethics complaint had been filed against him by fellow psychologist Sharon Gadberry, but the APA's Ethics Office had failed to act on it.[17] Mitchell then resigned from the APA in 2006, as did Kirk Hubbard, eliminating the possibility of subsequent sanctioning by the Ethics Committee.

THE HOFFMAN REPORT

In July 2015, after conducting more than 150 interviews, including some with dissident psychologists, and examining thousands of emails and other documents, Hoffman and his team completed a report of over 500 pages.[18] Most centrally, the independent review – informally known as the Hoffman Report – concluded that senior APA representatives, over a period of years, had secretly collaborated with Department of Defense officials to support policies that protected and preserved the ongoing participation of psychologists in coercive detention and interrogation operations.

For example, the detailed report alleged that "key APA officials, principally the APA Ethics Director joined and supported at times by other APA officials, colluded with important DoD officials to have APA issue loose, high-level ethical guidelines that did not constrain DoD in any greater fashion than existing DoD interrogation guidelines."[19] (As will become clear, this assessment has been contested by various parties.) The report also attributed the choices these individuals made to three important and interlinked motivations: to curry favor with the Department of Defense; to advance the APA's image from a public relations stance; and to promote opportunities for psychologists in national security settings. From a forward-looking perspective, the report also raised "serious concerns about the ability of APA officials – and APA itself – to act independently from the presidential administration in power, and from powerful government agencies that provide the profession of psychology with very substantial benefits."[20]

Much of this was familiar to those who had been paying attention from the outset, well over a decade earlier. But the findings seemed to catch many APA members, including some insiders, by surprise. Perhaps they couldn't believe that the dissidents had been justified in their outrage, or conceivably they hadn't imagined that the Hoffman team would actually be able to find such compelling evidence of the APA's behind-the-scenes collaboration with the military-intelligence establishment.

The Hoffman Report directed particular criticism at the APA's 2005 PENS Task Force. As dissidents had long argued, the seeming stacking of that group with military-intelligence representatives virtually guaranteed that the APA would officially endorse the continuing participation of psychologists in detention and interrogation operations. A key argument APA leaders had offered was that psychologists helped to keep these operations safe, legal, ethical, and effective – despite early credible reports that psychologists were among those involved in detainee torture and abuse.

Archived email exchanges obtained by the Hoffman team also provided details about how military psychologists Morgan Banks, Debra Dunivin, and Larry James collaborated with APA leaders, especially Stephen Behnke. Their coordinated efforts were seemingly aimed at guaranteeing that the APA's ethics policies didn't constrain the Pentagon's use of psychologists in its war-on-terror operations. For instance, as noted in Chapter 3, Dunivin guided APA leaders on the selection of military-intelligence personnel as members of the PENS Task Force, most strongly recommending Morgan Banks.[21] It appears that, once selected, Banks then sought to make sure that the PENS Report would support a Defense Department policy document that had already been drafted – by Banks and Dunivin themselves. At various times thereafter, Banks, Dunivin, and James joined forces with Behnke in developing and vetting statements and strategies that preserved the close alignment between APA and government policies. An early 2007 email from Behnke to Dunivin and Banks summed up the Ethics Office director's disdain for the dissident community: "Debra, unlike some of our colleagues whose ability to generate prattle on this subject is apparently endless, you and Morgan have full-time work that is hugely demanding and important."[22]

In contrast to the extensive documentation of links between the APA and the Department of Defense, the Hoffman Report gave substantially less attention to possible connections between the APA and the CIA. The report noted that "the collaboration between APA officials and government officials regarding the PENS process and related follow up events was dominated by APA–DoD interactions, with no evidence of significant CIA interactions regarding PENS."[23] However, Hoffman and his team also expressed uncertainty regarding the extent to which this contrast solely represented real differences between the two relationships, or whether, at least in part, it reflected the fact that the CIA is "an agency that trains people to keep things secret for a living."[24] Regardless, it's important to recognize that, lacking national security clearances, the investigators were unable to access potentially valuable documents held by various government agencies, including the CIA.[25]

But consequential linkages between the APA and the CIA *prior* to the PENS meeting were revealed in a different report – aptly titled *All the President's Psychologists* – that appeared on the *New York Times* website in April 2015, two months before the Hoffman Report was released.[26] Written by Coalition members Stephen Soldz and Steven Reisner along with Nathaniel Raymond, Scott Allen, Isaac Baker, and Allen Keller, this report was based on a thorough analysis of the hundreds of Gerwehr emails that James Risen had obtained while writing *Pay Any Price*. Soldz, Reisner, and their co-authors detailed several findings of relevance here.

Foremost, those emails show that, over a period of years, Geoff Mumford from the APA's Science Directorate had multiple contacts with the CIA's Kirk Hubbard. Hubbard was also among the non-disclosed attendees invited to the small meeting in July 2004 organized by Stephen Behnke to discuss issues facing psychologists in national security work. And as noted earlier, after the PENS meeting, Mumford sent Hubbard an email thanking him for his help in "getting this effort off the ground."[27]

Recall too that CIA contract psychologists Mitchell and Jessen, who designed the agency's torturous interrogation program, were participants at invitation-only national security-focused conferences co-sponsored by the APA in the years leading up to PENS. Mitchell maintained his APA membership during much of this period, not resigning from the association until 2006. The authors of *All the President's Psychologists* conclude by noting that their email review produced "no evidence that any APA official expressed concern over mounting reports of psychologist involvement in detainee abuse during four years of direct email communications with senior members of the US intelligence community."[28]

INITIAL RESPONSES TO THE REPORT

The Hoffman Report was presented to the APA's Board of Directors in early July 2015. The APA had committed to making the report publicly available, but it was anonymously leaked to the media several days ahead of the planned dissemination. The association immediately issued a lengthy press release that acknowledged the "findings of individual collusion and organizational failures" and presented an initial set of recommended policy changes.[29] Among these was a proposed policy "prohibiting psychologists from participating in interrogation of persons held in custody by military and intelligence authorities." The release also included an apology to APA members from then past president Nadine Kaslow: "The actions, policies and the lack of independence from government influence described in the Hoffman report represented a failure to live up to our core values. We profoundly regret, and apologize for, the behavior and the consequences that ensued. Our members, our profession and our organization expected, and deserved, better."[30]

The APA soon followed with an announcement that two senior staff members – CEO Norman Anderson and Deputy CEO Michael Honaker – were planning to retire by the end of 2015, and that Rhea Farberman, director of public and member communications for the APA, had resigned her position, effective at the end of that July. The press release described all three individuals in glowing terms.[31] No mention was made of any role or oversight responsibility they might have had in relation to the APA's collaboration with the military-intelligence establishment.

In contrast, Ethics Office director Stephen Behnke was summarily fired. In what turned out to be portent of things to come, his attorney – former Federal Bureau of Investigation (FBI) director Louis Freeh – warned, "Dr Behnke will consider all legal options in the face of this unfair, irresponsible and unfounded action by a select few APA board members."[32] It's worthy of note that now, seven years later, Behnke is apparently associated with Special Psychological Applications, a private consulting firm under the direction of Morgan Banks. The company, located in North Carolina not far from Fort Bragg, employs "doctoral level psychologists who have experience working for and/or with the military." Its clients include US military units and defense contractors.[33]

The Hoffman Report's disturbing findings provoked broad outrage and prominent coverage in the *New York Times*, the *Washington Post*, and other leading media outlets.[34] Physicians for Human Rights again called for a federal criminal probe into the APA's role in war-on-terror torture; one member of the organization's Board of Directors stated, "The APA's collusion with the government's national security apparatus is one of the greatest scandals in U.S. medical history."[35] In similar terms, human rights attorneys at the ACLU described the report as a "damning indictment of key APA leaders and staff," and wrote that it "provides a vivid illustration of how the government's decision to torture corrupted both individuals and institutions."[36] Psychologists for Social Responsibility offered guideposts for ameliorative action by the APA, while warning, "The APA's loss of legitimacy and credibility will remain a disturbing reality as long as the Association fails to fully confront and address the betrayal by its leadership and the harm it has caused."[37]

Before July had drawn to a close, three past presidents of the APA – Ronald Levant, Gerald Koocher, and Barry Anton – had written apologetically about their roles related to the scandal and the PENS Task Force in particular.[38] Collectively, they expressed regret on multiple fronts: for placing too much trust in APA senior staff; for restricting the PENS Task Force membership so that it relied too heavily on those with government connections; for ignoring conflicts of interest; for declaring an emergency PENS vote when pressured to do so by the APA's public affairs staff; for failing to support greater transparency in their efforts to protect the APA; and for ignoring warnings from dissident groups. At least indirectly, each of these apologies appeared to acknowledge the validity of key conclusions in the Hoffman Report.

But not everyone was on board with the burgeoning efforts to chart a course correction and re-prioritize do-no-harm ethics. Pushback quickly emerged from unsurprising quarters. For example, four of the individuals whose actions were criticized in the Hoffman Report – Morgan Banks, Debra Dunivin, Larry James, and Russ Newman – disseminated an open letter. In it they claimed that the report suffered from "prosecutorial bias and grandstanding rhetoric" and that it was filled with "a host of factual errors, unsupported inferences, and policy opinions masquerading as fact-based conclusions."[39]

The three military psychologists in the group also insisted that they had "devoted many years to ensuring humane conditions of confinement and to restraining and ending the use of abusive interrogation tactics."[40] However, as we'll see in the next chapter, a problem arises when words like "humane" and "abusive" are defined solely by the Department of Defense and its employees. Those definitions can allow for the use of tactics – for instance, extended solitary confinement, sensory deprivation, sleep deprivation, and the exploitation of fear and hopelessness – that may still cause significant psychological harm.[41] Two years later, in 2017, Banks, Dunivin, James, and Newman joined with fired Ethics Office director Stephen Behnke in filing a defamation lawsuit against Hoffman, his law firm, and the APA. The defendants have vigorously contested the plaintiffs' claims that they were defamed.

Thomas Williams, then the president of the APA's Society for Military Psychology (Division 19), also wrote an open letter condemning the Hoffman Report. Representing the division's leadership, he expressed dismay that the military psychologists named in the report had been harmed by "unsubstantiated and unbridled accusations."[42] His letter stated that

Banks, Dunivin, and James (among others) "have been maligned as nefariously engaging in 'collusion' when their true motivations, intent and the outcome of their actions in concert with the APA Staff with whom they worked, all point to *cooperation*." This could arguably be a flawed distinction. After all, collusion is generally defined as a particular type of cooperation: namely, "a secret agreement or cooperation especially for an illegal or deceitful purpose."[43] Nevertheless, Williams not only recommended that the APA leadership retract all "negative statements related to PENS and its membership." He also called upon the association to "provide an apology to any member of APA who is maligned in the Hoffman report."[44]

TREMORS IN TORONTO

It was only a month after publication of the Hoffman Report that the APA held its annual meeting in Toronto. The long weekend's panels, poster sessions, and parties were mostly routine convention fare. But other events linked to the report's disturbing revelations, especially a historic vote by the association's Council of Representatives, certainly were not.

On the Thursday night before that vote, Psychologists for Social Responsibility held a teach-in at St Andrew's Church, a few blocks from the convention site. In keeping with the gravity of the occasion, accentuated by the arched ceiling, towers, and many stained-glass windows, the group's president, Yosef Brody, focused on the challenges ahead in his welcoming remarks. He concluded by expressing his hope that this crisis would prove to be an opportunity to repair the profession's integrity while also reconsidering its collective purpose and how psychology might be changed for the better.

Several dissidents then came forward to share their own personal reflections. Among the issues highlighted were the urgency of the moment; the devastated lives of war-on-terror prisoners; and the pressing need for meaningful reform at the APA, greater attention to ethics education for all psychologists, and real accountability for anyone who had abetted abuse and torture. In my own observations, I recalled how two hundred years ago Dr Frankenstein had pursued a reckless path of science unmoored from values and ambition unrestrained by conscience, bringing to life a hideous monster, made of body parts collected from slaughterhouses, dissecting rooms, and graveyards. And I noted how, in the past decade, some leaders of the APA had seemingly helped to build a brutal beast of a different sort, and perhaps for much the same reason: the unbridled pursuit of greater power, influence, and prestige.[45]

The Council of Representatives meeting on Friday morning took place in front of an unusually large and sometimes boisterous crowd of onlookers. In a demonstration of unity and witnessing, dozens of these spectators wore black sashes, some reading "Hold APA Accountable" and others "No Torture in Our Name." A contingent of graduate students wore red T-shirts with "First, Do No Harm" written across them. In important ways, the sashes and shirts epitomized the devoted, low-budget, do-it-yourself, and contribute-whatever-you-can collaborative efforts that had characterized much of the growing dissident community's activism during this period.

The sashes, for example, were the creation of Naomi Podber, a City University of New York (CUNY) graduate student in psychology at that time.[46] Also a founding member of a protest street band, Podber had learned the importance of bold and graphic messaging.[47] Unable to attend the convention and looking for ways to combat a sense of helplessness and horror over the direction the APA had taken, Podber joined with several like-minded friends and the result was fifty hastily stenciled and screen-printed sashes.[48] They were transported to Toronto and then distributed by Susan Opotow and a colleague, two senior social justice scholars at CUNY.

The much-anticipated council business item that morning was a resolution that had been prepared and brought forward by Dan Aalbers, Scott Churchill, and Coalition members Steven Reisner and Jean Maria Arrigo, with assistance from several others. If the resolution passed, it would transform the association's stance toward US war-on-terror detention and interrogation operations. APA president-elect Susan McDaniel told those assembled, "We're here today to reset our moral compass and ensure that our organization is headed in the right direction."[49] During the lively debate that followed, Reisner emphasized that the resolution would "rectify ten years of deceitful and underhanded and secret collusion to impede the will of the membership." And council member Ali Mattu reminded everyone, "It is people of my race, of my ethnicity, of my faith, that were silenced and tortured by psychologists in the name of APA policies. And this is a time to act and correct our course."[50]

The proposed resolution included three key policy changes.[51] First, it sharply curtailed psychologists' involvement in national security interrogations: "Psychologists shall not conduct, supervise, be in the presence of, or otherwise assist any national security interrogations for any military or intelligence entities, including private contractors working on their behalf, nor advise on conditions of confinement insofar as these might facilitate such an interrogation." Two forms of continued participation were deemed acceptable. Psychologists were permitted to "provide consultation with regard to policy pertaining to information gathering methods which are humane so long as they do not violate the prohibitions of this Resolution and are not related to any specific national security interrogation or detention conditions." And the new restrictions did not apply to "domestic law enforcement interrogations or domestic detention settings where detainees are afforded all of the protections of the United States Constitution, including the 5th Amendment rights against self-incrimination ('Miranda' rights) and 6th Amendment rights to 'effective assistance' of legal counsel."[52]

Second, the resolution dispensed with definitions of torture and of cruel, inhuman, or degrading treatment or punishment tied to the "understandings" and "reservations" reflected in US law. The Bush Administration's "torture memos" had made it clear that these standards were changeable and manipulable in ways that made them inadequate as reliable protections against severe mistreatment. Instead, going forward these crucial definitions would be drawn solely from the United Nations (UN) Convention Against Torture and related international instruments.[53] The resolution emphasized that "when legal standards conflict, APA members are held to the highest of the competing standards."[54] And it reaffirmed that the prohibitions against psychologists' direct or indirect participation in torture or cruel, inhuman, or degrading treatment or punishment applied to all interrogation techniques and conditions of confinement, as well as to all persons regardless of who they were or where they were being held.

Third, the resolution clarified, based on the 2008 membership referendum described in the preceding chapter, that psychologists present at Guantanamo Bay and similar international sites were in violation of APA policy unless they were working directly on behalf of the detainees or providing treatment to military personnel.[55] Moreover, responsibility for determining whether or not a detention facility is meeting the required international standards would belong to the UN Committee against Torture or the UN Special Rapporteur on Torture and Other Cruel, Inhuman or Degrading Treatment or Punishment. The resolution also requested that the US government offer redeployment to any psychologists who were currently working at prohibited sites in violation of the APA's policy.

When it was finally time for the roll-call vote, the council overwhelmingly approved the resolution. The remarkable margin was 157 to 1, and it was immediately greeted with sounds of celebration and widespread applause. After years of delay and obstruction from internal and outside forces, the APA's leadership finally made a commitment to prioritize the profession's do-no-harm ethics even in national security settings.[56] The resounding victory was a truly momentous development, and the mood was clearly one of jubilation for the dissident community.

Interviewed just minutes later by Amy Goodman of *Democracy Now!*, a tearful Stephen Soldz explained, "This is the result of nearly a decade of effort by hundreds and thousands of people ... We've been spokespersons, but there have been many, many, many people involved in this ... It's a victory for the anti-torture movement ... The APA moves from the back of the pack to being a model for other parts of society."[57] When asked what it had taken to achieve this outcome, he summarized it this way: "For many of us, it was basically our life for the last decade ... writing hundreds of articles; organizing psychologists; making alliances with human rights groups; ... working with reporters; getting the public and the APA leadership to realize that this was a major issue, that this was a scandal that could not be allowed to stand."[58]

It was perhaps only fitting that the sole vote cast against the resolution belonged to retired Army colonel Larry James. He had been a member of the controversy-filled PENS Task Force in 2005 and before that he had served as the chief Behavioral Science Consultation Team (BSCT) psychologist at Guantanamo in 2003. At that time, the detention facility's standard operating procedures reportedly included a behavior management plan for newly arrived prisoners that was specifically designed to "enhance and exploit the disorientation and disorganization" they felt. It involved complete isolation for at least a month, no contact whatsoever with the chaplain or representatives from the International Committee of the Red Cross (ICRC), and only the barest minimum of basic comfort items such as a blanket,

towel, and bar of soap.[59] It might be surprising if James had no knowledge that prisoners were being treated in this way, but he has denied any responsibility for these conditions of confinement.

Also, as described earlier, eight years before the Toronto vote James flew from Guantanamo to San Francisco where, with much fanfare, he spoke to council members at the 2007 APA convention. At that time, the governing body was considering a proposed moratorium on psychologist involvement in national security interrogations, and James offered his ominous warning: "If we lose psychologists from these facilities, people are going to die."[60] It was a strange claim from an active duty officer, seemingly an assertion that some of his fellow soldiers in Cuba – those who weren't psychologists – would fatally injure prisoners there. Regardless, back then James' dramatic trip and appeal served the purpose APA officials apparently had in mind, and the moratorium resolution was defeated.

Things were very different for Larry James by the time of the 2015 convention. Although he didn't go quietly, it soon became clear that his persuasive powers within the council had largely evaporated. Minutes before the crucial vote in Toronto, he cautioned council members that passage of the APA's post-Hoffman resolution would lead to "dire negative consequences for all federal employees."[61] That warning failed to influence the votes of James' council colleagues. And today, more than seven years later, the dire consequences he had predicted are hard to find.

On Saturday afternoon, the day after the vote, the APA held a town hall meeting. Hundreds of convention-goers attended. Upon arriving, they were greeted by a large video screen that displayed a word cloud showing the results from a survey of how psychology graduate students felt about the Hoffman Report's disturbing findings. Two words loomed larger than all of the rest: "disappointment" and "disgust." "Embarrassment," "betrayal," "shame," "shock," and "sadness" were only somewhat smaller in size. For dissidents like myself, the students who gathered at the convention were reason for cautious optimism about the future of the APA and the profession.

On the stage were Nadine Kaslow and Susan McDaniel, the association's past president and president-elect respectively. They had led the special committee overseeing the Hoffman team's independent investigation. They began by commending the corrective steps that had been taken earlier that weekend, with Kaslow observing, "I've been on Council a very long time, and without a doubt, this was the most emotional vote I've ever wit-nessed."[62] McDaniel followed by recounting how the leadership had failed the membership, and she again apologized for the "actions, policies, and lack of independence from governmental influences" that the Hoffman Report had detailed.[63] The pair then opened the meeting for questions and comments from the audience, with six microphones placed around the spa-cious and packed room.

At one point, when Kaslow mentioned that many people had told her that they simply hadn't known about the wrongdoing described in the Hoffman Report, there was immediate pushback. Rejecting any suggestion that APA leaders were themselves unaware, Jean Maria Arrigo took to a mi-crophone and firmly stated, "I personally delivered evidence and testimony to people on the board in 2007. And not one person ever inquired of me." She was followed by Laurie Wagner, who noted that Ethics Office director Stephen Behnke wasn't the only one she felt deserved blame, emphasizing, "We had ten presidents and boards of directors who were continuing to actively allow psychologists to participate in detainee interrogations." And later, after reminding everyone of all the evidence that had been dissemi-nated over the past decade, Frank Summers insisted, "If you don't know, it's because you didn't want to know."[64]

When other speakers suggested that the Hoffman Report was a false narrative, or that the recriminations needed to stop, or that the APA de-served more credit for all it had accomplished in other areas, there was fur-ther pushback. Early-career psychologist Tiffany O'Shaughnessy stepped forward and explained, "I think that can be re-injuring to a lot of the people who haven't felt that APA has been fully accountable yet. So just thinking about how we're re-injuring a lot of folks in the room, a lot of folks from the Muslim community, from the Arab community who have really been and are still struggling." And not long after, a graduate student highlighted a troubling reality: "I haven't heard anyone apologize to the victims of the torture – to their families and their communities and to groups that tra-ditionally have very good reason to not trust psychologists and now have greater evidence not to have confidence in us."[65]

This was true. APA leaders had failed to offer an official apology to the predominantly Arab and Muslim detainees – or to members of Arab and Muslim communities within and outside the United States – for the calamitous harms perpetrated by war-on-terror excesses.[66] As the American Middle Eastern/North African Psychological Network wrote in an open letter shortly after the convention, "The erosion of ethical standards and protections at APA parallel the erosion of civil liberties, human rights, and protective policies in the United States since 9/11 that has disproportionately targeted minority groups."[67] It's also indisputable that, as philosophy professor Richard Matthews has highlighted, torture doesn't only assault the dignity of the isolated victim. It also attacks "the humanity of entire communities along gender, cultural, ethnic, familial, occupational, and generational lines."[68]

Conceivably having been warned of possible legal repercussions associated with such an apology, Kaslow and McDaniel seemed uncomfortable. But to their credit, they didn't duck the issue and both offered cautious apologies. Noting that the Hoffman Report did not hold the APA directly responsible for torture, Kaslow said, "We certainly are aware that we have not made this apology before … From hearing the impact of us not apologizing, from understanding that people have been seriously tortured and that that's absolutely abhorrent … we are genuinely apologizing for this." McDaniel said much the same: "It is clear that there has been, there are plenty of reports about very painful and disturbing things. And to the extent that there's any way that our ethical code or the collusion that happened might have enabled any of that, we deeply apologize." The apologies were greeted with loud approval and applause.[69]

However, amid the vocal popular support for these and other steps, there were also signs of growing opposition as the convention drew to a close. At the town hall, Jeremy Jinkerson, a graduate student pursuing a military career, lambasted the Hoffman Report, asking, "What I would like is an answer from APA leadership as to why we have allowed an independent review to serve as judge, jury, and executioner of our own members." Thomas Williams, the president of the APA's Society for Military Psychology (Division 19), similarly dismissed the alleged wrongdoing of psychologists as the actions of "one to two people" and asked, "What can you do to reassure American society that as threats are posed to our nation, that psychology will once again rise to the occasion to provide the appropriate support?"[70]

Even more extreme was an online diatribe, published on the same day as the historic council vote, in which two retired military colleagues of Morgan

Banks came to Banks's defense. They described the Hoffman Report as a "classic attack of cowards; pseudo-intellectuals sitting on the sidelines, jeering and criticizing the actual participants in the arena of life." They claimed that the APA had become "a willing co-conspirator to the likes of al Qaeda and ISIS." And they dismissed dissidents as "a small, but baying minority of APA members" who were spreading "baseless allegations."[71]

To disparage critics by questioning their patriotism is, of course, a familiar page from a well-worn playbook. What's more troubling is the fact that what seemed like an unhinged tirade was published on a website run by a group of anonymous APA members. Ironically, while choosing to hide their identities, they have asserted that their purpose is "to provide a forum for an open, transparent, and fact-based flow of information concerning those areas of the science and profession of psychology outside those that are primarily health care and treatment based."[72]

Even so, Coalition members and fellow dissidents didn't miss the opportunity to celebrate together in Toronto before heading our separate ways on the many flights back home from the convention. We left knowing that some very important reforms and measures of accountability had been achieved. Furthermore, the dissident community had demonstrated its effectiveness and resolve. It had fought off efforts to weaken the policy changes that were sought. And it had gained new supporters along the way. We weren't so naïve as to think that the struggle was over, but we realized that a significant role reversal had taken place. Rather than constantly trying to overcome resistance and move the APA forward, we would now be tested as to whether we could hold onto the ground we had gained.

The Empire Strikes Back

Disappointment arrived quickly for anyone who imagined that developments at the 2015 American Psychological Association (APA) convention in Toronto would usher in a consensual period of long overdue soul-searching, accountability, and further reform. Despite the near-unanimous adoption of the resolution prohibiting psychologists' involvement in national security detention and interrogation operations, the hopes of optimists were soon dashed by disgruntled factions comprising some of the key individuals who were arguably facilitators or bystanders during the years that the APA spent straying from the profession's do-no-harm principles.

These factions mounted what seemed to be a full-blown campaign to restore personal reputations and business-as-usual relations between the APA and the military-intelligence establishment, an offensive that continues to this day. They have apparently set their sights on discrediting not only the Hoffman Report itself, but also related APA reforms and the dissident psychologists who have led the call for change. In various forms, these efforts to turn back the clock have persisted for the past seven years.

In this chapter, I take a careful look at several examples of this possibly coordinated backlash, including rebuttal attempts from military operational psychologists, open letters of concern from past APA leaders, an anti-reform intervention from the Pentagon, retrograde resolutions brought to the APA's Council of Representatives, and defamation lawsuits, among other measures. As will become clear, to varying degrees it appears that each has relied on misrepresentations and the sowing of unwarranted doubt and confusion. I consider these forays in some depth and detail because, taken together, they usefully convey the magnitude of the challenges and obstacles that continue to encumber efforts to secure the prioritization of ethics and human rights over expediency and narrow guild interests.[1]

REBUTTAL ATTEMPTS FROM MILITARY PSYCHOLOGISTS

Of particular significance are two extensive parallel efforts to discredit the Hoffman Report that were undertaken shortly after its release, one by four psychologists involved in the behind-the-scenes collaboration detailed in the report and the other by a task force from the APA's Society for Military Psychology (Division 19).[2] The former group comprised retired military operational psychologists Morgan Banks, Larry James, and Debra Dunivin, along with Russ Newman, who had been director of the APA's Practice Directorate and was married to Dunivin at the time of the Psychological Ethics and National Security (PENS) meeting. The Division 19 task force was chaired by military operational psychologist Sally Harvey, who once compared her personal campaign against the Hoffman Report to the "never leave a fallen comrade behind" directive of the Army's Warrior Ethos.[3]

In a comprehensive critique, my Coalition for an Ethical Psychology colleagues Stephen Soldz and Steven Reisner have argued that the published commentaries from both of these groups "present distorted, selective, and disingenuous recastings of the Hoffman Report's central findings, the history of the PENS Task Force, and the roles of the Banks Commentary coauthors in this disastrous episode."[4] In their point-by-point refutation, Soldz and Reisner warn that what they see as numerous misrepresentations and omissions in the two commentaries serve to distract from the simple reality that the APA's collaboration with the Defense Department led to the adoption of permissive ethics policies and the preservation of roles for psychologists in settings where prisoner abuse was routine. They summarize their perspective on the apologists' strategy this way: "Such obfuscation must be regarded as an unsuccessful attempt to halt real progress in repairing the ethical foundations of psychology and promoting healing within the profession and the APA, following this decade-long ethics crisis."[5]

Given the commonalities shared by the commentaries of the Banks quartet and the Division 19 task force, I too will discuss them together here. Of greatest importance, both neglected to give serious attention to some of the most disturbing elements of the Hoffman Report's analysis of the APA's collaboration with the Defense Department. That is, what dissidents view as the covert agenda and secret correspondence, the manipulation and cover-up, and the strategic deception directed toward association members and the general public – all of which have been discussed in earlier chapters. These activities are thoroughly described in the Hoffman Report. The evidence assembled by Hoffman's investigatory team includes thousands of pages of relevant documents and email exchanges – between APA senior staff, the association's elected leaders, and representatives of the military-intelligence establishment – that defy easy refutation.

The seemingly incontrovertible nature of this paper trail may explain why these critics adopted a different and much narrower focus, with the Banks quartet arguing that "by the time of the PENS report all evidence showed that abusive interrogations within DoD had ended and were highly unlikely to resume."[6] With this claim they've sought to demonstrate that the Hoffman team was wrong to conclude that APA leaders, in order to curry favor with the Department of Defense, had adopted Pentagon-friendly ethics policies "without serious regard for the concerns raised that harsh and abusive techniques were occurring, and that they might occur in the future."[7] Yet, even if we accept the critics' restricted scope, in at least three important ways it is *their* stance – and *not* the Hoffman Report – that seems to misrepresent a crucial truth: war-on-terror prisoners continued to be subjected to psychological and physical abuse long *after* the PENS Report was released.

First, despite protestations otherwise, there's little doubt that the Defense Department's post-PENS policies continued to permit interrogation techniques and conditions of confinement that were *abusive* by international human rights standards and arguably by any reasonable understanding of the word.[8] Bear in mind as well that the insufficiently restrictive guidance of the PENS Report also applied in equal measure to the activities of Central Intelligence Agency (CIA) psychologists – and that contract psychologists James Mitchell and Bruce Jessen, among others, were still involved in the agency's abusive black site operations *after* PENS.[9]

But regardless of location, it's important to recognize that the reality of ill-treatment doesn't simply vanish because government officials declare certain procedures to be non-abusive. After all, when the Bush Administration approved the use of waterboarding, that didn't make it any less torturous. And when the Pentagon investigated allegations of detainee abuse, whether or not particular techniques were *authorized* didn't provide a meaningful answer to the question of whether prisoners were actually being harmed by these techniques.

For example, as Soldz and Reisner have highlighted, a 2004 Army Inspector General Report on detainee operations specifically limited its definition of abuse to instances of "wrongful death, assault, sexual assault, and theft."[10] Anything else approved by the Department of Defense – including prolonged isolation, sleep disruption or deprivation, and exposure to extreme temperatures – was, by definition, considered humane and non-abusive. Such methodological problems and other deficiencies also pervade other official reports that have examined prisoner abuse.[11] Soldz and Reisner have noted as well that pressure from above might have influenced those conducting these military investigations – especially after General Antonio Taguba was, according to his account, forced into early retirement following his own 2004 report documenting widespread and systemic abuses at Abu Ghraib.[12]

In this regard, law professor and public interest investigator Keith Rohman, whose work has included investigations of Abu Ghraib torture and the role of military contractor Blackwater in the mass shooting of Iraqi citizens, has emphasized that these Defense Department abuse investigations were faulty in significant ways. As he has described it, the problems range from "the choice of the investigators at the outset, to the selection of witnesses and the reliance on prior flawed reports, continuing through the failure to pursue important leads, and the inclusion of analytical errors."[13] Rohman's conclusion is telling: "The limited findings of the DoD reports appear pre-ordained."[14]

It appears that there were serious investigatory shortcomings at Guantanamo as well. While serving as a military defense counsel assigned to the Office of Military Commissions, Lieutenant Colonel David Frakt represented Guantanamo detainee Mohammed Jawad – whose circumstances were described earlier – in his 2008 military commission trial. Contrary to assertions by military psychologists that the use of abusive methods at Guantanamo had ended well before the PENS Task Force meeting in June 2005, an army intelligence officer testified that the "frequent flyer" program was still standard operating procedure for dozens of prisoners when he departed Guantanamo in April 2005.[15] The trial judge concluded that subjecting Jawad to this sleep deprivation technique constituted cruel and inhuman treatment.

In his later reflections about the inadequacy of accountability for prisoner abuse within the military, Frakt wrote, "The discovery in the Jawad case of significant new evidence of detainee abuse after multiple high-level investigations into detainee mistreatment strongly suggested either an intentional cover-up by Guantanamo officials or gross incompetence or willful blindness by the investigators."[16] After complaining about the government's failure to interview key eyewitnesses to Jawad's abuse, Frakt was told by the detention facility's legal office that detainees were not considered witnesses and were therefore not interviewed.

Even beyond the specific context of prisoner abuse, sole reliance on the Pentagon for accurate depictions of Guantanamo seems at best ill-considered and at worst an intentionally deceptive practice. Recall George Orwell's warning from decades ago: "The great enemy of clear language is insincerity. When there is a gap between one's real and one's declared aims, one turns as it were instinctively to long words and exhausted idioms, like a cuttlefish spurting out ink."[17] In a first-person account of his legal work representing dozens of Guantanamo prisoners, Clive Stafford Smith, co-founder of the United Kingdom–based human rights group Reprieve, has confirmed Orwell's observation.[18]

Consider three examples Stafford Smith provides of how the Defense Department manipulated language to disguise troubling realities at the island prison. First, apparently as a public relations strategy to quiet critics, the leadership at Guantanamo magically reduced the number of reported detainee suicide attempts by officially reclassifying them as cases of "manipulative self-injurious behavior." Second, for similar purposes, to decrease the number of "juveniles" imprisoned at Guantanamo, the Pentagon arbitrarily adopted *sixteen* as the cut-off age for designating someone as a juvenile detainee – even though the definition of a juvenile according to US and international law is someone under *eighteen* at the time of any alleged crime. And third, the initial designation of "not an enemy combatant," which might have led to demands for a prisoner's immediate release from Guantanamo, was soon changed to "*no longer* an enemy combatant"; this enabled the government to escape any charge that the prisoner had been detained unlawfully, while also allowing for continuing imprisonment, potentially until the end of the so-called war on terror.

But returning to the direct evidence for ongoing prisoner abuse long after the PENS Report was published in 2005, we shouldn't overlook the revised Army Field Manual (AFM), the operative guidance for Defense Department interrogations since 2006.[19] In their commentaries, the Banks quartet and the Division 19 task force cite this manual as evidence that post-PENS detention operations at Guantanamo were humane. But the AFM and particularly its controversial Appendix M authorize some techniques – including forms of sleep deprivation, extended solitary confinement, and sensory deprivation – that are recognized as cruel, inhuman, or degrading treatment under international law. All are permissible according to the Pentagon, but they are all abusive nonetheless.

The United Nations (UN) Committee against Torture and leading human rights organizations have raised serious objections to elements of Appendix M and have called for the United States to abolish some of its provisions.[20] Former government intelligence experts and interrogators agree with that assessment.[21] Similarly, law professor John Parry has characterized the field manual as a "combination of exhortations to comply with the Geneva Conventions and new methods that allow more psychological coercion and thus make compliance with the conventions more difficult."[22] And in the 2015 resolution following the Hoffman Report, the APA's Council of Representatives also concluded that the AFM-authorized techniques of solitary confinement and sleep deprivation constitute cruel, inhuman, or degrading treatment.[23]

Let's now turn to a second significant way in which the critiques of the Hoffman Report from Banks, James, Dunivin, and Newman and from the Division 19 task force seemingly misrepresented the reality and prevalence of post-PENS abuses. By focusing their attention on formal interrogations, these apologists for the Defense Department appeared to discount the accompanying abusive conditions of confinement that have characterized the daily lives of many prisoners at Guantanamo well beyond 2005.

These two components – interrogation and detention – are inherently inseparable. In fact, Defense Department guidelines for operational psychologists in Behavioral Science Consultation Teams (BSCT) – issued a full year *after* the PENS Report – specified that responsibilities included serving as command consultants for both interrogation and detention operations.[24] For interrogation purposes, they "evaluate the psychological strengths and vulnerabilities of detainees"; for detention purposes, they advise on "aspects of the environment that will assist in all interrogation and detention operations."[25] Importantly, according to the document, BSCT psychologists should understand that their client is the Department of Defense, and that their professional ethics code "does not supersede applicable US and international law, regulations, or DoD policy."[26]

This dual involvement for operational psychologists – advising on both interrogations and conditions of confinement – goes all the way back to Guantanamo's first year as a war-on-terror detention facility. As noted earlier, in 2002 then APA member John Leso co-authored a key memo about counter-resistance strategies. In addition to outlining three categories of increasingly harsh interrogation techniques, the memo recommended that "all aspects of the [detention] environment should enhance capture shock, dislocate expectations, foster dependence, and support exploitation to the fullest extent possible," including sleep deprivation and the removal of comfort items such as sheets, blankets, mattresses, and washcloths.[27]

The simple truth is that conditions of confinement at Guantanamo have arguably been abusive ever since the first day it opened. In 2007, Amnesty International, a past recipient of the Nobel Peace Prize, reported that most Guantanamo detainees were still held in "cruel conditions of isolation which flout international standards."[28] Drawing upon photographs and descriptions provided by detainees and their attorneys, the human rights organization also noted that a new camp was opened in late 2006 – long after the PENS Report – in which "detainees are confined for 22 hours a day to individual, enclosed, steel cells where they are almost completely cut off from human contact."[29]

Two years later, in 2009, the Center for Constitutional Rights issued a report suggesting that little had changed.[30] The report described how many prisoners at Guantanamo were still confined to their cells for at least twenty hours each day, with little or no human contact. Meals were eaten alone, with food delivered through a metal slot in the cell doors. Efforts to communicate with fellow prisoners in nearby cells sometimes led to disciplinary sanctions, including loss of privileges or beatings from guards. Essential items like a toothbrush and a blanket were designated as privileges. And in some of the cell blocks, the lights were kept on twenty-four hours a day. In short, the focus by critics of the Hoffman Report on *interrogation* practices obscures a broader and darker reality about the detention facility's abuses.

The psychologists denying Guantanamo's post-PENS mistreatment of prisoners also appear to overlook a related form of abuse: the force-feeding of detainees.[31] At various points in the detention facility's history, including within the past decade, significant numbers of prisoners have chosen to protest their conditions of confinement by going on hunger strikes – and psychologists have reportedly been involved in some of these force-feedings.[32] In an effort to hide this distressing reality from the public, in 2013 the Department of Defense decided that it would no longer disclose whether hunger strikes were taking place.[33]

According to international human rights authorities and experts, the Pentagon's policy on the force-feeding of these prisoners is unethical and constitutes, at the very least, inhuman and degrading treatment.[34] Furthermore, the specific methods used by Guantanamo staff, including shackling the detainee in a restraint chair, have been recognized by medical authorities as exceedingly harsh.[35] Physician and bioethics professor Steven Miles has described the procedures this way: "The persistence of the military's force-feeding policy in the face of international law, and the manner in which it is done, constitutes torture."[36] Again, it seems clear that the abuse of Guantanamo prisoners did *not* end prior to the APA's 2005 PENS Report.

Finally, the reports from the Banks quartet and the Division 19 task force appear to be misleading in a third way. By insisting that abusive practices had ended at Guantanamo before the PENS Task Force ever met, they fail to consider the psychologically devastating effects of indefinite detention, a reality for some Guantanamo detainees that persists today. Although these critics may actually believe that such circumstances fall short of psychological abuse, more knowledgeable experts disagree with them.

For instance, in 2013 Curt Goering, then the executive director of the Center for Victims of Torture, told a Senate committee, "The physical and psychological ramifications of indefinite detention rise to the level of cruel, inhuman, and degrading treatment (CID), a violation of US treaty obligations under the Convention Against Torture and Other Cruel, Inhuman or Degrading Treatment or Punishment (CAT) and in contravention of U.S. constitutional law."[37] He further explained that, even if other conditions of confinement are acceptable, "The very indeterminacy of indefinite detention, without charge or process for review and eventual determinate sentence or release, creates a degree of uncertainty, unpredictability and loss of control over the elemental aspects of one's life, causing severe harm in healthy individuals."[38]

At its 2014 meeting in Geneva, the UN Committee Against Torture echoed these points. The committee emphasized that indefinite detention at Guantanamo was a clear violation of international law, writing that, "notwithstanding the State party's position that these individuals have been captured and detained as 'enemy belligerents' and that under the law of war is permitted 'to hold them until the end of the hostilities,' the Committee reiterates that indefinite detention constitutes *per se* a violation of the Convention."[39] In sum, humane, non-abusive treatment has not ruled the day at Guantanamo post-PENS. In my view, to claim otherwise is an affront not only to the ethical practice of psychology but also to the hundreds of war-on-terror prisoners who have been the direct victims of past and ongoing abuse.

OPEN LETTERS FROM PAST APA LEADERS

Distinct from these two seemingly misleading commentaries by military operational psychologists, publication of the Hoffman Report also led to several open letters of concern from groups of individuals with past leadership roles in the APA. Collectively, these letters called attention to the possibility of bias in favor of the dissidents on the part of the investigators and expressed dissatisfaction with the process surrounding the report's preparation and dissemination. Certainly, an investigation that produces findings as disturbing and consequential as the Hoffman Report merits careful scrutiny – and it has certainly received its share. But it's also important to consider the extent to which a possible lack of objectivity – inadvertent or otherwise – might color the perspective of those who held positions of influence within the APA during the period examined by the report. As a result, their writing also deserves critical evaluation.

For example, a group of former chairs of the APA's Ethics Committee wrote an open letter in early 2016. They focused on accusations of bias that had been leveled against the Hoffman team by those implicated in the report. Noting that they didn't assume these allegations were necessarily true, the signers nonetheless called for "a process by which the Report is revisited in a thoughtful, meaningful and transparent manner."[40] Casting doubt on the report in this way, these former chairs offered to assist in such a reconsideration.

In evaluating the thrust of this letter, we should remember that, under the leadership of Stephen Behnke, the Ethics Office seemed to be a central hub for the entire covert endeavor that was described in the Hoffman Report – with extensive documentation provided in the report's six ancillary binders. These Ethics Committee chairs may well have been unaware of what transpired behind the scenes. But knowingly or not, several of them were arguably linked to one or more controversial decisions, including the "emergency" endorsement of the PENS Report in 2005, the years-long delay in revising Ethical Standard 1.02 to eliminate the just-following-orders Nuremberg defense, the failure to produce a timely casebook on ethical issues in national security settings as had been promised, and the determination that no ethics complaints against military-intelligence psychologists were justified.[41]

Another open letter was written in mid-2016 by several past presidents of the APA. They too raised doubts and concerns about the Hoffman Report and subsequent reform efforts. Noting that "there are very real and honest differences of opinion regarding ... what APA or its agents actually did that was either immoral, unethical, or illegal," the group warned that the report had caused "real damage ... to our Association as well as members and employees."[42] But even while acknowledging their positive contributions to the association and the profession, we shouldn't overlook certain potentially pertinent aspects of the histories of some of these signatories.

For instance, as a senior aide to US Senator Daniel Inouye, who chaired the Defense Appropriations Subcommittee, Patrick DeLeon spent much of his career building and coordinating relationships between the APA and the Pentagon.[43] Martin Seligman met with James Mitchell on multiple occasions; according to some reports, Mitchell subsequently relied on Seligman's theory of learned helplessness in developing the abusive "enhanced interrogation techniques" used at CIA black sites and elsewhere.[44] While Seligman has denied any knowledge of these activities, he has also referred to the ethics reform efforts of dissent psychologists as a "coup d'état" within the APA.[45] Joseph Matarazzo served on the board and owned a small financial stake in Mitchell Jessen & Associates, the firm that received $81 million to run the CIA's torture program; he has denied any knowledge of, or involvement in, those activities.[46] And Ron Fox was a member of the CIA's Professional Standards Advisory Committee, for which Mitchell was an occasional consultant.[47] None of these associations equate with responsibility for detainee abuse. Still, this background may provide useful context for the criticisms of the Hoffman Report that these past presidents have offered.

As one more example, a mid-2016 letter from the leadership of the APA's Division 42 – Psychologists in Independent Practice – announced an unusual "no confidence" vote in the reform-minded members of the APA's Board of Directors.[48] Yet again, it's worth considering some context. First, back in 2011, this division gave Behnke its distinguished public service award – despite what was alleged at that time about his role in the controversial PENS process and the disputes that followed. Second, as described earlier, in 2012 the division's board published a different open letter in which they "vehemently oppose[d]" the call for annulment of the PENS Report by the Coalition.[49] They accused the Coalition of spreading "false and biased information" and insisted that there was nothing wrong with the PENS process or with the APA's related policies. Third, one of the figures whose name appears dozens of times in the Hoffman Report – Gerald Koocher – was an officer of Division 42 at the time of their no-confidence resolution. Although he had apologized for his role when the Hoffman Report was first released, Koocher later reportedly changed his tune and insisted that "APA didn't do anything wrong."[50]

A PENTAGON INTERVENTION

The Pentagon didn't simply stand aside following the Hoffman Report and the reforms that it engendered within the APA. Following passage of the APA's post-Hoffman policy prohibiting military psychologists from involvement in interrogations or the care of Guantanamo detainees, in December 2015 psychologists were reportedly removed from these activities at the detention center.[51] But less than a month later, Brad Carson – the acting principal deputy undersecretary of defense – wrote a letter to the APA's president and CEO. The letter strongly encouraged reconsideration of these restrictions and requested assurances that the APA's new policy was *not* an "ethical mandate" that could put Guantanamo psychologists at professional risk. The same letter also claimed that the policy had become a source of anxiety for current and prospective military psychologists, and that it "could adversely affect the recruitment and retention of highly qualified psychologists."[52]

Carson's letter merits close consideration because it offers a valuable window into the kinds of seeming distortions that have been used to defend the role of psychologists in abusive detainee operations. For example, the APA's Ethics Code advises that "psychologists strive to benefit those with whom they work and take care to do no harm."[53] This expectation applies to *all* psychologists, regardless of their positions of employment or the nature of their activities. In his letter, Carson insisted that the Defense Department adheres to this same standard. But that isn't exactly true.

One key difference is that the relevant Pentagon directives apply a comparable do-no-harm guideline only for health professionals *who are providing treatment*. That is, this elevated standard apparently evaporates when it comes to military operational psychologists, who are *not* assigned healthcare roles when they're involved in detention and interrogation operations. For them, the instructions are less lofty: do not support operations "that would result in inhumane treatment or not be in accordance with applicable law."[54] As law professor John Parry and others have noted, the requirements of "humane treatment" and legality do not necessarily reach the standards set forth in the Geneva Conventions, nor do they necessarily override assertions of "military necessity."[55] In short, Carson appears to have misrepresented fundamental differences between conduct that's deemed appropriate for military operational psychologists and conduct that meets the profession's higher ethical standards.

Equally problematic was Carson's assertion that the Pentagon "understands the desire of the American psychology profession to make a strong statement regarding reports about the role of former military psychologists more than a dozen years ago."[56] Labeling the indisputable evidence of detainee abuse involving psychologists as mere "reports" clearly understates the facts. As previously discussed, these abuses have been well-documented, including in the 2008 Senate Armed Services Committee Report and reports from Physicians for Human Rights, the Constitution Project, and the Institute on Medicine as a Profession, among other sources.[57]

The claim that detainee mistreatment only occurred "more than a dozen years ago" by "former military psychologists" was seemingly also a misrepresentation. Again, as noted earlier, detainee abuse is not a thing of the past. It's ongoing even today when we consider that the UN Committee against Torture has determined that the current treatment of detainees at Guantanamo, including indefinite detention without trial, violates the Convention against Torture.[58] Additionally, Appendix M of the Army Field Manual allows the use of abusive interrogation techniques and conditions of confinement that violate psychological ethics.[59]

Carson's letter on behalf of the Department of Defense also argued that "withdrawing all government psychologists from patient care at Guantanamo would represent an abandonment by the psychology profession of the obligations of the U.S. Government under international and U.S. law." This stance appears to be wrong on at least two counts. First, according to Juan Méndez, a former UN special rapporteur on torture, "Existing [2015] APA policy regarding the role of medical professionals conforms to humane treatment standards under Geneva Conventions."[60] Moreover, the ethical obligation to avoid doing harm – and to avoid complicity in human rights abuses – reasonably precludes being part of a detention regime like Guantanamo, which the UN has repeatedly determined violates international law. Second, although unwelcome by the Pentagon and by some military operational psychologists, there's an obvious solution to Carson's concern: allow *independent* psychologists to provide care to detainees at Guantanamo. In fact, according to Méndez, the military's unwillingness to provide detainees with such access is itself a violation of international law.[61]

Finally, in what appears to be a particularly disingenuous section of the letter, Carson objected to the assessments from the UN Committee Against Torture and other affiliated human rights experts that the Guantanamo detention facility stood in violation of pertinent international law regarding the treatment of detainees.[62] He argued that the APA should ignore those judgments because "under the United Nations Charter, binding U.N. obligations are established by the U.N. Security Council, and not by a special rapporteur."[63] However, for its policy adopted in 2015 the APA specifically chose the UN Committee Against Torture and the appropriate rapporteurs for oversight, in part because alternatives of the sort suggested by Carson would be entirely impractical and likely ethically misguided. Carson presumably realized that the US government would simply veto any UN Security Council resolution that declared its own detention facility to be in violation of international law.

When all of these elements are considered together, this post-Hoffman letter from the Department of Defense looks like an effort to undermine the APA's reform agenda. The Pentagon wanted clear confirmation that, regardless of the association's policy changes, military psychologists wouldn't be subject to professional repercussions for serving at Guantanamo or any other military detention facility that failed to meet international standards. As it turns out, it seems Carson had already received those very assurances before he even sent his letter.

In a December 2015 conference call with Defense Department representatives, then APA president Nadine Kaslow reportedly explained that there was no need for such worries, because the association's policy resolutions were considered merely aspirational and therefore unenforceable from an Ethics Code perspective.[64] Almost three years later, in a September 2018 follow-up letter to the Pentagon, APA president Jessica Henderson Daniel confirmed this understanding in writing: "APA Council resolutions are aspirational statements and are not enforceable, unlike the requirements of our APA Ethical Principles of Psychologists and Code of Conduct (Ethics Code)."[65]

In September 2019, with this confirmation in hand, the Department of Defense issued new guidelines that specifically included "licensed doctoral-level clinical psychologists" as members of its "behavioral science support" teams.[66] According to the directive, these operational psychologists "observe, assess, and consult on" detainee operations and intelligence interrogations.

This seems to be a clear violation of the APA's policy prohibiting such involvement – but that policy has conveniently been deemed unenforceable by the association's leadership. In a thorough analysis of these more recent developments, Coalition colleague Stephen Soldz has expressed concerns that there may have been, yet again, "secret coordination between some officials within APA and the Defense Department."[67]

REGRESSIVE APA COUNCIL RESOLUTIONS

While the Pentagon has applied pressure from the outside, military psychologists within the APA have persisted in their efforts to discredit the Hoffman Report and turn back the clock on key reforms. Three years after the historic Toronto meeting, two regressive resolutions were brought before the APA's Council of Representatives at the 2018 annual convention in San Francisco. The first of these proposals – spearheaded by military psychologists Sally Harvey and Carrie Kennedy of Division 19 – called for the return of psychologists to Guantanamo in healthcare roles even though, as described earlier, the facility continued to operate in violation of international law.[68]

It's unclear why any Guantanamo prisoner today would want to confide in a military psychologist whose primary responsibility is to the US government. After all, psychologists were present throughout Guantanamo's history of abuse and torture. As a reminder, in the years immediately after 9/11, psychologists in healthcare roles were expected to provide patient assessments to interrogators for purposes of exploitation. Psychologists were also involved in creating detention conditions specifically designed to debilitate detainees. And in their patient notes, at least some healthcare professionals at Guantanamo neglected to inquire about or reference abuse and torture as possible explanations for a prisoner's psychological ill-health.[69]

Even after the APA instituted Guantanamo-related prohibitions in 2015, according to association policy it remained permissible for *independent* psychologists – those who work for organizations like the Red Cross or the Center for Victims of Torture, or psychologists who might work in tandem with attorneys representing detainees – to provide mental health care to detainees. It was also permissible for *military* psychologists, employed by the Department of Defense, to provide treatment to military personnel. So, at the time there was good reason to wonder whether this 2018 resolution to return military psychologists to Guantanamo – supposedly for the welfare of detainees – might actually be more about protecting careers and the Pentagon's image, interests, and agenda.

If approved by council members, the resolution would have eliminated any possibility that the Defense Department might reconsider its opposition to bringing in independent trauma-informed and torture-informed healthcare experts to support the prisoners who remain at Guantanamo. A consortium of human rights groups, including the American Civil Liberties Union (ACLU) and Physicians for Human Rights, warned that the Harvey-Kennedy resolution "turns a blind eye to history, undermines detainee welfare, and puts psychologists back at risk of being asked or ordered to participate in human rights abuses."[70] Ultimately, even though the proposal had support from the APA's Board of Directors and Ethics Committee, strong opposition from dissident psychologists, from groups within the APA such as the Society for the Psychological Study of Social Issues (APA's Division 9), and from concerned members of the council led to its resounding defeat.[71] But similar efforts to roll back reforms may still be forthcoming.

The second resolution at that 2018 APA meeting, also sponsored by Division 19's Sally Harvey with numerous co-signers, sought to remove the Hoffman Report from the association's website. The rationale they offered was that the report contained incorrect information and that, as a result, the APA's reputation was being harmed, military members of the APA were being wrongly considered "torturers," and students were being dissuaded from joining the military. The basis for these arguments is debatable, but the Council of Representatives reached a compromise: the Hoffman Report was retained on the APA website but links to online criticisms of the report were included as well. Renewed efforts to have the report removed entirely remain a possibility going forward.

DEFAMATION LAWSUITS

Since 2017, the campaign to discredit the Hoffman Report has also been waged in courtrooms around the country. Substantively identical defamation lawsuits have been filed in Ohio, Washington, DC, and Massachusetts.[72] The plaintiffs involved in all three are by now familiar names: former APA

employees Stephen Behnke and Russ Newman along with retired operational military psychologists Larry James, Morgan Banks, and Debra
Dunivin. The defendants are familiar too: David Hoffman, Hoffman's
law firm Sidley Austin, and the APA (with Stephen Soldz, a member of the
Coalition, added to the Massachusetts case).

To date, no case has been decided in the plaintiffs' favor. The Ohio case
was dismissed on jurisdictional grounds and appealed to the Ohio Second
District Court of Appeals, which upheld the trial court's ruling. In
Washington, DC, the parallel lawsuit was again dismissed by the Superior
Court.[73] The plaintiffs have appealed that ruling as well. Meanwhile, the
Massachusetts case has been stayed pending further developments.

Although legal filings in the dispute have been lengthy and sometimes
complex, in simple terms it appears that, as their primary complaint,
the plaintiffs have claimed that the Hoffman Report intentionally
mischaracterized their own actions, as well as key facts. In particular,
they've insisted that, contrary to the report's analysis, the ethical guidelines
approved by the PENS Task Force were neither loose nor designed to be
deferential to the Department of Defense's goals and preferences. And
they've further insisted that the exchanges the report described as a pattern
of secret collaboration – aimed at preserving psychologists' involvement
in detainee operations – were entirely proper and a normal part of
APA communications.

Regarding PENS, however, it is well-documented that the task force
and report adopted key elements of the Defense Department's own pre-
existing instructions for BSCT psychologists working at Guantanamo,
including the mantra "safe, legal, ethical, and effective." Arguably, the
deference here becomes even more apparent when one considers that some
of the techniques the Pentagon had deemed lawful – for example, physical
isolation for thirty days – seemingly violated psychologists' higher do-no-
harm ethical standards. Yet, despite a readily available public record at
that time, the PENS Report avoided all mention of the specific techniques
approved for use at Guantanamo, and whether they should be deemed off-
limits for the involvement of psychologists stationed there.

Turning to the nature of certain interactions among APA officials and
Defense Department representatives, the data retrieved by the Hoffman
team in support of their conclusions about covert collaboration included

binders with hundreds of pages of email exchanges, many of which were written by the plaintiffs themselves (several have been cited in preceding chapters).[74] In reviewing some of these materials, presiding DC Superior Court Judge Hiram Puig-Lugo concluded, "The purpose of the communications was to coordinate responses to public discussions about APA policies and to blunt criticisms related to treatment of detainees and interrogation practices."[75] He also added, "Curiously, the emails include phrases like 'Eyes Only,' 'Your eyes only,' 'Please delete after reading this,' and 'Please review and destroy.'"[76]

In dismissing the DC case, Puig-Lugo summarized matters succinctly when he wrote that the evidence provided by the plaintiffs – Banks, James, Dunivin, Behnke, and Newman – "fails to show that Defendants … pursued a preconceived outcome, relied on biased and unreliable sources that impacted the conclusions of the investigation and purposely avoided the truth."[77] But he went further than that. The plaintiffs had submitted numerous affidavits from their supporters, perhaps in an effort to demonstrate to the court that these sworn statements were independent confirmations of their defamation claims. However, in places several of these affidavits used almost precisely the same language, and this didn't go unnoticed by the judge. Offering verbatim examples of repeated phrases – for example, "preconceived narrative" – in his ruling against the plaintiffs, he highlighted the striking extent to which the purportedly independent affidavits "echo each other in tenor and vocabulary."[78]

With no victories in court, it might seem that the lawsuit route has been futile and has served no purpose for the plaintiffs. Yet this isn't necessarily so. The DC Superior Court held that dismissal of the case was required by the jurisdiction's ban on "strategic lawsuits against public participation" (commonly referred to by the acronym "SLAPP"). As the judge explained, the purpose of this law is to "deter meritless claims" that seek to "harass the defendant" or "punish or prevent the expression of opposing points of view."[79] But if further appeals or other legal action by the plaintiffs take months or even years to wend their way through the courts, the persistent looming threat of legal entanglements for outspoken dissidents could still have a chilling effect – one that wouldn't necessarily be unwelcomed by the military-intelligence establishment.

Even though the SLAPP ban has prevailed thus far in court, that hasn't prevented other efforts apparently aimed at silencing those who offer critical appraisals outside the courtroom. Two examples are instructive. First, in June 2017, University of Colorado professor Mitchell Handelsman published "A Teachable Ethics Scandal" in the journal *Teaching of Psychology*.[80] The article used the Hoffman Report to help explain various factors that can complicate the process of making ethical decisions. Not long after the article appeared online, it seems that former APA president Gerald Koocher – who had received extensive attention in the Hoffman Report – played a role in the publisher's decision to retract it, on the grounds that the paper failed to give adequate attention to the ongoing defamation lawsuits and related criticisms of the report.[81] In turn, this potential threat to academic freedom led Psychologists for Social Responsibility and other dissident psychologists to publicize and protest the retraction decision, and that decision was seemingly reversed.[82] Instead, the editor added a note to the article, cautioning readers that Handelsman's piece was solely his own opinion, and that anyone using it for teaching purposes should stay apprised of unfolding developments.[83]

Second, in a related instance in 2017, three unidentified military psychologists filed an ethics complaint with the APA against Coalition member Steven Reisner. They accused him of making false and deceptive statements in his extensive and influential efforts to help expose and end the involvement of psychologists in war-on-terror abuse and torture. Embracing a standard that would stifle debate on many essential questions, the complainants insisted that only psychologists with specific training in interrogation and related areas of operational psychology and "military culture" had the expertise necessary to comment on ethical issues in these domains. In his response to the Ethics Committee, Reisner warned that the complaint was, foremost, "an effort at intimidation and retaliation for my public and professional advocacy regarding important policy issues of concern to the profession and to the broader community."[84] The case was dismissed by the Ethics Office – but not before it required a detailed rebuttal from Reisner, who received assistance from the New York Civil Liberties Union and the Center for Justice and Accountability.

RESISTING THE ONSLAUGHT

The examples offered in this chapter have shown the wide range of strategies used in unsuccessful attempts – thus far – to reverse crucial APA ethics reforms. Taken as a whole, this ongoing campaign reveals the extent to which a predictable cast of characters has arguably seized upon any opportunity to undermine the efforts of those working to ensure that the APA prioritizes the profession's do-no-harm foundations over other considerations. But, in my view, they can only succeed by rewriting history.

When the CIA decided to use torturous "enhanced interrogation techniques" at its infamous black sites, we've seen that the agency gave multi-million dollar contracts to two psychologists – one was a member of the APA – who had retired from the military just months earlier. We've also seen that some active-duty military psychologists at Guantanamo were cogs in a detention and interrogation machine once described by the International Committee of the Red Cross (ICRC) as "tantamount to torture."[85] Indeed, as noted earlier, a Bush Administration official refused to refer a Guantanamo detainee for trial because she concluded that his treatment met the legal definition of torture.[86] And UN independent human rights experts have warned that indefinite detention without due process – as now exists at Guantanamo – is itself cruel, inhuman, and degrading.[87]

It's within this context that we have a simple core conclusion from the Hoffman Report: over this period, key leaders of the APA and representatives of the military-intelligence establishment worked together – often behind the scenes – to ensure that psychologists would be able to continue their involvement in detainee operations at Guantanamo and other war-on-terror detention facilities where abuses occurred.[88] They accomplished this, in part, by pushing APA policies in directions aligned with the government's preferences. There's no question that this collaboration succeeded for a very long time, despite the significant concerns that were repeatedly raised by dissident psychologists and human rights advocates alike. When its full extent was finally revealed by the Hoffman Report in 2015, the APA's Council of Representatives instituted policy reforms intended to thereafter prohibit both the participation of psychologists in national security interrogations and the involvement of military psychologists with prisoners held at Guantanamo and other unlawful sites.[89]

Those who are accustomed to power and deferential treatment often react poorly to evidence that undermines their authority or calls into question the choices they've made. That appears to be what has happened here. A vocal cadre of psychologists – some with ties to the detention and interrogation operations promoted by Bush, Cheney, and Rumsfeld – opted to pursue an aggressive anti-Hoffman offensive. The report's revelations may have threatened their reputations, their influence within the APA, and perhaps their standing within the military-intelligence establishment itself. But I believe any narrative that portrays these individuals as solely the victims of baseless allegations should be met with skepticism.

This campaign has brought together some of the very people and forces that seemingly undermined the will of the APA's membership and the profession's do-no-harm principles in the past. Despite any efforts to persuade otherwise, evidence suggests that the covert collaboration detailed in the Hoffman Report was real, the adverse consequences for psychology have been real, and the harm suffered by the victims of abuse and torture is real and potentially everlasting. For over a decade, APA members witnessed what seems to have been a tragic failure of leadership, one of perhaps historic proportions. The ongoing attacks on both the Hoffman Report and today's reform-minded APA members are vivid reminders of just that. In my view, giving the helm back to those who arguably ran the ship aground – and then let it sit rotting for years – is an alarming prospect.

At the same time, we shouldn't lose sight of the larger picture. Although influential, the military operational psychologists described in this and preceding chapters are representatives of a small contingent within the profession of psychology. Their numbers are even small within the field of military psychology. They may be motivated by a strong desire to protect the country, but their area of specialization includes within its scope some activities that can be seen as ethically suspect and precarious for psychologists – namely, national security operations designed to harm or exploit, where targets have no informed consent protections and where interventions are often classified and not readily accessible to external ethical oversight.

Such practices diverge sharply from the principles and expectations that guide the daily work of almost all psychologists – including most military psychologists – who serve as healthcare providers, researchers, teachers, or consultants. It's therefore important that we not let this small

137

contingent create false divisions in their search for broader support. The real divide isn't between psychologists who are employed by the military and those who work in the civil sector. Nor is it between psychologists who are healthcare practitioners and those who work in non-clinical areas. The divide that really matters is the one between psychologists who recognize the urgent need for accountability and reform and those who seemingly rationalize the harms, insist that no wrongdoing took place, and would like to see business as usual prevail.

Ultimately, the indisputable connections linking psychologists to the abuse of US war-on-terror prisoners bring a central question to the fore: what activities *should* be ethical for psychologists – and other health professionals – in potentially fraught national security contexts? That's the focus of the next chapter.

Operational Psychology:
The Good, the Bad, and the Ugly

DISPENSING WITH DO NO HARM?

Before 9/11, the fundamental precept "first, do no harm" might have been considered uncontroversial. But during the years that followed the terrorist attacks, efforts to expand the realm of psychological practice quickly took hold. Ever since, new career avenues in non-clinical, non-traditional roles have been aggressively promoted by military operational psychologists and their supporters. They've claimed that protecting the country from future attacks should and must supersede any commitment to avoiding harm to the individuals who are the targets of a psychologist's interventions. As we've seen, in some cases this presumption was taken to horrific extremes.

The APA's *Ethical Principles of Psychologists and Code of Conduct* has long recognized doing no harm and benefiting society as two distinct and sometimes conflicting positive values. The code's Principle A – Beneficence and Nonmaleficence – states that "psychologists strive to benefit those with whom they work and take care to *do no harm*" (emphasis added).[1] Concurrently, Principle B – Fidelity and Responsibility – states that "psychologists … are aware of their professional and scientific *responsibilities to society* and to the specific communities in which they work" (emphasis added).[2]

Tension between these values is largely absent for clinicians whose work focuses on the well-being of their individual clients. In other domestic settings, however, situations arise where the strict avoidance of harm by a psychologist can be more difficult to achieve. For example, in forensic contexts where work is conducted on behalf of the court, a psychologist's evaluation or recommendation can result in someone winding up worse off than before the proceedings began. A parent may lose custody of a child, an applicant's claim for disability relief may be denied, or a criminal defendant's insanity plea may be refuted. But it's important to note that in cases like these, it is rarely, if ever, either a requirement or the specific intent of the psychologist to cause anyone harm.

In contrast, US government authorities knowingly sought to cause harm to war-on-terror prisoners in their custody – and psychologists, often following orders from their superiors, contributed in various ways to this dehumanizing process. Still, operational psychologists have defended activities of this kind by asserting that they recognize the importance of both Principle A and Principle B. In this regard, military psychologists Carrie Kennedy and Thomas Williams have acknowledged that among the most difficult cases in the national security domain are those "in which the psychologist's input may have significant negative consequences for the individual."[3] But this statement glosses over the harmful *intent* that characterized operations at Central Intelligence Agency (CIA) and Department of Defense detention facilities. Moreover, as the preceding chapters have shown, some members of the operational psychology community have seemingly chosen to minimize or even deny the reality of years-long government-authorized abuses at Guantanamo and elsewhere.

Relevant here is the concept of "dual loyalty," sometimes referred to as "mixed agency." Most often, it applies to situations where health professionals have conflicting duties to their patients on the one hand and to third parties – typically their employers – on the other. During times of war, the dilemma can arise for doctors employed by their country's military. In this context, for example, the health professional may face a decision as to whether or not injured soldiers are healthy enough to return to the battlefield, knowing that the military's goals would be well-served by their re-engagement. The choice reflects a potentially difficult and ethically fraught balancing act – but it's one in which doctor and patient are on the same side of the struggle and presumably share a commitment to the larger mission.

When applied to the so-called war on terror and prisoner ill-treatment, things get messier. The dual loyalty concept has been extended in some quarters to include the activities of health professionals involved in facilitating harsh detention and interrogation operations.[4] Proponents have argued that psychologists face a daunting but legitimate ethical challenge when they're expected to simultaneously protect detainees from harm *and* help obtain actionable intelligence from them.

In the simplest terms, this kind of situation can pit basic human rights against national security interests. That trade-off is quite different from the scenario involving the doctor and injured soldier, in no small measure because the prisoners and the operational psychologists at CIA black sites and Guantanamo did *not* share the same allegiances to country or cause. Furthermore, the historical record is clear: dual loyalty was arguably a misnomer at facilities where the loyalty of operational psychologists appeared to flow in only one direction – downhill, in support of brutal mistreatment and psychological torment.[5]

Despite the public's growing awareness of widespread detainee mistreatment, the Psychological Ethics and National Security (PENS) Task Force – dominated by members who were themselves operational psychologists – nevertheless concluded in 2005 that the Ethics Code of the American Psychological Association (APA) was "fundamentally sound in addressing the ethical dilemmas that arise in the context of national security-related work."[6] The many apparent shortcomings of the PENS Report were described in Chapter 3. But its tacit endorsement of the controversial standard permitting psychologists to follow government orders that violated their ethical code was, on its own, a near-lethal blow against principled psychological ethics in national security settings. In the years since, some operational psychologists have asserted that the Ethics Code wasn't really designed to address the dilemmas that can arise in these contexts, and that there are frequent conflicts between psychological ethics on the one hand and organizational and legal demands on the other.[7]

This recognition of incompatibility could have stirred doubts about the ethical legitimacy of certain activities within the operational psychology community. Instead, some psychologists who practice in this domain have called for the Ethics Code to be modified, or even discarded. One argument they've offered is that they can't afford to have their hands tied given their ability to contribute to keeping Americans safe. Another is that if the profession and its Ethics Code don't evolve, psychology will lose its relevance in today's changing world.[8]

Recall the assertion from former PENS Task Force member Michael Gelles and his colleague Charles Ewing, who wrote in 2003 that it would be wrong to hold psychologists in national security settings accountable to an ethics code that has "little if any relevance to their vital government functions."[9] Adopting an even more extreme stance, operational psychologist Mark Staal, a former president of the APA's Society for Military Psychology (Division 19), has seemingly dismissed the very idea that psychologists should have their own professional code of conduct, writing, "Either an activity is ethical, or it isn't. If ethical, then psychologists should be allowed to provide their expertise to whatever problem or issue is presented."[10]

Permissive views like these, which to a significant extent diminish the do-no-harm priority of traditional psychological ethics, also appear in the writing of other operational psychologists and their allies. As mentioned previously, prior to the PENS meeting then APA president-elect Gerald Koocher told task force members that in order to protect "innocents," the goal of some psychologists' work will involve "contributing to the incarceration, debilitation, or even death of the potential perpetrator."[11] Michael Matthews, another former president of the APA's Society for Military Psychology, has recommended a role for psychologists in training soldiers in "adaptive killing," to help them more readily overcome the natural aversion to taking another life and the tendency to feel guilty about having done so.[12]

Psychology professor William O'Donohue and several of his colleagues have advocated what appears to be an even more extreme view. In a 2014 article they contended that, in order to protect the innocent, there are circumstances where it would actually be unethical and immoral for a psychologist *not* to participate in torture.[13] In a penetrating rebuttal, Jean Maria Arrigo and her co-authors with military-intelligence and ethics backgrounds have highlighted serious flaws with this lesser-evil argument.[14] Among its shortcomings, O'Donohue's analysis seems to ignore all of the following: the profound harm that torture causes to democratic institutions and the citizens that rely on them; the endangerment of other soldiers who face a greater risk of torture when international humanitarian law is abandoned; and the increased radicalization of many more potential terrorists.

Three other significant deficiencies are also present in O'Donohue's analysis. First, there's the inaccurate assertion that we lack compelling evidence that psychologists have participated in war-on-terror torture. This is a baffling claim given the extensive documentation of such involvement, as detailed in earlier chapters here. Second, O'Donohue fails to provide any evidence that the euphemistically named "enhanced interrogation techniques" have proven effective in obtaining actionable intelligence that prevented mass casualties. Third, regardless of the professional ethics in question, no evidence is offered to support the assumption that psychologists have any specialized skills likely to make torture tactics more "effective" than they would otherwise be.

Although unwelcome in some operational psychology circles, there is an option that doesn't involve either expanding or rejecting the profession's Code of Ethics – namely, strengthening the code by clarifying the kinds of activities that are professionally off-limits. As described in Chapter 4, the APA took a valuable step in this direction when, over the objections of some influential operational psychologists, Ethical Standard 1.02 was finally modified in 2010. The revision eliminated the highly problematic just-following-orders defense and included the addition that "under no circumstances may this standard be used to justify or defend violating human rights."[15]

ADVERSARIAL OPERATIONAL PSYCHOLOGY IS UNETHICAL

A decade ago, members of the Coalition for an Ethical Psychology – along with colleagues in other professions, including some with extensive military and intelligence experience – began working on what has proved to be a long-term project. Our goal was to develop a preliminary framework that we believed would be useful in distinguishing the types of national security operations that should be ethical for psychologists to participate in from those that should *not* be.[16] In an initial 2012 publication, we named the former realm "collaborative operational psychology" and the latter "adversarial operational psychology."[17] That article led to the subsequent publication of a four-part exchange with critics of our framework.[18] Then, in 2015, Coalition members organized a workshop to further explore and refine these ideas. Participants included health professionals, social scientists, and military and intelligence professionals, among others. The meeting produced a document titled "The Brookline Principles on the Ethical Practice of Operational Psychology."[19] This, in turn, led to a second four-part exchange with critics in a series of journal articles.[20]

With this background in mind, let's now turn to a discussion of the activities that we consider adversarial operational psychology. According to the framework, there are three conditions under which it's unethical for a psychologist to be involved in a national security operation. We believe that any one of these three is usually sufficient reason to rule out ethical participation by psychologists.

First, psychologists should *not* directly participate in a national security operation designed to cause significant pain and suffering to individuals or groups. Especially given the harmful intent of such an operation, here the ethical requirement that a psychologist "take care to do no harm" isn't legitimately balanced against some purported societal benefit.[21] Instead, it's obliterated entirely. A clear-cut case would be consultation to, or participation in, an interrogation in which a prisoner is intentionally subjected to physical or psychological abuse, even if it doesn't reach the level of torture. Another example would be involvement in an intelligence operation in which deceit and deception are intentionally used to discredit or humiliate political opponents.

Second, psychologists should *not* directly participate in a national security operation where the targets of the operation have not, to a reasonable degree, provided their voluntary informed consent. As established by the Nuremberg Code after World War II, this ethical restriction applies most clearly to experimentation involving human subjects.[22] In this regard, it's noteworthy that the CIA's black-site "enhanced interrogation techniques" were described by Physicians for Human Rights as "experiments in torture," and a key Senate report on detainee treatment described how military officers at Guantanamo referred to that facility as "America's Battle Lab" for new detention and interrogation techniques.[23] The APA's Ethics Code extends this informed consent requirement to assessment, therapy, counseling, and consulting services. The code's Principle E – Respect for People's Rights and Dignity – also emphasizes that "psychologists respect the dignity and worth of all people, and the rights of individuals to privacy, confidentiality, and self-determination."[24]

Third, psychologists should *not* directly participate in a national security operation in which the activities are not reasonably subject to ethical oversight and possible sanction by external professional boards. Without the availability of such monitoring by independent, unbiased experts and subsequent accountability for wrongdoing, ethical violations can persist indefinitely without remedy. This oversight problem becomes especially apparent in cases where research projects and other operations are highly classified and therefore inaccessible to those without requisite security clearances. From the perspective of psychological ethics, then, participation in projects that are beyond professional oversight and accountability is inherently objectionable.

It should be clear that the participation of psychologists in abusive war-on-terror detention and interrogation operations qualifies as adversarial operational psychology – and is therefore unethical according to this framework – on all three counts (again, any one of these criteria would be sufficient). Prisoners were intentionally subjected to significant harm, voluntary informed consent from detainees was entirely lacking when subjecting them to abuse and experimentation, and the secrecy surrounding these activities made external ethical oversight and meaningful professional accountability difficult to achieve.

It's important to recognize, however, that the vast majority of psychologists working for the US military and other national security agencies are *not* involved in adversarial operational psychology. The largest number of them are engaged in clinical practice or applied research related to the provision of mental health care to our soldiers and veterans. Other psychologists participate in collaborative operational psychology rather than adversarial operational psychology, where none of the three criteria described above is violated. Examples of collaborative operational psychology include personnel assessment and selection for specific duties, various types of training and evaluation programs, and non-covert research that focuses on improving performance. In general, the targets of intervention in all of these cases are willing participants who share a commitment to the psychologist's mission. These activities are not immune from ethical pitfalls, but they're not intrinsically in opposition to psychologists' long-standing code of conduct.

The potential damage caused by adversarial operational psychology extends well beyond the harm to its direct victims, including the prisoners abused and tortured in US war-on-terror operations. For example, a much broader negative consequence is the weaponization of a discipline rooted in advancing human welfare and knowledge. The protection of *universal* human rights likely becomes secondary, at best, when the military-intelligence establishment becomes the decision-maker as to what's ethically appropriate for psychologists to do or not do. Almost inevitably, prioritizing care and compassion will give way to participation in operations often characterized by coercion and assault.

In much the same way, psychological science – the study of human behavior – can be at risk of diversion and degradation by the massive funding resources of the Defense Department and other national security agencies. Within academia, psychologists and faculty in other disciplines may be drawn away from basic and applied research in areas central to improving the human condition. Additionally, as philosophy professor Tamsin Shaw has described, "When the defense industry supplies hundreds of millions of dollars a year to support research (both basic and applied) that is related to military psychology, there is always a potential conflict of interest between supplying results that the military wants and producing objective science."[25]

As well, when psychologists become participants in classified military-intelligence research projects, the basic procedures that advance scientific inquiry – transparency, data-sharing, and peer review – are often jettisoned and even the identities of the researchers themselves are sometimes never made public.[26] Emblematic of the pressures toward this reorientation was former APA president Martin Seligman's call to arms in 2003: "The civilized world is at war with Jihad Islamic terrorism. It takes a bomb in the office of some academics to make them realize that their most basic values are now threatened ... If we win this war, we can go on to pursue the normal goals of science."[27]

By violating widely held expectations about the healing role of psychologists in our society, adversarial operational psychology can also jeopardize the public's trust in the profession. When healthcare practitioners and researchers alike are viewed with suspicion and distrust, it diminishes their capacity to contribute knowledge and expertise in helping people better cope with the challenges they face in their lives.

PUSHBACK FROM OPERATIONAL PSYCHOLOGISTS

Not surprisingly, those psychologists whose work has involved or may involve them in adversarial operational psychology – whether for the military, intelligence agencies, or defense contractors – have strenuously objected to our analysis and to the recommendations that follow from it. Their first line of defense has routinely involved efforts to discredit us. For instance, operational psychologist Mark Staal has portrayed my colleagues and me as motivated by "personal and political bias" and as conducting a "misinformation campaign."[28] Going even further, operational psychologist Thomas Williams has described us as "too often thinly veiled in the shadows of distorted, disingenuous, and discredited diatribes." In an appeal to his colleagues, he's written that "we must ensure we are able to dislodge the opposition to operational psychology from within our profession."[29] Responses like these are counterproductive, in part because they postpone and distract from more serious discussion and debate.[30] However, three substantive criticisms that have been raised about our proposed framework merit greater attention here.

First, defenders of psychologists' involvement in adversarial operational psychology have appealed to "military necessity," arguing that essential operations simply can't succeed without the active participation and unique training of psychologists.[31] This claim, however, is at best considered a hypothesis rather than a confirmed truth, and history provides good reason to doubt its validity. Certainly, despite assurances, it now seems clear that the involvement of psychologists failed to keep interrogations "safe, legal, ethical, and effective," and that torture and abuse, facilitated by psychologists, did not produce reliable intelligence.[32]

In short, at this point there's no convincing evidence that time-honored standards for psychological ethics must be loosened, contorted, or abandoned as a matter of military necessity – even to achieve legitimate goals in the national security arena. And if it were demonstrated that a critical operation required intentional abuse – or even torture – in order to succeed and save lives, it still doesn't directly follow that psychologists must be involved in its design or implementation.

Second, supporters of adversarial operational psychology have argued that the US government – for example, the Department of Defense or the CIA – is their actual client, and that principles of psychological ethics must be understood with that client-provider relationship in mind.[33] Using this logic, however, can lead to the problematic claim that do-no-harm constraints are of relatively little consequence when it comes to the treatment of prisoners, because what really matters is whether or not the psychologist's activities have faithfully avoided harm to the agency for which they work. In turn, this formulation can open the door to all kinds of intentionally abusive interventions, as long as government authorities support them.

This same strained formulation can then be used to argue that voluntary informed consent actually hinges on whether the *government* has given permission for the psychologist to take certain actions, not whether a *detainee* has consented to the sharing of his health records with interrogators, or whether he has agreed to be subjected to sleep deprivation or other abuses. It seems apparent that this sort of reversal runs counter to prioritizing the protection of basic human rights.

Third, defenders of psychologists' involvement in activities that qualify as adversarial operational psychology have repeatedly emphasized that psychologists have an ethical obligation to benefit society.[34] As noted earlier, this is certainly true. But as former APA Ethics Office director Stephen Behnke wrote back in 2006, "Whenever a psychologist fulfills a responsibility to society, the psychologist does so abiding by Principle A in the APA Ethics Code, 'Do no harm.'"[35] In addition, it's a false equivalence to suggest that doing the bidding of the Pentagon or the CIA – especially when it involves causing harm to individuals and violating their human rights – is the same thing as benefiting society more broadly.[36] We can hope that government policies in national security contexts consistently enhance the common good. But it would be foolish to simply take that for granted.

After all, it's hard to make the case that the mistreatment of war-on-terror prisoners has proven beneficial to anyone, especially given the damage it has done to the country's image and influence.[37] Furthermore, by their very nature, psychological ethics are universalistic – they don't favor the well-being of one society and its members over another. This perspective can, at times, create irreconcilable conflicts with military operations that are much narrower in regard to whom they seek to aid. To this point, in a 2009 interview Bryce Lefever – a military operational psychologist and a former member of the PENS Task Force – revealingly explained, "America is my client; Americans are who I care about … I have no fondness for the enemy, and I don't feel like I need to take care of their mental health needs."[38]

PROFESSIONAL PRACTICE GUIDELINES FOR OPERATIONAL PSYCHOLOGY?

As I write in mid-2022, a new development bears directly on ethical issues related to operational psychology. Mark Staal – who, as previously noted, has seemingly expressed some doubts about the need for a code of ethics specific to psychologists – is now leading a task force that includes several other operational psychologists. The group is seeking to gain the APA's official approval for a set of "professional practice guidelines" that they've proposed for those involved in operational psychology.[39] As one can imagine, their proposed guidelines don't look anything like the framework that I've outlined here. A brief examination of the draft guidelines formulated by this task force is informative – and worrisome – in several ways.

What may be most striking about the draft guidelines, which seek to "encourage the practice and continued development of operational psychology," is what they fail to include.[40] There's no mention of the disturbing history of operational psychologists' involvement in detainee abuse, aside from a passing and rather cryptic reference to "past controversies."[41] There's also no mention of relevant international laws, including essential documents such as the Convention against Torture (CAT) and related instruments. And there's no mention of key APA policies that prohibit operational psychologists and other military psychologists from being present at unlawful detention sites such as Guantanamo Bay and from participating in national security interrogations.[42] This does not seem to be an oversight. Rather, these omissions appear to reflect a strategy more akin to whitewashing past wrongdoing and ignoring pre-existing constraints on the practice of operational psychology.

The proposed guidelines are also replete with vague statements that lack sufficient substance and clarity. For instance, the draft guidelines state that operational psychologists "support intelligence and military operations."[43] No descriptions of ethically permissible and impermissible forms of support are provided. Similarly, according to the draft guidelines, operational psychologists "take reasonable steps to promote welfare and avoid or minimize harm when it is foreseeable."[44] But what counts as "reasonable" and "foreseeable," who decides, and how? The proposed guidelines also state that "operational psychologists strive to avoid participating in practices that are illegal or unjust, or that unnecessarily infringe upon or violate others' rights."[45] But here too, what's the difference between striving to avoid and actually avoiding? And again, how is the determination made – and by whom – that it's necessary to infringe upon or violate someone's rights? These are all examples from the text, and it appears that much more is hidden than is revealed.

In presenting the draft guidelines, the authors note that they are "unaware of any potential financial benefit resulting from the development or implementation of the guidelines."[46] This may well be true. But if we look at the larger picture for psychologists involved in adversarial operational psychology, it seems that their military careers – and their post-retirement work as defense contractors – are likely to become more secure if these proposed practice guidelines are approved by the APA. So, it's not as though there are no financial considerations at stake in the outcome of the deliberations that lie ahead.[47] As part of the APA's approval process, the draft guidelines authors must respond to feedback they've received during a public comment period. As a result, the updated version of the guidelines is likely to be different, quite possibly in important ways. But this original version is very useful in assessing how expansive and permissive Staal and his task force may want the guidelines to be.

WHAT IS TO BE DONE?

In sum, because adversarial operational psychology arguably violates professional psychology's core ethics, the case against it is strong and the arguments in its favor are weak. Had the leadership of the APA recognized this years ago, the best path forward for the association after the 9/11 attacks might have been clearer, and perhaps much of the damage that followed could have been avoided. It seems obvious that blurring the boundaries between psychologists' ethical practice and certain forms of military-intelligence work represents a serious threat to the profession of psychology. In fact, the adversarial versus collaborative operational psychology distinction aims to protect the many psychologists involved in national security work who practice in accordance with traditional psychological ethics and international law but are directed or recruited to instead become purveyors of harm.

I therefore believe we should be wary of those who, whether motivated by values, career opportunities, patriotism, or other considerations, adopt a "gloves off" mentality when it comes to military-intelligence applications of psychology. We've seen the tremendous harm that this stance has caused. Nevertheless, perhaps untroubled by the history, there are psychologists within the APA who seemingly continue to actively promote this perspective – with firm support from the national security establishment. For at least some operational psychologists, former Army Surgeon General Kevin Kiley's description of psychology as "an important weapons system" remains a guiding light despite its apparent disregard of ethical considerations.[48]

It's a separate question as to whether the activities that characterize adversarial operational psychology are ethical for *non-psychologists*. Some may be. But it's the view of Coalition members and like-minded others that individuals who participate in this realm should be prohibited from holding licenses as *practicing psychologists*, and that they should not be allowed to hold positions as *psychologists* in academia, in research organizations, or in professional associations.[49] Instead, if they choose to do so, they can become *intelligence professionals* with expertise in psychology. This approach does entail significant career consequences, and we recognize that it merits further scrutiny and discussion among all stakeholder groups, as well as revision or elaboration as appropriate.

Given that adversarial operational psychology conflicts with fundamental dimensions of psychological ethics, it's important that the relatively small community of military-intelligence psychologists engaged in these activities not gain unwarranted acceptance and influence by claiming common cause with other psychologists – operational and otherwise – whose work doesn't encroach on the same ethical red lines. Yet this seems to be exactly what they are trying to achieve when Mark Staal insists, for example, that a negative view of adversarial operational psychology has "global implications … for the practice of applied professional psychology across public safety, law enforcement, and other organizational consulting domains."[50]

Staal's claim ignores the fact that our framework focuses solely on the national security sector and that this sector has important characteristics – for psychologists, at least – that are not typically found elsewhere. These include, for example, the exceedingly extensive background checks that are necessary to obtain requisite security clearances, the clear government directives that the profession's Code of Ethics does *not* supersede Department of Defense policy, and the heightened protections from civil prosecution or disciplinary action in light of the relative paucity of investigative journalists, citizen action groups, independent attorneys, and oversight boards that might spur legal action or ethics complaints.[51]

To be sure, there are legitimate debates to be had about various aspects of psychological ethics, and the so-called war on terror has brought some of them into sharper focus. But the profession's concerns about protecting society cannot justify the rubber-stamping of whatever national security operations the military-intelligence establishment chooses to pursue. As Coalition members Stephen Soldz, Jean Maria Arrigo, and Brad Olson have highlighted, "To allow psychology to be subsumed under military or intelligence exigencies would ... erode the essential counterweight provided by autonomous professions in modern civil societies."[52] Or, to put it another way, in my view adversarial operational psychology isn't merely some sort of slippery slope – it's more like an avalanche that can overwhelm professional ethics and bury human rights.

8

Lessons Learned and the Road Ahead

BEYOND INDIVIDUAL WRONGDOING

As I write this final chapter of *Doing Harm*, we're now a year past the twentieth anniversary of the September 11, 2001, terrorist attacks. The destruction wrought by that day and by the so-called war on terror that followed have had profound and lasting effects on millions of lives, in the United States and around the world. My focus here has been much narrower: examining the disturbing consequences of these events in relation to professional psychology in the United States and particularly the American Psychological Association (APA).

The abuse and torture of prisoners in US custody would have been unconscionable even if health professionals had played no role whatsoever. But because psychologists were involved and the APA adopted a supportive stance toward government-authorized detention and interrogation operations, these immoral excesses were arguably given the patina of decency and necessity. Indeed, we've seen that there's reason to believe that the participation of health professionals and the acquiescence of the APA made the cruel, inhuman, and degrading treatment of detainees more likely to occur and persist. And tragically, if elected officials in Washington, DC, or concerned citizens opposed to US war-on-terror policies wanted validation for their stance from a respected voice, they had to look elsewhere than the world's largest organization of psychologists to find it.

Today, the APA's turbulent journey since 9/11 is still unfinished business, and we don't know whether the association will demonstrate a steadfast commitment to human rights and professional ethics when the Pentagon and the Central Intelligence Agency (CIA) next come calling. Important ethics reforms that limit the role of psychologists in national security operations – finally adopted in 2015 after years of dissident activism and advocacy – still remain as official APA policy. But they are undoubtedly fragile. With support from the military-intelligence establishment, APA members eager to undo these changes haven't abandoned their fight. The ultimate outcome of their efforts is uncertain, but the significance of what's at stake is not.

It seems apparent that the actions of key individuals – and the inaction of many bystanders – played significant roles in the APA's failure to stand as a bulwark against war-on-terror abuses. However, the destructive influences of broader organizational patterns and powerful societal forces merit our careful attention as well. With this recognition in mind, in this chapter I attempt to explain how these factors are critical for a full understanding of the APA's two-decade struggle and its current precarious circumstances. Of particular note, these same considerations apply to challenges faced by a wide range of civil society organizations in the United States. I then conclude with recommendations for steps the APA's leadership should take in order for the association to establish and maintain a firm and demonstrable commitment to psychological ethics and human rights going forward.

THE DYNAMICS OF INSTITUTIONAL BETRAYAL

An organization engages in "institutional betrayal" when, through acts of either commission or omission, it violates the trust and expectations of the people who rely on it for their well-being or identity. Psychologist Jennifer Freyd and her colleagues have identified a variety of forms that this betrayal typically takes: creating conditions where harm becomes more likely; failing to take steps to prevent harm from occurring; denying or disguising the harm that has already taken place; refusing to hold the perpetrators of harm accountable; erecting obstacles that make it more difficult to report harm; and using threats or retaliation against those who do report or publicize the harm.[1] In regard to the APA, at least some of these tactics should seem familiar from preceding chapters.

One particularly pernicious form of institutional betrayal goes by the acronym "DARVO" for deny, attack, and reverse victim and offender.[2] In these instances, those found to have engaged in wrongdoing deny their role as perpetrators and instead portray themselves as the victims of their critics' unfair accusations. It seems that DARVO, too, has been a weapon used at various times by the APA's leadership and by members who worked to preserve the involvement of psychologists in ethically suspect war-on-terror operations.

Freyd has also studied what she calls "betrayal blindness."[3] The phenomenon refers to the dissonance-reducing tendency – among victims, perpetrators, and witnesses alike – to be unaware, dismissive, or forgetful of the betrayal they've experienced, committed, or observed. To put it another way, if we wish that something hadn't happened, sometimes we try to imagine that it didn't. Related research suggests that the more strongly individuals identify with and depend upon an organization, the more likely they are to see their own identities as imperiled by threats to the organization.[4] When that threat takes the form of alleged organizational wrongdoing, it's not surprising that betrayal blindness will characterize the response of some members. As we've seen, this seems true for the APA. At both the leadership and the general membership levels, there's been an unwillingness to fully recognize, acknowledge, and address the association's apparent misconduct.[5]

But the APA's institutional betrayal is far from unique. We see it elsewhere, in many shades and contexts. In the business world, public reports have identified now familiar cases where executives concerned about company profits engaged in acts of negligence or cover-up, violating the public's expectations of good corporate citizenship. For decades, tobacco companies concealed evidence of the addictive and cancer-causing effects of cigarettes.[6] For just as long, asbestos industry giants withheld information about the heightened risks of cancer and other diseases from their workers and customers.[7] Over many years, auto companies denied dangerous manufacturing defects, and in some cases tried to silence whistleblowers.[8] And the oil and gas industry did much the same in regard to climate change, promoting profit-generating misinformation long after the adverse consequences of fossil fuel use had been recognized.[9]

Instances like these are deeply troubling, even if we recognize and accept the reality that profit-seeking is a driving force in the corporate world.

In important ways, then, betrayal is both more unexpected and more painful when the institutions at fault present themselves as communities committed to a higher purpose. Yet disturbing reports are not hard to find here either. Belying its message of spiritual sustenance and fellowship, for years the Catholic Church has been engulfed in scandal, with thousands of priests and clergy credibly accused of child sexual abuse.[10] Likewise, the ongoing menace of widespread sexual assault in the US military – and the broken system of accountability that allows it to persist – contradicts representations of camaraderie in the nation's service.[11] And the sexual abuse scandals at prominent schools over the past decade have undercut the image of universities as safe havens for the pursuit of higher education and personal growth.[12]

It seems we can now add the APA to this latter category. One might even argue that there's something especially demoralizing and outrageous when institutional betrayal involves a profession – and its 100,000-member association – that has an avowed commitment to providing care, to defending human rights, and, above all, to doing no harm. After publication of the Hoffman Report, Freyd and her colleagues turned their attention specifically to the APA case, explaining how the harm resulting from betrayal has affected not only the association and its members, but also the profession of psychology and the abused war-on-terror detainees.[13]

Given the breadth and magnitude of this damage, it's important to consider whether there are organization-level factors that, in one way or another, made it more likely that institutional betrayal would occur at the APA. Ideally, greater awareness of these features should help to prevent a recurrence. From my own perspective, I believe three factors proved to be especially consequential for the APA: the prioritization of guild ethics, the overweighting of reputation management, and the seemingly dysfunctional nature of the association's leadership structure and norms. Let's examine each in turn, recognizing that all of them are potential risk factors for other organizations as well.

First, the APA's apparent betrayal of the profession's core values can be tied to what Ken Pope has identified as the association's transition from a focus on "professional ethics" to "guild ethics."[14] According to Pope, professional ethics are a code of conduct designed to protect the public against practitioners who misuse their expertise and influence to pursue self-interested goals. Guild ethics are very different from that because they are foremost intended to facilitate members' careers while insulating them from accountability for their transgressions. The distinction is clear: when faced with controversy, does the organization respond with efforts to protect its members or does it try to help those who have allegedly been harmed by them? For the APA, this difference has had profound consequences, especially given that many state licensing boards rely on the association's Ethics Code when reviewing complaints from the public.

Pope has also warned that guild ethics can masquerade as professional ethics and can "find ways around even the most absolute, unambiguous prohibitions, discover loopholes in seemingly solid standards, and offer the appearance but not the reality of fair, just, and meaningful mechanisms of accountability."[15] It may only be during times of organizational crisis that the underlying reality truly becomes visible. At other times, the lack of clarity can persist indefinitely because organizations that operate under guild ethics or professional ethics don't necessarily differ from each other in the skills, ideals, or accomplishments of their members. In short, the diminished standards associated with guild ethics can hold sway within an organization even while the public – and some members of the group itself – continue to think that elevated professional ethics are the guiding principles.[16]

For the APA, the shift from professional ethics to guild ethics appears to have started well before 9/11. But the trend accelerated and reached its zenith with the association's deference to Pentagon and CIA war-on-terror preferences despite the divergences from traditional psychological ethics. As previously discussed, the change to Ethical Standard 1.02 that was adopted in 2002, making it permissible to follow orders that would otherwise violate the Ethics Code, may be the clearest instance of a broader trend. At that time, the revised 1.02 diminished the likelihood of sanctions for ethical wrongdoing. In turn, this reduced risk served to expand opportunities for military-intelligence psychologists, who could thereafter participate in detention and interrogation operations in a less ethically constrained manner – and with APA leaders seemingly ready to defend them.

A second organization-level factor that arguably contributed to the APA's institutional betrayal is the high priority given to protecting the association's reputation at the expense of meaningful transparency and accountability. Of particular relevance here is the rich history of scholarship in sociology that has focused on how people – individuals and groups alike – craft statements designed to help them escape the adverse consequences that might otherwise result from their wrongdoing. A brief review of this literature shows how it directly resonates with the APA's various post-9/11 tactics.

Over a half-century ago, Marvin Scott and Stanford Lyman wrote about what they called "accounts" – statements that are made "to explain untoward behavior and bridge the gap between actions and expectations."[17] They focused on two specific types of accounts: justifications and excuses. With justifications, they explained, "one accepts responsibility for the act in question, but denies the pejorative quality associated with it"; with excuses, "one admits that the act in question is bad, wrong, or inappropriate but denies full responsibility."[18]

In their analysis, Scott and Lyman credited the work of fellow sociologists Gresham Sykes and David Matza, who, a decade earlier, had developed an inventory of "techniques of neutralization."[19] Sykes and Matza highlighted five techniques as the core justifications that youthful offenders used when defending their delinquent acts: denying responsibility for the wrongdoing; denying that anyone was actually injured by it; claiming that the injured party was the real wrongdoer; claiming that those who criticize them were being unfair; and insisting that their actions were governed by higher principles. Some of these self-serving accounts certainly fit the assertions of APA leaders that I've detailed in earlier chapters.

This early scholarship was extended by others to analyzing organizations rather than individuals. Sociologist Stanley Cohen, for example, applied elements of these frameworks in examining how governments engage in denial when faced with revelations of human rights abuses and related atrocities.[20] Cohen identified four elements to this denial: "*cognition* (not acknowledging the facts), *emotional* (not feeling, not being disturbed), *morality* (not recognizing wrongness or responsibility), and *action* (not taking active steps in response to knowledge)."[21] He also explained that when these governments are forced to manufacture accounts for their transgressions, their aim isn't necessarily to persuade the public that what they did was right, but rather to encourage the view that their explanations are at least credible and reasonable. Cohen summarized official statements as "a mixture of blatant lies, half-truths, evasions, legalistic sophistries, ideological appeals and credible factual objections."[22] The parallels with the APA's own pronouncements seem apparent.

Other scholars have also directed their attention to the strategic use of accounts by corporations and other organizations in responding to the public disclosure of their malfeasance.[23] The goal of these efforts is to preserve or reestablish perceived legitimacy in the eyes of both internal and external actors. Based on his research in this area, sociologist Mark Suchman has offered a useful definition of organizational legitimacy: "a generalized perception or assumption that the actions of an entity are desirable, proper, or appropriate within some socially constructed system of norms, values, beliefs, and definitions."[24]

Achieving the goal of perceived legitimacy becomes a source of conflict when specific actions are deemed legitimate by some stakeholders but illegitimate by others.[25] This is certainly true for the APA, where representatives of the military-intelligence establishment have defended psychologist involvement in harsh detention and interrogation operations while dissidents have argued that such work is unethical. For many years, it appears that the APA tried to have it both ways, doing the bidding of the Pentagon and the CIA while downplaying or hiding this accommodation from concerned members and the public. The extent to which this may still be happening is not entirely clear.

In this regard, it has often been frustrating for the dissident community to see how APA leaders seemingly take advantage of the broader membership's lack of close attention to particular issues. This limited engagement makes it much easier for the leadership to distort the truth in self-protective and reputation-enhancing ways. Several instances of this tactic have already been described in preceding chapters, but one more example is worth recounting here because it captures this reputation management strategy so well.

In June 2009, the APA Board of Directors sent a letter to all association members, expressing regret and alarm over evidence that psychologists had been involved in detainee abuse.[26] The letter gave the impression that this disturbing reality was somehow newsworthy, rather than something that had been clear as day for years. The letter also emphasized that the Ethics Committee was hard at work tackling Standard 1.02, even though the council's initial call for revision had come in 2005, *four years* earlier. And the letter suggested that the APA would continue to speak out strongly against torture and abuse, even though the actual record shows that the APA's public criticism of Bush-era detention and interrogation policies was much more the exception than the rule. Still, most members who read the letter probably found it persuasive and reassuring – in other words, a reputation management success.

Suchman has also noted that when faced with a crisis of legitimacy, organizations typically try to formulate "a normalizing account that separates the threatening revelation from larger assessments of the organization as a whole."[27] Consistent with other scholarship in this area, he explains that, depending upon the situation, these normalizing accounts may primarily rely on denials ("It never happened"), excuses ("We're not to blame"), or justifications ("We had good reason"). As we've seen, at varying times APA leaders have turned to all three.

Prime examples in the excuse category have been variations of the false claim that psychologist involvement in war-on-terror abuses was limited to the actions of "a few bad apples." CIA psychologists James Mitchell and Bruce Jessen (who themselves have denied wrongdoing) are routinely cited in this way to create cover and distance for both the APA and the Department of Defense. For instance, in a published letter responding to a 2017 *Washington Post* essay that I had written about the APA's ethics scandal, the association's CEO Arthur Evans, Jr, wrote that the profession of psychology shouldn't be confused with "the actions of two rogue psychologists who designed and implemented the CIA's notorious detainee torture program during the George W. Bush administration."[28] In a similar manner, in a wide-ranging interview two years later, Rosie Phillips Davis, the APA's president at that time, responded to a question about prisoner abuse by insisting, "We had two psychologists who were not APA members who designed the program … It was not APA as an organization."[29] Sadly, face-saving assertions like these have been familiar fare throughout the entire duration of the APA's ethics debacle.

The third organization-level factor implicated in the APA's institutional betrayal revolves around the association's leadership structure and norms. Psychologists Dan Aalbers and Thomas Teo have identified several important and worrisome characteristics. For example, they've described the APA's unelected senior staff members as "the power behind the throne."[30] These senior staffers typically have long tenures; Ethics Office director Stephen

Behnke held his position for fifteen years before his abrupt dismissal in 2015. This kind of longevity, they explain, can convey a sense of ownership and provide the capacity to engage in "bureaucratic sabotage" in order to preserve policies that these staffers helped to establish – even when doing so defies the will of the membership.[31]

By contrast, the association's president only serves a one-year term, along with additional single years as president-elect and past-president. However, it's important not to overlook the influence of "lifers" among the APA's elected leaders as well. Over a period of years or even decades, some members find ways to rotate from one position to another, serving on the Board of Directors, or the Council of Representatives, or the executive committees of various APA divisions, or in some other role. Gerald Koocher, for instance, has held an elected leadership position within the APA for most of the past quarter-century.

Aalbers and Teo have also identified another significant problem with the nature of the APA's elected governing body, emphasizing that "the structure of the APA ensures that the Council members are under-informed, over-worked and required to make decisions without deliberation."[32] The full council meets only for a few days, twice each year, and the lengthy agenda established beforehand by the leadership makes it clear that limited discussion and quick agreement are highly valued process norms. Those members who express reservations about a policy recommendation are likely to be viewed as "narcissists who place their individual judgements above the careful deliberations of highly qualified individuals."[33]

These troubling features of the APA's council meetings are characteristics often associated with "groupthink," a destructive phenomenon that's been studied by psychologists for decades, beginning with Irving Janis.[34] Groupthink refers to the ineffective, costly, and misguided decisions made by a group when it focuses too much on achieving harmony and consensus and not enough on encouraging dissenting views and open debate. Among the most well-known tragedies linked to groupthink was NASA's launch of the space shuttle *Challenger* in January 1986. Facing various pressures, authorities chose to ignore concerns raised by some engineers about the heightened dangers given the unusually low temperatures that day. A minute after lift-off, the shuttle exploded, killing all seven astronauts on board – and severely damaging the country's space program.[35]

Groupthink pressures to conform are likely to be especially strong when those in positions of power exert tight control over the proceedings and are convinced that their own views are right and righteous. Individuals who assume the role of "mindguards" further serve to keep everyone in line. They block the presentation of contrary information and minimize opportunities for the expression of dissenting perspectives. This in turn can lead to self-censorship among those who harbor doubts, and it may even lead to their departure from the group.

Related to the embrace of leadership norms that actively discourage dissent, the APA's guidelines for council members include an expectation of primary loyalty and fidelity to the association itself. Voting for what's deemed best for the APA can therefore take precedence over what's morally right or what's in the public interest. This gives tremendous power to those within the APA who are viewed as the final arbiters of what's most beneficial to the association. Ultimately, Aalbers and Teo are pessimistic about lasting change within the APA as long as the bureaucracy and associated norms described here remain unchanged. They specifically note, "Unless the APA transforms its governing body into a deliberative one, and unless it returns decision-making power to the elected leadership, a return to a strong relationship between the DoD and APA may be inevitable."[36]

Bryant Welch, a member of the Coalition for an Ethical Psychology who previously spent many years employed by the APA and led its Practice Directorate, has expressed similar concerns about the internal workings of the association.[37] In particular, he has emphasized how, under the leadership of the late former CEO Raymond Fowler, the APA "was transformed into a conflict-avoidant culture characterized by narcissism and self-congratulatory fawning that was carefully cultivated and readily manipulated by a few key leaders who used it for personal gain."[38] The abstract value of "working together" was promoted to such an extent that even substantive criticism from council members of the APA's policies or agenda was deemed mean-spirited and contrary to the customary and preferred way of doing business. Although Fowler retired in 2003, some of his devoted followers remained in the association's highest echelons. They preserved much of the same culture, despite the need for serious discussion and debate about US war-on-terror excesses and the involvement of psychologists in some of the worst cases.

In sum, the APA's focus on guild ethics and reputation management, along with its problematic governance structure and norms, all pointed to heightened risks of institutional betrayal. And they continue to do so. But an equally powerful force that I believe has ensnared the APA is the pervasive lure of militarism, and I turn to that topic next.

THE LURE OF MILITARISM

In Washington, DC, there's always near-unanimous bipartisan support for the ever-growing US defense budget. That annual budget, now well over $700 billion, exceeds the expenditures of the next seven largest countries combined – and it doesn't even fully account for the hundreds of billions spent annually on the CIA and other intelligence agencies, the maintenance of our nuclear weapons, and the Department of Veterans Affairs.[39]

Beyond these staggering absolute figures, this level of funding comes with an additional significant cost: the failure to meet other pressing needs. In a memorable address, shortly after becoming president of the United States in 1953, General Dwight Eisenhower warned, "Every gun that is made, every warship launched, every rocket fired signifies, in the final sense, a theft from those who hunger and are not fed, those who are cold and are not clothed."[40] He would likely be astounded by how things look today. Yet, appeals to patriotism and images of doom at the hands of foreign enemies continue to drive this spending even though strong arguments have been made that many of these so-called national security dollars could be better spent protecting us in other ways.[41]

To its credit, over the years the APA has taken public stands confronting the perils and injustices associated with a wide range of issues that are removed from traditional conceptions of national security. Examples include advocacy in regard to climate change, poverty, racism, gun violence, consumerism, immigration, reproductive rights, LGBTQ rights, and the COVID-19 pandemic.[42] Nevertheless, when the focus shifts to conquering the third of what Martin Luther King, Jr, called the "giant triplets of racism, extreme materialism, and militarism," all too often the APA and US psychology have seemingly turned silent – or worse.[43]

During federal budget discussions in the nation's capital, at times the association has warned against cuts to domestic programs, especially those that would diminish practice opportunities for psychologists.[44] But the APA rarely speaks out against the enormous funding that's routinely provided to the military-intelligence establishment. Indeed, the APA frequently sponsors testimony before defense appropriations committees calling for *more* funding for psychological research with military and intelligence applications.[45]

So even though the APA, as a bastion of scientific knowledge about human behavior, could play an important role in cautioning against unchecked militarism, that doesn't really happen. Apparent deference to the will and whim of the Bush Administration – which arguably put the APA on the wrong side of history and morality – is just the most obvious example. The association's leaders, it seems, were overly eager to find ways to support the burgeoning "war on terror," even when it meant twisting the profession's ethical principles into nearly unrecognizable forms. The APA's accommodations may well have contributed to the acceptance of brutality and inhumanity that few would have imagined possible.

It's inevitable that psychologists – and practitioners, educators, and researchers in other disciplines as well – will sometimes face potential ethical dilemmas when called upon to use their expertise for avowed national security purposes. When placed in this circumstance after 9/11, the APA tried to have it both ways – publicly claiming allegiance to do-no-harm ethics while working behind the scenes to find ways for psychologists to continue participating in detainee operations where abuse was not uncommon. In so doing, I believe the APA held tightly to the misguided and grandiose conviction that the profession should try to embrace almost every opportunity to expand its sphere of influence. The association could instead have used its knowledge and reputation to promote alternatives to the choices of Bush, Cheney, and Rumsfeld. But it seems that entrepreneurs, careerists, and yea-sayers were allowed to carry the day.[46]

At the same time, it's important to recognize that, historically, psychology hasn't been alone in its support for ill-considered and often clandestine participation in ethically suspect US military-intelligence operations. Anthropology's past century provides some relevant comparisons. In a letter published in *The Nation* in 1919 just after the end of World War I, Franz Boas – considered by many the father of American anthropology – condemned unnamed fellow anthropologists, writing that "a person ... who uses science as a cover for political spying ... prostitutes science in an unpardonable way and forfeits the right to be classed as a scientist."[47] The governing council of the American Anthropological Association responded quickly, censuring Boas for conduct deemed detrimental to the profession. It wasn't until 2005 that the association rescinded and repudiated that censure motion.[48]

Examples of other dubious endeavors by anthropologists prior to the "war on terror" have included their participation in the War Relocation Authority that oversaw the internment of Japanese Americans during World War II, the US Army's Project Camelot, which involved anthropologists in counterinsurgency work in Latin America under the guise of scientific research, and their involvement in advancing the US war effort in Vietnam through similar counterinsurgency research.[49] Roberto Gonzalez, Hugh Gusterson, and David Price of the Network of Concerned Anthropologists have noted that this "episodic militarization" of the field has brought with it "three recurring fundamental ethical problems: secrecy, harm, and manipulation."[50]

A more recent war-on-terror case was the Pentagon's controversial Human Terrain System (HTS). First developed in 2005, the program embedded anthropologists as intelligence assets in operations in Afghanistan and Iraq.[51] The objective was to provide US soldiers with ready access to expert socio-cultural knowledge in order to facilitate the Army's counterinsurgency efforts and related military missions. The ethical issues raised by such work seem clear. One HTS anthropologist explained her own participation in the program this way: "The reality is there are people out there who are looking for bad guys to kill … I'd rather they did not operate in a vacuum."[52]

In 2009, spurred to take action by a dissident faction of anthropologists including Gonzalez, Gusterson, and Price, a committee of the American Anthropological Association deliberated and reached a clear conclusion: "When ethnographic investigation is determined by military missions, not subject to external review, where data collection occurs in the context of war, integrated into the goals of counterinsurgency, and in a potentially coercive environment – all characteristic factors of the HTS concept and its application – it can no longer be considered a legitimate professional exercise of anthropology."[53] The government quietly discontinued the HTS program in 2014. According to the Army, the operational advice of civilian anthropologists was simply no longer needed.[54]

As a practical matter, the prospect of ethics-based tensions between the military-intelligence establishment and professional psychology are likely to be even more fraught and consequential. Unlike for anthropology and other social science disciplines, the Department of Defense and the Department of Veterans Affairs are among the single largest employers of psychologists.[55] Moreover, these departments and related national security agencies provide many internships for graduate students and significant funding for psychological research.[56] For-profit defense contractors offer employment opportunities to psychologists as well. In some cases, these businesses are owned or operated by psychologists, including retired military operational psychologists who have held influential roles within the APA.[57]

Especially relevant to this context, Bryant Welch has identified two specific factors that also have contributed to what appears to be the outsized influence of those with military-intelligence connections within the APA. First, he has highlighted the role played by former APA president Patrick DeLeon over many years. DeLeon was a longtime senior aide to Daniel Inouye, the late senator from Hawaii who was among the most powerful figures on Capitol Hill when it came to authorizing military and intelligence expenditures. Through DeLeon, the APA was able to develop and maintain highly valued goodwill and accommodation from Inouye's office in regard to funding for psychological research with defense applications.

Second, for decades there have been close ties between the APA and the Human Resources Research Organization (HumRRO).[58] Initially focused on research that included the development of techniques for "psychological warfare," HumRRO was founded in 1951 by psychologist Meredith Crawford with sole funding from the Pentagon. Years later, the company became an independent nonprofit corporation, but much of its budget in recent years has continued to come from diverse defense-related projects, including research investigating trends in military recruitment, selection criteria for Predator and Reaper drone operators, and the design of "overwhelmingly lethal" combat systems.[59]

In the late 1950s, Crawford became the APA's treasurer and he remained an influential figure within the association for decades – all while also serving as a member of HumRRO's Board of Trustees. Thereafter, it became routine for HumRRO executives to assume leadership positions at the APA. Over the past decade, William Strickland, a former president of the APA's Society for Military Psychology, served terms as an elected member of the APA's Council of Representatives and Board of Directors while simultaneously employed as HumRRO's president and CEO. And in 2016, Nathalie Gilfoyle, then the APA's general counsel, assumed the position of vice chair and secretary of HumRRO's Board of Trustees months before she retired from the association.[60] Even though these overlapping roles are lawful and have been unconcealed, they have raised concerns nonetheless.

For example, in a paper presented at the 2017 meeting of the International Society of Military Ethics, Coalition member Jean Maria Arrigo and retired special forces officer Dutch Franz described what they see as the problematic nature of often-overlooked connections between the APA and HumRRO. They referenced the conflicts of loyalty that are likely to arise, the inside information that can flow from the APA to HumRRO, and the reality that those individuals who hold leadership positions in both organizations can "steer the APA towards policies that support outside business interests not aligned with the APA mission and traditional psychological ethics." According to Arrigo and Franz, "The embedding of HumRRO personnel in high-level APA governance and staff positions is an investment in opportunities for networking, recruiting, marketing, and policymaking, cloaked in APA's good name as a professional association."[61]

To be clear, the APA's history of overzealousness when it comes to opportunities for collaboration with the military hasn't been limited to its support for misguided war-on-terror detention and interrogation operations. Another noteworthy example was the association's questionable promotion of the Army's Comprehensive Soldier Fitness (CSF) program over a decade ago. The developers of CSF, including former APA president Martin Seligman, were enthusiastic that the program, which has cost hundreds of millions of dollars, would build resilience among US soldiers and thereby significantly reduce the incidence of PTSD and suicide among American troops. In January 2011, the APA devoted the entirety of its monthly flagship journal, *The American Psychologist*, to singing the praises of CSF. Seligman was one of the co-editors of this special issue.[62]

But regardless of the intentions, it appears that a potentially serious problem should have been salient for the APA and other interested parties from the very outset: CSF was never pilot-tested to see if it actually worked before quickly rolling it out and making the experimental program mandatory for over one million soldiers. When outcome data were eventually collected and analyzed to assess csf's effectiveness, *independent* evaluations – including one from the prestigious National Academy of Sciences Institute of Medicine – concluded that the overhyped program failed to achieve its stated goals.[63] In short, here too the APA had rushed to lend its support to a venture bringing together the US military and professional psychology while seemingly ignoring significant questions about both the science and the ethics involved.[64]

HOLDING ON, AND LETTING GO

The theologian Forrest Church wrote, "When cast into the depths, to survive we must first let go of things that will not save us. Then we must reach out for things that can."[65] In many ways, this is exactly the right prescription for the APA, if the association wants to overcome its years characterized by apparent institutional betrayal and thereby regain the legitimacy it has lost. The APA's mission of "advancing psychology to benefit society and improve people's lives" certainly doesn't require it to turn away from matters of national security. But it does necessitate the prioritization of ethics and human rights over expediency and opportunity. There are a range of steps the APA can take in this direction.[66]

Acknowledgment of wrongdoing and sincere efforts at restitution matter. In 2015, after the release of the Hoffman Report, key APA leaders sent a letter of apology on behalf of the association to the general membership.[67] The letter acknowledged that the APA failed to adopt a clear and consistent anti-torture stance, that appropriate checks and balances were lacking within the organization, and that concerns raised by dissidents and others should not have been discounted. A similar letter was sent to international psychologists, expressing regret for the potential damage to the profession worldwide.[68] These were important steps. But at that time, the APA leadership did not offer an official apology to the direct victims of the "war on terror" and their communities.[69] Now, seven years later, what I believe is a serious omission still awaits correction.

Of course, torture survivors need and deserve more than an apology. They're also entitled under international law to compensation and support for their rehabilitation, and accountability for those who contributed to their harm.[70] The APA can use its much-touted influence in Washington, DC, to help make this happen. The association is also well-positioned – with both trauma expertise and financial resources – to assist former prisoners and their families interested in obtaining mental health care. Recurring contributions to nonprofit organizations that provide such services could become part of the APA's regular annual giving.[71] Beyond the benefits to survivors, these various actions would serve to demonstrate an ongoing commitment by the APA to remembering and repairing past trans-gressions – and to avoiding them in the future.

In recognition of 2022 as the twenty-fifth anniversary of the United Nations (UN) International Day in Support of Torture Victims, the executive committee of the Society for the Study of Peace, Conflict, and Violence (APA's Division 48) endorsed a statement I drafted that calls upon the APA's leadership to take these two ameliorative steps. I am currently spearheading a campaign that invites other organizations to add their endorsements to this call for apology and reparations from the association.[72] To date, several leading human rights groups – including Amnesty International USA, the Center for Constitutional Rights, the Center for Victims of Torture, and Physicians for Human Rights – have signed on. In addition, several other divisions within the APA are now endorsers as well. However, to the best of my knowledge, members of the APA's Board of Directors have offered no response whatsoever. An observation that psychologist Ellen Gerrity has made seems apt here: "Those who are tortured say that they are told again and again that no one cares or will ever care about what has happened to them. Part of the torturer's objective is to isolate and instill despair."[73]

There are also related ways that APA leaders can communicate their firm opposition to detainee abuse and torture. The association can join dozens of human rights groups – and former detainees – that have forcefully advocated for the closure of Guantanamo and an end to the indefinite detention of the prisoners still there.[74] As recently as January 2021, special rapporteur on torture Nils Melzer and other UN experts described the facility as a "disgrace" and "a place of arbitrariness and abuse, a site where torture and ill-treatment was rampant and remains institutionalised, where the rule of law is effectively suspended, and where justice is denied."[75] They noted as well that "the prolonged and indefinite detention of individuals, who have not been convicted of any crime by a competent and independent judicial authority operating under due process of law, is arbitrary and constitutes a form of cruel, inhuman, and degrading treatment, or even torture."[76]

In striking contrast to his predecessor, US president Joe Biden has expressed a desire to close Guantanamo as part of his administration's agenda. [77] To its credit, the APA sent a letter to the White House in May 2021 communicating support for these efforts.[78] But the letter doesn't acknowledge the role that psychologists have played in the abuses at the detention center, and it hasn't been followed by more forceful advocacy. Making Guantanamo's closure a higher and more public priority would signal loudly that respect for human dignity and professional ethics have overcome considerations of political and economic expediency at the APA. The association can go a step further and also call for the removal of Appendix M from the Army Field Manual, the current basis for interrogation operations. As described earlier, the appendix still permits psychologically abusive techniques, including extended isolation, sleep deprivation, and sensory deprivation.

But the prospects for significant progress by the APA on these and related fronts seem questionable at best unless the association makes significant and lasting internal adjustments in the way it operates. Furthermore, as Ken Pope has aptly noted about organizations struggling to end a crisis, time isn't likely to be on the side of the reformers: "As time passes, the urgency of reform fades and the urge to externalize accountability, outsource responsibility, and backtrack takes hold. Powerful incentives inside and outside the organization, as well as organizational character, culture, and other factors that caused the crisis and allowed it to metastasize reassert themselves, often with renewed force and determination."[79]

Regrettably, this pattern appears to be playing out already. For example, the APA's leadership has arguably failed to take sufficient action over the past five years in responding to a 2017 report from its own "blue ribbon" Ethics Commission.[80] Following the Hoffman Report's revelations, this seventeen-member panel was established "to examine the APA's ethics processes and recommend changes."[81] Among other recommendations, the commission's report called for the APA to "articulate a core set of organizational ethical principles and standards" recognizing psychologists as protectors of human rights, develop a process for "adopting policies that are enforceable without being written into the Ethics Code," enhance the APA's "institutional conflict of interest policies," and engage in a recurring "ethics audit, conducted by an external organization with such expertise."[82] All of these changes, discussed in detail in the full report, make good sense in light of the APA's post-9/11 history. To date, it appears that they still await effective implementation. That should happen, and without further delay.[83]

Perhaps even more troubling is the fact that the APA has apparently decided to take significant steps in direct *opposition* to the recommendations from the Ethics Commission. Specifically, the commission recommended several procedural changes aimed at making the APA's processing and adjudication of ethics complaints more thorough and more effective.[84] However, in 2018, mere months after receiving the report, the association announced that the Ethics Office would instead *reduce* its engagement in these matters and would "only accept complaints against an APA member psychologist if there is no alternative forum to hear the complaint."[85]

The rationale offered by the APA is that the public will be better served in this way because the association lacks the investigatory and sanctioning powers that other oversight bodies possess. There may be some truth to this assessment, but the claim appears to ignore a serious consequence of this policy shift. The APA's seeming abdication of enforcement responsibilities means that individuals and organizations potentially much less concerned about psychological ethics will now be the ones adjudicating complaints about such wrongdoing. As Ken Pope has observed, the human resources department at a private corporation, the inspector general's office at a government agency, or the military's chain of command are all examples where the profession's ethics may not be adequately prioritized when a grievance is filed against a psychologist.[86]

There's also a clear need for the APA to evaluate, address, and regularly monitor its relationship with the military-intelligence establishment.[87] Particular attention should be given to ensuring that commitments to psychological ethics and human rights are not subverted by national security interests. Had such safeguards been in place prior to 9/11, it's possible that the APA would have made very different and much better choices in its response to the "war on terror." Moving forward, it seems likely that adequate oversight will require the increased involvement of human rights organizations and experts. The APA's track record suggests that the association may be ill-equipped to go it alone in resisting pressure or manipulation by the military or intelligence agencies.

In this context, as described earlier, Coalition member Jean Maria Arrigo has pointed to particularly thorny problems that can arise when APA members employed by for-profit defense contractors assume leadership positions in the association. In a letter to the American Association for the Advancement of Science Committee on Scientific Freedom and Responsibility, Arrigo and Dutch Franz emphasized that "defense contractors are necessarily profit-driven actors accountable only to the performance measures outlined in the (possibly classified) contract and the financial benefit of the contracting company."[88] Since those outcomes may at times be inconsistent with the APA's mission, they have recommended that the APA – and similar civil-sector organizations – refrain from allowing defense contractor employees to hold governance positions.

At the same time, significant resources should be devoted to education and training in order for the APA to establish a firm commitment to human rights and psychological ethics in national security contexts, and beyond. Substantial knowledge of these topics – including relevant international standards – should be a requirement for the association's staff and for members who hold positions in governance. Learning opportunities in these specialized areas should also be made more readily available to all APA members, to students pursuing careers in psychology, and to the public as well.[89] All of these education initiatives would benefit from the participation of human rights organizations and independent scientific associations.[90] Building a profession and a citizenry with greater awareness on these fronts could be an important reparative act for the APA. As psychologist Philip Cushman has reminded us, "When one does not know how to reason through an ethical dilemma, and has not had the experience of and guidance in doing so, fear and confusion increase. At that point, the impulse to conform, comply, or create loopholes becomes increasingly difficult to resist."[91]

These and other remedial steps seem essential for the APA to adequately disentangle itself from the oversized influence of the military-intelligence establishment. Without creating that greater autonomy, the association may never fulfill its vision as "an effective champion of the application of psychology to promote human rights."[92] Encouraging this transformation shouldn't be seen as disparaging the valuable contributions of military psychologists, including those whose clinical work and research are focused on providing care to our soldiers and veterans. The stresses of military service are daunting, ranging from lengthy family dislocations to combat experiences that involve exposure to unspeakable brutality and the risk of injury and death. Even after returning home from the battlefield, heightened dangers of PTSD, substance use, and suicide remain. Certainly, those who serve – and those professionals devoted to their well-being – deserve support and appreciation.

But I believe the APA – and the profession of psychology more broadly – does a disservice when it loses its moral compass, scientific rudder, and independent voice in the military-intelligence arena. Almost a decade ago, the Coalition emphasized that the APA's apparent uncritical embrace and unquestioning accommodation to national security interests "has facilitated harm to vulnerable populations by supporting policies that lack adequate protection against abusive treatment; has badly damaged the reputation of US psychology both domestically and internationally; has diminished the APA's commitment to advance psychology for the purpose of promoting health, education and human welfare; and has compromised the integrity of the relationship between professional psychology and the security sector."[93]

All of these consequences still linger today. Having now moved past the twentieth anniversary of Guantanamo's opening, where dozens of prisoners still remain, the struggle to create an APA focused on ethics and human rights is far from over. The military operational psychologists who've defended the APA's accommodation to national security interests during the "war on terror" don't represent military psychology as a whole. But they seemingly have no intention of relinquishing their influential roles within the association, and the APA's leadership arguably has an uninspiring history when it comes to opposing ethically suspect aspirations promoted by the military-intelligence establishment. It is also sobering that without greater transparency and accountability, recommendations for righting the APA's course will likely remain unrealized. If that proves to be the case, then the accomplishments of the association and its members in other areas will be substantially diminished.

Even as uncertainty about the APA's future persists, *Doing Harm* should leave little doubt about one point: the path taken by the APA since the 9/11 terrorist attacks demonstrates, yet again, the importance of dissident voices and collective action in bringing attention and change to organizations and institutions that have strayed from their calling. This will be true going forward as well. As one who has been outspoken about what I see as the association's failures and fictions, I hope the American Psychological Association will be up to the challenge of looking inward and examining fundamental questions. Among the most important is whether the intentional infliction of harm should ever be part of a psychologist's ethical work.

NOTES

Introduction

1 At the time of my writing, thirty-six detainees still remain from a total of 780 once held at Guantanamo; hundreds more were imprisoned by US forces at other overseas locations. For further background on the arrival of prisoners at Guantanamo and their links to terrorism, see: "Shackled Detainees Arrive in Guantanamo," CNN.com, January 11, 2002, https://edition.cnn.com/2002/WORLD/asiapcf/central/01/11/ret.detainee.transfer/index.html; Karen Greenberg, *The Least Worst Place: Guantanamo's First 100 Days* (New York: Oxford University Press, 2009); Associated Press, "Guantanamo Inmates Say They Were 'Sold,'" NBC News, May 31, 2005, https://www.nbcnews.com/id/wbna8049868; Ken Ballen and Peter Bergen, "The Worst of the Worst?," *Foreign Policy*, October 20, 2008, https://foreignpolicy.com/2008/10/20/the-worst-of-the-worst-4/; Human Rights First, "Closing Guantanamo," December 20, 2018, https://www.humanrightsfirst.org/resource/closing-guantanamo.

2 Mark Denbeaux and Joshua Denbeaux, "Report on Guantanamo Detainees: A Profile of 517 Detainees through Analysis of Department of Defense Data," *Seton Hall Law Review* 41, no. 4 (2011): 1211–29, https://scholarship.shu.edu/shlr/vol41/iss4/2.

3 "Defense Department Briefing," C-SPAN, January 11, 2002, https://www.c-span.org/video/?168158-1/defense-department-briefing.

4 Ibid.

5 There are numerous excellent books that provide illuminating accounts about the post-9/11 period, the "war on terror," and torture. Examples include Jane Mayer, *The Dark Side: The Inside Story of How the War on Terror Turned into a War on American Ideals* (New York: Doubleday, 2008); Philippe Sands, *Torture Team: Rumsfeld's Memo and the Betrayal of American Values* (New York: Palgrave Macmillan, 2008); Joshua E.S. Phillips, *None of Us Were Like This Before: American Soldiers and Torture* (New York: Verso, 2010); Larry Siems, *The Torture Report: What the Documents Say about America's Post-9/11 Torture Program* (New York: OR Books, 2011); Mark Fallon, *Unjustifiable Means: The Inside Story of How the CIA, Pentagon, and US Government Conspired to Torture* (New York: Regan Arts, 2017); Spencer Ackerman, *Reign of Terror: How the 9/11*

Era Destabilized America and Produced Trump (New York: Viking Press, 2021); Cathy Scott-Clark and Adrian Levy, *The Forever Prisoner* (New York: Atlantic Monthly Press, 2022).

6 "Text: Vice President Cheney on NBC's 'Meet the Press,'" *Washington Post*, September 16, 2001, https://www.washingtonpost.com/wp-srv/nation/specials/attacked/transcripts/cheney091601.html.

7 United States Senate and House Select Committees on Intelligence, *Joint Inquiry into Intelligence Community Activities Before and After the Terrorist Attacks of September 11, 2001*, September 26, 2002, https://fas.org/irp/congress/2002_hr/092602black.html.

8 For example, see "Memorandum for Alberto R. Gonzales, Counsel to the President, and William J. Haynes II, General Counsel of the Department of Defense, Re: Application of Treaties and Laws to al Qaeda and Taliban Detainees," January 22, 2002, https://www.justice.gov/sites/default/files/olc/legacy/2009/08/24/memo-laws-taliban-detainees.pdf.

9 For example, see: Amnesty International, "Memorandum to the US Government on the Rights of People in US Custody in Afghanistan and Guantanamo Bay," April 2002, https://web.archive.org/web/20021024083213/http://web.amnesty.org/aidoc/aidoc_pdf.nsf/index/AMR510532002ENGLISH/$File/AMR5105302.pdf; Human Rights Watch, "U.S.: Guantanamo Kids at Risk," April 23, 2003, https://www.hrw.org/news/2003/04/23/us-guantanamo-kids-risk.

10 Throughout *Doing Harm*, I often refer to individuals as "dissident" psychologists. I use this designation if, in my judgment, through their advocacy, writing, or other activities, they made clear their opposition to the APA's permissive stance toward psychologists' involvement in war-on-terror detention and interrogation operations. I also make frequent reference to my Coalition colleagues, but *Doing Harm* is my independent work and I have not sought their endorsement of the account it presents.

11 Democracy Now!, "Psychological Warfare? A Debate on the Role of Mental Health Professionals in Military Interrogations at Guantanamo, Abu Ghraib and Beyond," August 11, 2005, https://www.democracynow.org/2005/8/11/psychological_warfare_a_debate_on_the.

12 Gerald Koocher, "Speaking against Torture," *Monitor on Psychology* 37, no. 2 (2006): 5, http://www.apa.org/monitor/feb06/pc.aspx.

13 Carol Goodheart, "APA in the Age of Outrage," *Monitor on Psychology* 41, no. 1 (2010): 5, https://www.apa.org/monitor/2010/01/pc.

14 Larry James, *Fixing Hell: An Army Psychologist Confronts Abu Ghraib* (New York: Grand Central Publishing, 2008), 251.

15 David H. Hoffman, Danielle J. Carter, Cara R. Viglucci Lopez, Heather L. Benzmiller, Ava X. Guo, S. Yasir Latifi, and Daniel C. Craig, *Report to the Special Committee of the Board of Directors of the American Psychological Association: Independent Review Relating to APA Ethics Guidelines, National Security*

Interrogations, and Torture, rev. ed. (Chicago: Sidley Austin LLP, 2015), https://www.apa.org/independent-review/revised-report.pdf.

16 American Psychological Association, "Letter to APA Membership from Nadine J. Kaslow and Susan H. McDaniel," news release, July 11, 2015, https://www.apa.org/independent-review/final-report-message; American Psychological Association, "Letter to APA Membership from Susan H. McDaniel and Nadine J. Kaslow," news release, July 24, 2015, https://www.apa.org/independent-review/letter-members-apology.pdf.

17 James Risen, *Pay Any Price: Greed, Power, and Endless War* (New York: Houghton Mifflin Harcourt, 2014).

Chapter One

1 American Psychological Association, *Return of Organization Exempt from Income Tax (Form 990)* (Washington, DC: American Psychological Association, 2019), https://www.apa.org/pubs/info/reports/2019-form-990.pdf.

2 American Psychological Association, "APA Divisions," n.d., accessed July 7, 2022, https://www.apa.org/about/division.

3 American Psychological Association, "About APA," n.d., accessed May 3, 2022, https://www.apa.org/about.

4 American Psychological Association, *Ethical Principles of Psychologists and Code of Conduct* (Washington, DC: American Psychological Association, 2017), 3, https://www.apa.org/ethics/code/ethics-code-2017.pdf.

5 Ibid., 3.

6 American Psychological Association, "APA Responds to Terrorist Attacks," *Monitor on Psychology* 32, no. 10 (2001), https://www.apa.org/monitor/nov01/aparesponds.

7 For example, see Roy J. Eidelson, Gerard R. D'Alessio, and Judy I. Eidelson, "The Impact of September 11 on Psychologists," *Professional Psychology: Research and Practice* 34, no. 2 (2003): 144–50, https://doi.org/10.1037/0735-7028.34.2.144.

8 Peter Waldman and Hugh Pope, "'Crusade' Reference Reinforces Fears War on Terrorism Is against Muslims," *Wall Street Journal*, September 21, 2001, https://www.wsj.com/articles/SB1001020294332922160; Todd Purdum, "After the Attacks: The White House; Bush Warns of a Wrathful, Shadowy and Inventive War," *New York Times*, September 17, 2001, https://www.nytimes.com/2001/09/17/us/after-attacks-white-house-bush-warns-wrathful-shadowy-inventive-war.html.

9 Siri Carpenter, "Behavioral Science Gears Up to Combat Terrorism," *Monitor on Psychology* 32, no. 10 (2001): 54, https://www.apa.org/monitor/nov01/gearsup.

10 Norine Johnson, "We, The People," *Monitor on Psychology* 32, no. 10 (2001): 5, https://www.apa.org/monitor/nov01/pc.

11 Carpenter, "Behavioral Science Gears Up," 54; Ronald F. Levant, "Psychology Responds to Terrorism," *Professional Psychology: Research and Practice* 33, no. 5 (2002): 507–9, https://doi.org/10.1037/0735-7028.33.5.507.

12 For example, see Ian Lustick, *Trapped in the War on Terror* (Philadelphia: University of Pennsylvania Press, 2006).

13 Sara Martin, "Thwarting Terrorism," *Monitor on Psychology* 33, no. 1 (2002), https://www.apa.org/monitor/jan02/terrorism.

14 Carpenter, "Behavioral Science Gears Up," 54.

15 Rebecca Clay, "Military Psychologists Respond to Attacks," *Monitor on Psychology* 32, no. 10 (2001), https://www.apa.org/monitor/nov01/militarypsych.

16 Radical Psychology Network, "American Psychological Association's Response to Terrorism," November 5, 2001, http://www.radpsynet.org/admin/response.html.

17 Frank Summers, "Making Sense of the APA: A History of the Relationship between Psychology and the Military," *Psychoanalytic Dialogues* 18, no. 5 (2008): 614–37, https://www.tandfonline.com/doi/abs/10.1080/10481880802297665.

18 Ibid.

19 Ibid.

20 Jonathan Alter, "Time to Think about Torture," *Newsweek*, November 4, 2001, https://www.newsweek.com/time-think-about-torture-149445; Jim Rutenberg, "Torture Seeps into Discussion by News Media," *New York Times*, November 5, 2001, https://www.nytimes.com/2001/11/05/business/torture-seeps-into-discussion-by-news-media.html.

21 For example, see Leadership Conference on Civil Rights, "Racial Profiling and the September 11 Attacks," October 24, 2001, https://civilrights.org/2001/10/24/racial-profiling-and-the-september-11-attacks/; American Civil Liberties Union, "Statement of Gregory T. Nojeim, Associate Director, ACLU Washington National Office," December 14, 2001, https://www.aclu.org/press-releases/threats-civil-liberties-post-september-11-secrecy-erosion-privacy-danger-unchecked.

22 United States Senate Committee on the Judiciary, "Testimony of Attorney General John Ashcroft," December 6, 2001, http://www.justice.gov/archive/ag/testimony/2001/1206transcriptsenatejudiciarycommittee.htm.

23 "Text: President Bush Addresses the Nation," *Washington Post*, September 20, 2001, https://www.washingtonpost.com/wp-srv/nation/specials/attacked/transcripts/bushaddress_092001.html.

24 Boston Area Psychologists for Peace and Justice, "Psychology's Response to Terrorism (Letter to the Editor)," *Monitor on Psychology* 33, no. 2 (2002): 4, https://www.apa.org/monitor/feb02/letters.html.

25 American Psychological Association, "Resolution on Torture," 2002, https://www.apa.org/about/policy/chapter-4b.

26 Scott Shane, "2 U.S. Architects of Harsh Tactics in 9/11's Wake," *New York Times*, August 11, 2009, https://www.nytimes.com/2009/08/12/us/12psychs.html.

27 Martin E.P. Seligman, "The Hoffman Report, the Central Intelligence Agency, and the Defense of the Nation: A Personal View," *Health Psychology Open* (July–December 2018): 1–9, https://www.ncbi.nlm.nih.gov/pmc/articles/PMC6125854/.

28 Katherine Eban, "Rorschach and Awe," *Vanity Fair*, July 17, 2007, https://www.vanityfair.com/news/2007/07/torture200707.

29 Seligman, "The Hoffman Report," 2.

30 American Psychological Association, "Hats Off to Our Psychology Advocates," *Monitor on Psychology* 33, no. 11 (2002): 64, https://www.apa.org/monitor/dec02/ppup.

31 American Psychological Association, "APA President Zimbardo Headliner for APA Meeting with National Security Council Staff," *Science Policy Insider News*, July 2002, https://web.archive.org/web/20131027041130/http://www.apa.org/about/gr/science/spin/2002/07/also-issue.aspx.

32 Hoffman et al., *Independent Review*, 53.

33 For more information, see United States Holocaust Memorial Museum, *The Nuremberg Trials*, n.d., accessed May 22, 2022, https://www.ushmm.org/collections/bibliography/the-nuremberg-trials.

34 Evelyn Shuster, "Fifty Years Later: The Significance of The Nuremberg Code," *New England Journal of Medicine* 337 (1997): 1436–40, https://www.nejm.org/doi/full/10.1056/nejm199711133372006; for a detailed analysis of the Nazi doctors and their experiments, see Robert J. Lifton, *The Nazi Doctors: Medical Killing and the Psychology of Genocide* (New York: Basic Books, 1986); for other key documents on research ethics, see: National Commission for the Protection of Human Subjects of Biomedical and Behavioral Research, *The Belmont Report: Ethical Principles and Guidelines for the Protection of Human Subjects of Research* (Bethesda, MD: The Commission, 1978); World Medical Association, "World Medical Association Declaration of Helsinki: Ethical Principles for Medical Research Involving Human Subjects," *JAMA: Journal of the American Medical Association* 310, no. 20 (2013): 2191–4, https://doi.org/10.1001/jama.2013.281053.

35 United Nations, *Universal Declaration of Human Rights* (December 10, 1948), https://www.un.org/en/about-us/universal-declaration-of-human-rights.

36 For valuable summaries, see Rebecca Gordon, *American Nuremberg: The U.S. Officials Who Should Stand Trial for Post-9/11 War Crimes* (New York: Hot Books, 2016); American Red Cross, "International Humanitarian Law and Human Rights," April 2011, https://www.redcross.org/content/dam/redcross/atg/PDF_s/Family___Holocaust_Tracing/IHL_HumanRights.pdf.

37 Lisa Hajjar, "Why the Right Not to Be Tortured Is Important to You," *Studies in Law, Politics, and Society* 48 (2009): 107, https://doi.org/10.1108/S1059-4337(2009)0000048007.

38 International Committee of the Red Cross, *Geneva Conventions of 12 August 1949*, https://www.icrc.org/en/doc/assets/files/publications/icrc-002-0173.pdf.

39 International Court of Justice, *Nuremberg Trial Archives*, 2018, https://www.icj-cij.org/public/files/library-of-the-court/library-of-the-court-en.pdf.

40 Ibid.

41 United Nations General Assembly, *Convention Against Torture and Other Cruel, Inhuman or Degrading Treatment or Punishment*, December 10, 1984, https://www.ohchr.org/en/professionalinterest/pages/cat.aspx.

42 University of Minnesota Human Rights Library, "U.S. Reservations, Declarations, and Understandings, Convention Against Torture and Other Cruel, Inhuman or Degrading Treatment or Punishment, Cong. Rec. S17486-01 (daily ed., Oct. 27, 1990)," http://hrlibrary.umn.edu/usdocs/tortres.html.

43 Ibid.

44 Ibid.

45 George J. Annas, "Human Rights Outlaws: Nuremberg, Geneva, and the Global War on Terror," *Boston University Law Review* 87, no. 2 (2007): 427–66, https://www.bu.edu/law/journals-archive/bulr/volume87n2/documents/ANNASV.2.pdf.

46 American Psychological Association, "Resolution: Opposition to Torture," 1986, https://www.apa.org/about/policy/chapter-14.

47 United Nations, *Convention against Torture*.

48 Anthony J. Pinizzotto, Susan E. Brandon, and Geoffrey K. Mumford, "Countering Terrorism: Integration of Practice and Theory," February 28, 2002, https://www.apa.org/news/press/releases/2002/11/countering-terrorism.pdf; American Psychological Association, "Countering Terrorism: Integrating Theory and Practice," *Science Policy Insider News*, March 2002, https://www.apa.org/about/gr/science/spin/2002/03/terrorism.

49 APA Practice Organization, "Duty to Protect," *Good Practice* (Fall 2013): 2–5, https://www.apaservices.org/practice/good-practice/duty-to-protect.pdf.

50 Pinizzotto et al., "Countering Terrorism," 17.

51 American Psychological Association, "APA Works with CIA and RAND to Hold Science of Deception Workshop," *Science Policy Insider News*, July 2003, https://www.apa.org/about/gr/science/spin/2003/07/also-issue.

52 Ibid.

53 Jeffrey Kaye, "APA Scrubs Pages Linking It to CIA Torture Workshops," *Shadowproof*, May 16, 2010, https://shadowproof.com/2010/05/16/apa-scrubs-pages-linking-it-to-cia-torture-workshops/.

54 American Psychological Association, "The Science of Deception: Integration of Theory and Practice," news release, August 2003, http://web.archive.org/web/20030802090354/http://www.apa.org/ppo/issues/deceptscenarios.html; See also Susan E. Brandon, "The Science of Deception: Integration of Theory and Practice," January 12, 2004, https://assets.documentcloud.org/documents/2065302/scienceofdeceptionworkshopreport.pdf.

55 The full text of this email appears in Stephen Soldz, Nathaniel Raymond, Steven Reisner, Scott A. Allen, Isaac L. Baker, and Allen S. Keller, *All the President's Psychologists: The American Psychological Association's Secret Complicity with the White House and US Intelligence Community in Support of the CIA's 'Enhanced'*

Interrogation Program, April 2015, 40, https://s3.amazonaws.com/s3.
documentcloud.org/documents/2069718/report.pdf.

56 Martha Davis, "Recruiting Research Psychologists for National Security
Applications," *The Psychology and Military Intelligence Casebook on
Interrogation Ethics*, October 10, 2008, http://www.pmicasebook.com/
PMI_Casebook/Case_-_Davis.html.

57 American Psychological Association, "Lies and the Lying Liars Who Tell
Them," *Science Policy Insider News*, July 2004, https://web.archive.org/
web/20040818164248/https://www.apa.org/ppo/spin/704.html.

58 Scott Gehwehr, "Interpersonal Deceptive Practices," *Science Policy Insider News*,
July 2004, https://www.apa.org/about/gr/science/spin/2004/07/gerwehr.

59 American Psychological Association, *Ethical Principles*, 11.

60 Ewen MacAskill, "CIA Threats to Detainees' Families Exposed," *The Guardian*,
August 24, 2009, https://www.theguardian.com/world/2009/aug/24/cia-
report-unauthorised-techniques-threats.

61 American Psychological Association, "Redline Comparison of APA Ethical
Principles of Psychologists and Code of Conduct, December 1992 and
December 2002," n.d., accessed May 3, 2022, https://www.apa.org/ethics/
code/92-02codecompare.pdf.

62 American Psychological Association, "Redline Comparison"; see also
Mandy Conrad, "Moving Upstream in the Post-Hoffman Era: When Ethical
Responsibilities Conflict with the Law," *Professional Psychology: Research and
Practice* 50, no. 6 (2019): 407–18, http://dx.doi.org/10.1037/pro0000109.

63 Kenneth S. Pope, "A Human Rights and Ethics Crisis Facing the World's Largest
Organization of Psychologists," *European Psychologist* 24, no. 2 (2019): 180–94,
https://psycnet.apa.org/fulltext/2018-62354-001.pdf.

64 For example, see Stephen Behnke, "Detainee Interrogations: American
Psychological Association Counters, but Questions Remain," *Psychiatric Times*
25, no. 10 (2008), https://www.psychiatrictimes.com/view/detainee-interrogations-
american-psychological-association-counters-questions-remain.

65 Kenneth S. Pope, "Are the American Psychological Association's Detainee
Interrogation Policies Ethical and Effective?," *Zeitschrift fur Psychologie / Journal
of Psychology* 219, no. 3 (2011): 153, https://econtent.hogrefe.com/doi/10.1027/
2151-2604/a000062.

66 American Psychological Association, "Redline Comparison."

67 Ibid.

68 We met on November 7, 2011, and this summary is based on my notes from that
meeting.

69 American Psychological Association, "Redline Comparison."

70 Ibid.

71 For example, see Nathaniel Raymond, Scott Allen, Vincent Iacopino, Allen
Keller, Stephen Soldz, Steven Reisner, and John Bradshaw, *Experiments in
Torture: Evidence of Human Subject Research and Experimentation in the*

'Enhanced' Interrogation Program, June 2010, https://phr.org/wp-content/uploads/2010/06/Experiments_in_Torture.pdf.

72 Bryant Welch, "The American Psychological Association and Torture: The Day the Tide Turned," *Huffington Post*, August 21, 2009, https://www.huffpost.com/entry/the-american-psychologica_b_242020.

73 Clark McCauley, "Jujitsu Politics: Terrorism and Responses to Terrorism," in *Collateral Damage: The Psychological Consequences of America's War on Terrorism*, eds. Paul Kimmel and Chris Stout (Westport, CT: Praeger Publishers, 2006), 45–65.

74 Paul Kimmel, personal communication with the author, November 11, 2021.

75 David H. Hoffman, Danielle J. Carter, Cara R. Viglucci Lopez, Heather L. Benzmiller, Ava X. Guo, S. Yasir Latifi, and Daniel C. Craig, *Report to the Special Committee of the Board of Directors of the American Psychological Association: Independent Review Relating to APA Ethics Guidelines, National Security Interrogations, and Torture, Binder 2* (Chicago: Sidley Austin LLP, 2015), 1435, https://www.apa.org/independent-review/binder-2.pdf.

76 Bryant Welch, "The American Psychological Association and Torture: How Could It Happen?," *International Journal of Applied Psychoanalytic Studies* 14, no. 2 (2017): 116–24, https://doi.org/10.1002/aps.1519.

77 Paul Kimmel and Chris Stout, eds., *Collateral Damage: The Psychological Consequences of America's War on Terrorism* (Westport, CT: Praeger Publishers, 2006). For other valuable psychological analyses of terrorism, see: Fathali Moghaddam and Anthony Marsella, eds., Understanding Terrorism: Psychosocial Roots, Consequences, and Interventions (Washington, DC: American Psychological Association, 2004), https://doi.org/10.1037/10621-000; Clark McCauley and Sophia Moskalenko, *Friction: How Conflict Radicalizes Them and Us*, rev. ed. (New York: Oxford University Press, 2016).

78 Molly Moore, "Villagers Released by American Troops Say They Were Beaten, Kept in 'Cage,'" *Washington Post*, February 11, 2002, https://www.washingtonpost.com/archive/politics/2002/02/11/villagers-released-by-american-troops-say-they-were-beaten-kept-in-cage/6cce7fd9-bcb6-4490-ad08-901ffddd1bc5/.

79 Rajiv Chanrasekaran and Peter Finn, "U.S. Behind Secret Transfer of Terror Suspects," *Washington Post*, March 11, 2002, https://www.washingtonpost.com/archive/politics/2002/03/11/us-behind-secret-transfer-of-terror-suspects/b4345faf-7a26-47d2-838f-ee0881b66c2f/.

80 Dana Priest and Barton Gellman, "U.S. Decries Abuse But Defends Interrogations," *Washington Post*, December 26, 2002, https://www.washingtonpost.com/archive/politics/2002/12/26/us-decries-abuse-but-defends-interrogations/737a4096-2cf0-40b9-8a9f-7b22099d733d/.

81 Ibid.

82 Jesse Bravin and Gary Fields, "How Do U.S. Interrogators Make a Captured Terrorist Talk?," *Wall Street Journal*, March 4, 2003, https://www.wsj.com/articles/SB104673282554097688o.

83 Carlotta Gall, "U.S. Military Investigating Death of Afghan in Custody," *New York Times*, March 4, 2003, https://www.nytimes.com/2003/03/04/world/threats-responses-prisoners-us-military-investigating-death-afghan-custody.html.

84 April Witt, "U.S. Probes Death of Prisoner in Afghanistan," *Washington Post*, June 24, 2003, https://www.washingtonpost.com/archive/politics/2003/06/24/us-probes-death-of-prisoner-in-afghanistan/8e605dba-50d7-442a-a6b5-17a76da5fa2b/; see also "Court Upholds CIA Contractor's Detainee Abuse Conviction," AFP, August 11, 2009, https://web.archive.org/web/20120130071733/http://www.google.com/hostednews/afp/article/ALeqM5gSo6iRtgbNNlDhDyO_VcZEmT45MQ.

85 Rebecca Leung, "Abuse of Iraqi POWs by GIs Probed," *60 Minutes II*, April 27, 2004, https://www.cbsnews.com/news/abuse-of-iraqi-pows-by-gis-probed/; Seymour Hersh, "Torture at Abu Ghraib," *New Yorker*, May 10, 2004, https://www.newyorker.com/magazine/2004/05/10/torture-at-abu-ghraib.

86 David S. Cloud, Carla Anne Robbins, and Greg Jaffe, "Red Cross Found Widespread Abuse of Iraqi Prisoners," *Wall Street Journal*, May 7, 2004, https://www.wsj.com/articles/SB108384106459803859; "Red Cross Saw 'Widespread Abuse,'" BBC News, May 8, 2004, http://news.bbc.co.uk/2/hi/americas/3694521.stm; see also Scott Horton, "Busting the Torture Myths," *Daily Beast*, April 27, 2009, https://www.thedailybeast.com/busting-the-torture-myths.

87 "The Interrogation Documents: Debating U.S. Policy and Methods," July 13, 2004, National Security Archive at George Washington University, https://nsarchive2.gwu.edu/NSAEBB/NSAEBB127/index.htm#additional.

88 For example, see *Memorandum for Alberto R. Gonzales, Re: Standards of Conduct for Interrogation under 18 USC §§ 2340-2340A*, August 1, 2002, https://www.justice.gov/olc/file/886061/download.

89 Dana Priest and R. Jeffrey Smith, "Memo Offered Justification for Use of Torture," *Washington Post*, June 8, 2004, https://www.washingtonpost.com/archive/politics/2004/06/08/memo-offered-justification-for-use-of-torture/17910584-e7c3-4c8c-b2d1-c986959ebc6a/.

90 Neil Lewis, "Red Cross Finds Detainee Abuse in Guantanamo," *New York Times*, November 30, 2004, https://www.nytimes.com/2004/11/30/politics/red-cross-finds-detainee-abuse-in-guantanamo.html.

91 Neil Lewis, "Fresh Details Emerge on Harsh Methods at Guantanamo," *New York Times*, January 1, 2005, https://www.nytimes.com/2005/01/01/us/fresh-details-emerge-on-harsh-methods-at-guantanamo.html.

92 For further discussion of propaganda and its effects, see: E.J. Dionne, Jr, "Inevitably, the Politics of Terror: Fear Has Become Part of Washington's Power Struggle," *Brookings Institution*, May 25, 2003, https://www.brookings.edu/opinions/inevitably-the-politics-of-terror-fear-has-become-part-of-washingtons-power-struggle/; Arash Javanbakht, "The Politics of Fear: How Fear Goes Tribal, Allowing Us to Be Manipulated," *The Conversation*, January 11, 2019, https://theconversation.com/the-politics-of-fear-how-fear-goes-tribal-allowing-

us-to-be-manipulated-109626; Garth S. Jowett and Victoria O'Donnell, *Propaganda & Persuasion*, 5th ed. (Los Angeles: Sage, 2012); Arthur Lupia, and Jesse Menning, "When Can Politicians Scare Citizens into Supporting Bad Policies?," *American Journal of Political Science* 53, no. 1 (2009): 90–106, http://www.jstor.org/stable/25193869; Richard M. Perloff, *The Dynamics of Persuasion*, 3rd ed. (New York: Lawrence Erlbaum Associates, 2008); Kirk Waldroff, "Fear: A Powerful Motivator in Elections," news release, American Psychological Association, October 13, 2020, https://www.apa.org/news/apa/2020/fear-motivator-elections.

93 Solomon E. Asch, "Studies of Independence and Conformity: I. A Minority of One Against a Unanimous Majority," *Psychological Monographs: General and Applied* 70, no. 9 (1956): 1–70, https://doi.org/10.1037/h0093718; Solomon E. Asch, "Opinions and Social Pressure," *Scientific American* 193, no. 5 (1955): 31–5; Solomon E. Asch, *Social Psychology* (Englewood Cliffs, NJ: Prentice-Hall, 1955); Solomon E. Asch, "Effects of Group Pressure on the Modification and Distortion of Judgments," in *Groups, Leadership and Men*, ed. Harold Guetzkow (Pittsburgh, PA: Carnegie Press, 1951): 177–90.

94 Asch, "Opinions and Social Pressure," 34.

95 Stanley Milgram, "Behavioral Study of Obedience," *Journal of Abnormal and Social Psychology* 67, no. 4 (1963): 371–8; Stanley Milgram, *Obedience to Authority: An Experimental View* (New York: Harper & Row, 1974).

96 Milgram, *Obedience to Authority*, 189; see also Herbert C. Kelman and V. Lee Hamilton, *Crimes of Obedience: Toward a Social Psychology of Authority and Responsibility* (New Haven, CT: Yale University Press, 1989).

97 For further background on the relevant work of these scholars, see: Morton Deutsch, *Distributive Justice: A Social-Psychological Perspective* (New Haven, CT: Yale University Press, 1985); Morton Deutsch, "Psychological Roots of Moral Exclusion," *Journal of Social Issues* 46, no. 1 (1990): 21–5, https://doi.org/10.1111/j.1540-4560.1990.tb00269.x; Susan Opotow, "Moral Exclusion and Injustice: An Introduction," *Journal of Social Issues* 46, no. 1 (1990): 1–20, https://doi.org/10.1111/j.1540-4560.1990.tb00268.x; Susan Opotow, "Drawing the Line: Social Categorization, Moral Exclusion, and the Scope of Justice," in *Conflict, Cooperation, and Justice: Essays Inspired by the Work of Morton Deutsch*, eds. Barbara Benedict Bunker and Jeffrey Z. Rubin (San Francisco: Jossey-Bass, 1995), 347–69; Susan Opotow, "Social Injustice," in *Peace, Conflict and Violence: Peace Psychology for the 21st Century*, eds. Daniel J. Christie, Richard V. Wagner, and Deborah DuNann Winter (New York: Prentice-Hall, 2001), 102–9; Ervin Staub, *The Roots of Evil: The Origins of Genocide and Other Group Violence* (New York: Cambridge University Press, 1989); Ervin Staub, "Moral Exclusion, Personal Goal Theory, and Extreme Destructiveness," *Journal of Social Issues* 46, no. 1 (1990): 47–64, https://doi.org/10.1111/j.1540-4560.1990.tb00271.x.

98 Albert Bandura, "Selective Activation and Disengagement of Moral Control," *Journal of Social Issues* 46, no. 1 (1990): 27–46, https://doi.

org/10.1111/j.1540-4560.1990.tb00270.x; Albert Bandura, "Moral Disengagement in the Perpetration of Inhumanities," *Personality and Social Psychology Review* 3, no. 3 (1999): 193–209, https://doi.org/10.1207/s15327957pspr0303_3; Albert Bandura, *Moral Disengagement: How People Do Harm and Live with Themselves* (New York: Worth Publishers, 2016).

Chapter Two

1 Mark Denbeaux and Joshua Denbeaux, "Report on Guantanamo Detainees: A Profile of 517 Detainees through Analysis of Department of Defense Data," *Seton Hall Law Review* 41, no. 4 (2011): 1211–29, https://scholarship.shu.edu/shlr/vol41/iss4/2; Mark Denbeaux, Sean Camoni, Paul W. Taylor, and Philip Taylor, "Rumsfeld Knew: DoD's 'Worst of the Worst' and Recidivism Claims Refuted by Recently Declassified Memo," Seton Hall University School of Law Research Paper No. 2003598, March 2011, https://papers.ssrn.com/sol3/papers.cfm?abstract_id=2003598; Carol Rosenberg, "New Guantanamo Intelligence Upends Old 'Worst of the Worst' Assumptions," *Miami Herald*, September 30, 2016, https://www.miamiherald.com/news/nation-world/world/americas/guantanamo/article105037571.html.
2 Alfred W. McCoy, "Cruel Science: CIA Torture and U.S. Foreign Policy," *New England Journal of Public Policy* 19, no. 2, Article 15 (2005), http://scholarworks.umb.edu/nejpp/vol19/iss2/15; Alfred W. McCoy, *Torture and Impunity: The U.S. Doctrine of Coercive Interrogation* (Madison: University of Wisconsin Press, 2012).
3 Central Intelligence Agency, *KUBARK Counterintelligence Interrogation Manual*, July 1963, https://nsarchive2.gwu.edu/NSAEBB/NSAEBB27/docs/doc01.pdf.
4 Central Intelligence Agency, *Human Resource Exploitation Manual*, 1983, https://nsarchive2.gwu.edu/NSAEBB/NSAEBB122/CIA%20Human%20Res%20Exploit%20A1-G11.pdf.
5 United States Senate Select Committee on Intelligence, *Committee Study of the Central Intelligence Agency's Detention and Interrogation Program*, 2014, https://www.intelligence.senate.gov/sites/default/files/publications/CRPT-113srpt288.pdf.
6 Lewis Carroll, *Through the Looking-Glass and What Alice Found There* (Chicago: W.B. Conkey Co., 1900).
7 *Memorandum for Alberto R. Gonzales, Counsel to the President, Re: Standards of Conduct for Interrogation under 18 U.S.C. §§ 2340-2340A*, August 1, 2002; for an extensive compilation of the "torture memos" and related government documents, see Karen J. Greenberg and Joshua L. Dratel, eds., *The Torture Papers: The Road to Abu Ghraib* (New York: Cambridge University Press, 2005); see also Jake Romm, "No Home in This World: The Case against John Yoo before the International Criminal Court," *International Criminal Law Review* 20, no. 5 (2020): 862–907.

8 United Nations General Assembly, *Convention against Torture and Other Cruel, Inhuman or Degrading Treatment or Punishment*, December 10, 1984, https://www.ohchr.org/en/professionalinterest/pages/cat.aspx.

9 For example, for details about these techniques see International Committee of the Red Cross, ICRC *Report on the Treatment of Fourteen "High Value Detainees" in CIA Custody*, February 2007, https://web.archive.org/web/20210227135103/https://www.nybooks.com/media/doc/2010/04/22/icrc-report.pdf; United States Senate Committee on Armed Services, *Inquiry into the Treatment of Detainees in U.S. Custody*, 2008, https://www.armed-services.senate.gov/imo/media/doc/Detainee-Report-Final_April-22-2009.pdf; United States Senate Select Committee on Intelligence, *Committee Study of the Central Intelligence Agency's Detention and Interrogation Program*, 2014, https://www.intelligence.senate.gov/sites/default/files/publications/CRPT-113srpt288.pdf; Antonio M. Taguba, *Article 15-6 Investigation of the 800th Military Police Brigade*, 2004, https://www.thetorturedatabase.org/files/foia_subsite/pdfs/DODDOA000248.pdf; Physicians for Human Rights, *Break Them Down: Systematic Use of Psychological Torture by US Forces*, 2005, https://humanrights.ucdavis.edu/resources/library/documents-and-reports/physicians_for_human_rights; Larry Siems, *The Torture Report: What the Documents Say About America's Post-9/11 Torture Program* (New York: OR Books, 2011); Mark Denbeaux, "How America Tortures," *Seton Hall Public Law Research Paper*, 2019, https://papers.ssrn.com/sol3/papers.cfm?abstract_id=3494533.

10 For further background and documentation on the various techniques listed here, see: Physicians for Human Rights, *Break Them Down*; International Committee of the Red Cross, *Report of the International Committee of the Red Cross (ICRC) on the Treatment by the Coalition Forces of Prisoners of War and Other Protected Persons by the Geneva Conventions in Iraq During Arrest, Internment and Interrogation*, February 2004; Brendan O'Neill, "After Guantanamo," BBC News, January 25, 2005, http://news.bbc.co.uk/2/hi/uk_news/magazine/4203803.stm; Neil Lewis, "Broad Use of Harsh Tactics Is Described at Cuba Base," *New York Times*, October 17, 2004, https://www.nytimes.com/2004/10/17/politics/broad-use-of-harsh-tactics-is-described-at-cuba-base.html; Human Rights Watch, *"Enduring Freedom": Abuses by U.S. Forces in Afghanistan*, March 2004, https://www.hrw.org/reports/2004/afghanistan0304/afghanistan0304.pdf; Amnesty International, USA: *Human Dignity Denied: Torture and Accountability in the 'War on Terror,'* October 2004, https://www.amnesty.org/download/Documents/92000/amr511452004en.pdf; Suzanne Goldenberg and James Meek, "Papers Reveal Bagram Abuse," *The Guardian*, February 17, 2005, https://www.theguardian.com/world/2005/feb/18/usa.iraq; Carol Leonnig and Dana Priest, "Detainees Accuse Female Interrogators," *Washington Post*, February 10, 2005, https://www.washingtonpost.com/archive/politics/2005/02/10/detainees-accuse-female-interrogators/1e472805-5bf4-4144-ac5a-f46a1968c9dd/; Josh White and Scott Higham, "Use of Dogs to

Scare Prisoners Was Authorized," *Washington Post*, June 11, 2004, https://www.washingtonpost.com/archive/politics/2004/06/11/use-of-dogs-to-scare-prisoners-was-authorized/6b684726-a282-4b0d-a25a-3693108e69c1/; Office of Inspector General, Central Intelligence Agency, *Special Review: Counterterrorism Detention and Interrogation Activities*, (September 2001–October 2003) (Report No. 2003-7123-IG), May 7, 2004, https://www.hsdl.org/?view&did=34272.

11 Institute on Medicine as a Profession, *Ethics Abandoned: Medical Professionalism and Detainee Abuse in the War on Terror* (New York: The Institute, 2013), https://hrp.law.harvard.edu/wp-content/uploads/2013/11/IMAP-EthicsTextFinal2.pdf.

12 *Memorandum for William J. Haynes II, General Counsel of the Department of Defense, Re: Military Interrogation of Alien Unlawful Combatants Held Outside the United States*, March 14, 2003, https://www.aclu.org/sites/default/files/pdfs/safefree/yoo_army_torture_memo.pdf.

13 *Memorandum for John Rizzo, Acting General Counsel of the Central Intelligence Agency, Re: Interrogation of al Qaeda Operative*, August 1, 2002, https://www.hsdl.org/?view&did=37518.

14 *Memorandum for John A. Rizzo, Senior Deputy General Counsel, Central Intelligence Agency, Re: Application of United States Obligations under Article 16 of the Convention against Torture to Certain Techniques That May Be Used in the Interrogation of High Value al Qaeda Detainees*, May 30, 2005, https://www.hsdl.org/?view&did=37511.

15 For relevant government documents, see: United States Senate, CIA *Detention and Interrogation Program*; United States Senate Committee on Armed Services, *Inquiry into the Treatment of Detainees in U.S. Custody*, 2008, https://www.armed-services.senate.gov/imo/media/doc/Detainee-Report-Final_April-22-2009.pdf.

16 Katherine Eban, "Rorschach and Awe," *Vanity Fair*, July 17, 2007, https://www.vanityfair.com/news/2007/07/torture200707; United States Senate, CIA *Detention and Interrogation Program*.

17 International Committee of the Red Cross, *The Geneva Conventions of 1949 and Their Additional Protocols*, January 1, 2014, https://www.icrc.org/en/document/geneva-conventions-1949-additional-protocols.

18 For descriptions of SERE training and techniques, see "Statement of Jerald F. Ogrisseg, Former Chief, Psychology Services, 336th Training Group, United States Air Force Survival School," *Treatment of Detainees in U.S. Custody: Hearing Before the Committee on Armed Services* (June 17, 2008), https://irp.fas.org/congress/2008_hr/treatment.pdf; United States Senate, *Treatment of Detainees*.

19 For example, see: Charles A. Morgan, III, *Expert Report: Suleiman Abdullah Salim, et al v. James E. Mitchell and John Jessen* (E.D. Wash. No.15-0286-JLQ, November 21, 2016), https://www.aclu.org/sites/default/files/field_document/211-6._exhibit_6_7.14.17.pdf.

20 *Memorandum for John Rizzo Re: Interrogation of al Qaeda Operative*.

21 CIA Office of Medical Services, *OMS Guidelines on Medical and Psychological Support to Detainee Rendition, Interrogation, and Detention*, 2004, 7, https://www.aclu.org/sites/default/files/torturefoia/released/103009/cia-olc/2.pdf.

22 Ibid., 7.

23 Charles Church, "What Politics and the Media Still Get Wrong about Abu Zubaydah," *Just Security*, August 1, 2018, https://www.lawfareblog.com/what-politics-and-media-still-get-wrong-about-abu-zubaydah; Spencer Ackerman, "U.S. Captured, Tortured, and Cleared Him. He's Still in GITMO," *Daily Beast*, May 3, 2021, https://www.thedailybeast.com/us-captured-tortured-and-cleared-abu-zubaydah-hes-still-in-gitmo.

24 United States Senate, *CIA Detention and Interrogation Program*, xii.

25 Eban, "Rorschach and Awe."

26 Ibid.

27 United States Senate Select Committee on Intelligence, *Committee Study of the Central Intelligence Agency's Detention and Interrogation Program*, 2014, https://www.intelligence.senate.gov/sites/default/files/publications/CRPT-113srpt288.pdf; Associated Press, "CIA Destroyed Tapes Despite Court Orders," NBC News, December 12, 2007, https://www.nbcnews.com/id/wbna22217926; United States Senate, *CIA Detention and Interrogation Program*.

28 James Mitchell and Bill Harlow, *Enhanced Interrogation: Inside the Minds and Motives of the Islamic Terrorists Trying to Destroy America* (New York: Crown Publishing Group, 2016).

29 Cathy Scott-Clark and Adrian Levy, *The Forever Prisoner* (New York: Atlantic Monthly Press, 2022).

30 United States Senate, *CIA Detention and Interrogation Program*.

31 Katherine Hawkins, "State Secrets That Aren't Secret," *Project on Government Oversight*, September 10, 2021, https://www.pogo.org/analysis/2021/09/state-secrets-that-arent-secret/.

32 United States Senate, *CIA Detention and Interrogation Program*.

33 Scott-Clark and Levy, *The Forever Prisoner*, 335; Scott Shane, "2 U.S. Architects of Harsh Tactics in 9/11's Wake," *New York Times*, August 11, 2009, https://www.nytimes.com/2009/08/12/us/12psychs.html.

34 United States Government, "Indemnification Agreement with Mitchell Jessen & Associates," November 8, 2007, https://www.thetorturedatabase.org/files/foia_subsite/cia_37.pdf; Associated Press, "CIA Granted Waterboarders $5M Legal Shield," CBS News, December 17, 2010, https://www.cbsnews.com/news/ap-cia-granted-waterboarders-5m-legal-shield/.

35 Suleiman Abdullah Salim, Mohamed Ahmed Ben Soud, Obaid Ullah (as personal representative of Gul Rahman), Plaintiffs, v. James Elmer Mitchell and John "Bruce" Jessen, Defendants. No. CV-15-0286-JLQ, United States District Court, E.D. Washington, DC, October 13, 2015, https://www.aclu.org/sites/default/files/field_document/salim_v._mitchell_-_complaint_10-13-15.pdf; American Civil Liberties Union, "Salim v. Mitchell – Lawsuit against Psychologists Behind CIA

Torture Program," August 17, 2017, https://www.aclu.org/cases/salim-v-mitchell-lawsuit-against-psychologists-behind-cia-torture-program.

36 For example, see: Sherri Fink and James Risen, "Psychologists Open a Window on Brutal C.I.A. Interrogations," *New York Times*, June 21, 2017, https://www.nytimes.com/interactive/2017/06/20/us/cia-torture.html; Mitchell and Harlow, *Enhanced Interrogation*; United States Senate, CIA *Detention and Interrogation Program*.

37 Sherri Fink, "2 Psychologists in C.I.A. Interrogations Can Face Trial, Judge Rules," *New York Times*, July 28, 2017, https://www.nytimes.com/2017/07/28/us/cia-interrogations-torture-psychologists.html; Suleiman Abdullah Salim et al. v. James Elmer Mitchell and John "Bruce" Jessen, NO. 2:15-cv-286-JLQ, Document 190 (Wash., June 12, 2017), https://www.aclu.org/sites/default/files/field_document/190._defs_response_to_plaintiffs_msj_6.12.17_1.pdf.

38 American Civil Liberties Union, "On Eve of Trial, Psychologists Agree to Historic Settlement in ACLU Case on Behalf of Three Torture Victims," August 17, 2017, https://www.aclu.org/press-releases/cia-torture-psychologists-settle-lawsuit.

39 United States Department of the Army, Office of the Surgeon General, *Final Report: Assessment of Medical Operations for OEF, GTMO, and OIF*, April 13, 2005, 19-7, http://humanrights.ucdavis.edu/resources/library/documents-and-reports/detmedopsrpt.pdf; United States Army, "OTSG/MEDCOM Policy Memo 06-029: Behavioral Science Consultation Policy," October 20, 2006, https://humanrights.ucdavis.edu/projects/the-guantanamo-testimonials-project/testimonies/testimonies-of-standard-operating-procedures/behavioral_science_consultation_policy_memo_2006.pdf; see also Peter Slevin and Joe Stephens, "Detainees' Medical Records Shared," *Washington Post*, June 10, 2004, https://www.washingtonpost.com/archive/politics/2004/06/10/detainees-medical-files-shared/1d32be44-ea28-47ba-96cf-014c754a499c/; Leonard Rubenstein, Christian Pross, Franklin Davidoff, and Vincent Iacopino, "Coercive US Interrogation Policies: A Challenge to Medical Ethics," *JAMA: Journal of the American Medical Association* 294, no. 12 (2005): 1544–9, https://pubmed.ncbi.nlm.nih.gov/16189368/.

40 Scott-Clark and Levy, *The Forever Prisoner*, 291–2; United States Senate, *Treatment of Detainees*, 142.

41 Jason Leopold, "Accused of Enabling Torture, a US Military Psychologist Says He Was Doing the Opposite," *Vice*, July 15, 2015, https://www.vice.com/en/article/wja8ky/accused-of-enabling-torture-a-us-military-psychologist-says-he-was-doing-the-opposite.

42 United States Senate, *Treatment of Detainees*, 50–3.

43 Ibid., 52.

44 Leonard S. Rubenstein, "First, Do No Harm: Health Professionals and Guantanamo," *Seton Hall Law Review* 37, no. 3 (2007): 741, https://scholarship.shu.edu/cgi/viewcontent.cgi?article=1144&context=shlr.

45 For detailed background on the interrogation of al-Qahtani, see: Roy J. Eidelson, "'No Cause for Action': Revisiting the Ethics Case of Dr. John Leso," *Journal of Social and Political Psychology* 3, no. 1 (2015): 198–212, https://jspp.psychopen.eu/index.php/jspp/article/view/4849/4849.pdf; Mark Fallon, *Unjustifiable Means: The Inside Story of How the CIA, Pentagon, and US Government Conspired to Torture* (New York: Regan Arts, 2017); Steven H. Miles, "Medical Ethics and the Interrogation of Guantanamo 063," *American Journal of Bioethics* 7, no. 4 (2007): 1–7; United States Army, *Army Regulation 15-6: Final Report: Investigation into FBI Allegations of Detainee Abuse at Guantanamo Bay, Cuba Detention Facility*, April 1, 2005, https://www.thetorturedatabase.org/files/foia_subsite/pdfs/schmidt_furlow_report.pdf; United States Senate, *Treatment of Detainees*; Adam Zagorin and Michael Duffy, "Inside the Interrogation of Detainee 063," *Time*, June 20, 2005, https://time.com/3624326/inside-the-interrogation-of-detainee-063/.

46 United States Department of Defense, *Exhibit 63 to Army Regulation 15-6 Investigation into Detainee Abuse at Guantanamo Bay*, January 11, 2005, https://web.archive.org/web/20170119030708/http://www.dod.gov/pubs/foi/Reading_Room/Detainee_Related/Exhibit_63_to_AR15_6GTMO_Investigation.pdf.

47 Ibid.

48 For background on the deeply flawed military commissions, see Jess Bravin, *The Terror Courts: Rough Justice at Guantanamo Bay* (New Haven, CT: Yale University Press, 2013); Lisa Hajjar, *The War in Court: Inside the Long Fight Against Torture* (Oakland: University of California Press, 2022); Alka Pradham and Scott Roehm, "Nuremberg Prosecutor Says Guantanamo Military Commissions Don't Measure Up," *Just Security*, August 24, 2021, https://www.justsecurity.org/77835/nuremberg-prosecutor-says-guantanamo-military-commissions-dont-measure-up/; Anthony Romero, "Guantanamo's 9/11 Show Trials," *The Guardian*, May 7, 2012, https://www.theguardian.com/commentisfree/cifamerica/2012/may/07/guantanamo-911-show-trial; Steve Vladeck, "It's Time to Admit That the Military Commissions Have Failed," *Lawfare*, April 16, 2019, https://www.lawfareblog.com/its-time-admit-military-commissions-have-failed.

49 David Luban, "Torture Evidence and the Guantanamo Military Commissions," *Just Security*, May 26, 2021, https://www.justsecurity.org/76640/torture-evidence-and-the-guantanamo-military-commissions/.

50 Bob Woodward, "Guantanamo Detainee Was Tortured, Says Official Overseeing Military Trials," *Washington Post*, January 14, 2009, https://www.washingtonpost.com/wp-dyn/content/article/2009/01/13/AR2009011303372.html.

51 Carol Rosenberg and Charlie Savage, "Panel Backs Transfer of Mentally Ill Guantanamo Detainee Suspected of 9/11 Role," *New York Times*, February 4, 2022, https://www.nytimes.com/2022/02/04/us/politics/guantanamo-detainee-transfer.html; Carol Rosenberg, "'20th Hijacker' Is Returned to Saudi Arabia for Mental Health Care," *New York Times*, March 7, 2022, https://www.nytimes.com/2022/03/07/us/politics/saudi-arabia-911-hijacker.html.

52 Larry James, *Fixing Hell: An Army Psychologist Confronts Abu Ghraib* (New York: Grand Central Publishing, 2008), 49.

53 United States Army Joint Task Force Guantanamo, "Camp Delta Operating Procedures (SOP)," March 28, 2003, https://nsarchive2.gwu.edu/torturingdemocracy/documents/20030327.pdf.

54 American Psychological Association, "Recognizing Groundbreaking Efforts," *Monitor on Psychology* 35, no. 9 (2004): 12, http://www.apa.org/monitor/octo4/efforts.aspx.

55 Associated Press, "Military Confirms Secret Guantanamo Lockup," NBC News, February 6, 2008, https://www.nbcnews.com/id/wbna23037067.

56 James, *Fixing Hell*.

57 Ibid., 41.

58 Ibid., 66.

59 United Nations General Assembly, "Declaration on the Protection of all Persons from Enforced Disappearance" (Resolution 47/133), December 18, 1992, https://www.un.org/en/genocideprevention/documents/atrocity-crimes/Doc.7_Declaration%20on%20the%20Protection%20of%20all%20Persons%20from%20Enforced%20Disappearance.pdf.

60 Ibid., 66.

61 David Rose, *Guantanamo: The War on Human Rights* (New York: New Press, 2004), 133.

62 For example, see Constitution Project, *The Report of The Constitution Project's Task Force on Detainee Treatment*, 2013, https://detaineetaskforce.org/pdf/Chapter-6_Role-of-Medical-Professionals.pdf; Institute on Medicine as a Profession, *Ethics Abandoned: Medical Professionalism and Detainee Abuse in the War on Terror* (New York: The Institute, 2013), https://hrp.law.harvard.edu/wp-content/uploads/2013/11/IMAP-EthicsTextFinal2.pdf; Santiago Wills, "The Role of Health Professionals in Detainee Interrogation," *The Atlantic*, November 11, 2012, https://www.theatlantic.com/health/archive/2012/11/the-role-of-health-professionals-in-detainee-interrogation/263812/; Al Halmandy et al. v. Obama et al. – "Government Status Report on Return of Jawad to Afghanistan," August 24, 2009, https://www.aclu.org/legal-document/al-halmandy-et-al-v-obama-et-al-government-status-report-return-jawad-afghanistan.

63 Matt Apuzzo, Sherri Fink, and James Risen, "How U.S. Torture Left a Legacy of Damaged Minds," *New York Times*, October 8, 2016, https://www.nytimes.com/2016/10/09/world/cia-torture-guantanamo-bay.html.

64 For further background, see David J.R. Frakt, "Mohammed Jawad and the Military Commissions of Guantanamo," *Duke Law Journal* 60 (2011): 1367–411, https://scholarship.law.duke.edu/cgi/viewcontent.cgi?article=1497&context=dlj; David Frakt, "Closing Argument at Guantanamo: The Torture of Mohammed Jawad," *Harvard Human Rights Journal* 22, no. 1 (2009): 1–24, https://papers.ssrn.com/sol3/papers.cfm?abstract_id=2103825; David Frakt, "Closing Argument at Guantanamo II: The Torture of Mohammad Jawad, Continued," *Pen America*,

May 17, 2013, https://pen.org/closing-argument-at-guantanamo-ii-the-torture-of-mohammad-jawad-continued/.

65 Josh Meyer, "Guantanamo Prosecutor Quits," *Los Angeles Times*, September 25, 2008, https://www.latimes.com/archives/la-xpm-2008-sep-25-na-gitmo25-story.html; Darrel Vandeveld, "Declaration in Support of Mohammed Jawad's Petition for Habeas Corpus," January 12, 2009, https://humanrights.ucdavis.edu/projects/the-guantanamo-testimonials-project/testimonies/testimonies-of-prosecu-tion-lawyers/vandeveld-declaration-january-12-2009.

66 American Civil Liberties Union, "Saki Bacha v. Obama et al. – Judge's Order Granting Jawad's Petition For Habeas Corpus," August 24, 2009, https://www.aclu.org/legal-document/saki-bacha-v-obama-et-al-judges-order-granting-jawads-petition-habeas-corpus; Sena Garven, "Welcome New Members!," *Military Psychologist* 27, no. 1 (2012): 14–16.

67 For further details about Slahi's mistreatment, see Sherri Fink, "Where Even Nightmares Are Classified: Psychiatric Care at Guantanamo," *New York Times*, November 12, 2016, https://www.nytimes.com/2016/11/13/world/guantana-mo-bay-doctors-abuse.html; Mohamedou Ould Slahi, *Guantanamo Diary*, Restored Edition (New York: Back Bay Books, 2017); Ben Taub, "Guantanamo's Darkest Secret," *The New Yorker*, April 15, 2019, https://www.newyorker.com/magazine/2019/04/22/guantanamos-darkest-secret; United States Senate, *Treatment of Detainees*, 135–45.

68 United States Senate, *Treatment of Detainees*, 141.

69 Jess Bravin, "The Conscience of a Colonel," *Wall Street Journal*, March 31, 2007, https://www.wsj.com/articles/SB117529704337355155; Jess Bravin, "Pentagon Forbids Marine to Testify," *Wall Street Journal*, November 8, 2007, https://www.wsj.com/articles/SB119448421393585946.

70 Carol Rosenberg, "The Legacy of America's Post-9/11 Turn to Torture," *New York Times*, September 12, 2021, https://www.nytimes.com/2021/09/12/us/politics/torture-post-9-11.html.

71 Mark A. Staal and James A. Stephenson, "Operational Psychology Post-9/11: A Decade of Evolution," *Military Psychology* 25, no. 2 (2013): 97, http://dx.doi.org/ 10.1037/h0094951; see also Thomas J. Williams, James J. Picano, Robert R. Roland, and Morgan L. Banks, "Introduction to Operational Psychology," in *Military Psychology: Clinical and Operational Applications*, eds. Carrie H. Kennedy and Eric A. Zillmer (New York: Guilford Press, 2006), 193–214.

72 Tim Golden and Don van Natta, Jr, "The Reach of War; U.S. Said to Overstate Value of Guantanamo Detainees," *New York Times*, June 21, 2004, https://www.nytimes.com/2004/06/21/world/the-reach-of-war-us-said-to-overstate-value-of-guantanamo-detainees.html; Andy Worthington, *The Guantanamo Files: The Stories of 774 Detainees in America's Illegal Prison.* (London: Pluto Press, 2007).

73 Advocates for U.S. Torture Prosecutions, *Shadow Report to the United Nations Committee Against Torture on the Review of the Periodic Report of the United States of America*, September 29, 2014, http://hrp.law.harvard.edu/wp-content/

uploads/2014/10/CAT-Shadow-Report-Advocates-for-US-Torture-Prosecutions.
pdf; John Eligon, "Advisers on Interrogation Face Legal Action by Critics,"
New York Times, April 27, 2011, https://www.nytimes.com/2011/04/28/nyregion/
psychologist-advisers-on-questioning-terror-suspects-face-ire.html.

74 There are many valuable sources for further information, including the fol-
lowing: Metin Basoglu, Maria Livanou, and Cvetana Crnobaric, "Torture vs
Other Cruel, Inhuman, and Degrading Treatment: Is the Distinction Real or
Apparent?," *Archives of General Psychiatry* 64, no. 3 (2007): 277–85, https://
jamanetwork.com/journals/jamapsychiatry/fullarticle/482225; Mark A.
Costanzo and Ellen Gerrity, "The Effects and Effectiveness of Using Torture
as an Interrogation Device: Using Research to Inform the Policy Debate,"
Social Issues and Policy Review 3, no. 1 (2009): 179–210; Otto Doerr-Zegers,
Lawrence Hartmann, Elizabeth Lira, and Eugenia Weinstein, "Torture:
Psychiatric Sequelae and Phenomenology," *Psychiatry* 55, no. 2 (1992): 177–84;
Joseph El-Khoury, Riwa Haidar, and Andres Barkil-Oteo, "Psychological
Torture: Characteristics and Impact on Mental Health," *International Journal
of Social Psychiatry* (2020): 1–7, https://doi.org/10.1177%2F0020764020961800;
Ellen Gerrity, Terence M. Keane, and Farris Tuma, eds., *The Mental Health
Consequences of Torture* (New York: Springer, 2013); David Luban and Henry
Shue, "Mental Torture: A Critique of Erasures in U.S. Law," Georgetown
University Law Center, 2011, https://core.ac.uk/download/pdf/70374172.pdf;
Alfred W. McCoy, *A Question of Torture: CIA Interrogation, from the Cold War
to the War on Terror* (New York: Henry Holt and Company, 2006); Nils Melzer
and Steven J. Barela, "The Méndez Principles: Beware Crossing the Line to
Psychological Torture," *Just Security*, June 25, 2021, https://www.justsecurity.
org/77115/the-mendez-principles-beware-crossing-the-line-to-psychologi-
cal-torture/; Steven H. Miles, *Oath Betrayed: Torture, Medical Complicity, and
the War on Terror* (New York: Random House, 2006); Steven H. Miles, *The
Torture Doctors: Human Rights Crimes & the Road to Justice* (Washington,
DC: Georgetown University Press, 2020); Physicians for Human Rights, *Break
Them Down*; Pau Pérez-Sales, *Psychological Torture: Definition, Evaluation and
Measurement* (London: Routledge, 2017); Darius Rejali, *Torture and Democracy*
(Princeton, NJ: Princeton University Press, 2009); Hernan Reyes, "The Worst
Scars Are in the Mind: Psychological Torture," *International Review of the Red
Cross* 89, no. 867 (2007): 591–617, https://www.icrc.org/en/doc/assets/files/other/
irrc-867-reyes.pdf; Elaine Scarry, *The Body in Pain: The Making and Unmaking
of the World* (New York: Oxford University Press, 1985); United Nations, *Istanbul
Protocol: Manual on the Effective Investigation and Documentation of Torture
and Other Cruel, Inhuman, or Degrading Treatment or Punishment* (New York:
United Nations, 2004), https://phr.org/wp-content/uploads/2020/11/istan-
bul-protocol_opt.pdf; United Nations, *Report of the Special Rapporteur: Torture
and Other Cruel, Inhuman or Degrading Treatment or Punishment*, 2020, https://
documents-dds-ny.un.org/doc/UNDOC/GEN/G20/070/73/PDF/G2007073.pdf?

OpenElement; Beth Van Schaak and Ron Slye, "Teaching Torture," Santa Clara Law Digital Commons, 2009, https://digitalcommons.law.scu.edu/cgi/viewcontent.cgi?article=1623&context=facpubs.

75 Miles, *The Torture Doctors*, 123; see also Miles, *Oath Betrayed*.

76 See International Committee of the Red Cross, *Treatment by the Coalition Forces*; International Committee of the Red Cross, *ICRC Report on the Treatment of Fourteen "High Value Detainees" in CIA Custody*, February 2007, https://web.archive.org/web/20210227135103/https://www.nybooks.com/media/doc/2010/04/22/icrc-report.pdf; Joshua E.S. Phillips, *None of Us Were Like This Before: American Soldiers and Torture* (New York: Verso, 2010); Physicians for Human Rights and Human Rights First, *Leave No Marks: Enhanced Interrogation Techniques and the Risk of Criminality*, August 2007, https://phr.org/wp-content/uploads/2007/08/leave-no-marks-1.pdf; United States Senate, *Treatment of Detainees*; United States Senate, *CIA Detention and Interrogation Program*.

77 David Luban and Katherine S. Newell, "Personality Disruption as Mental Torture: The CIA, Interrogational Abuse, and the U.S. Torture Act," in *Interrogation and Torture: Integrating Efficacy with Law and Morality*, eds. Steven J. Barela, Mark Fallon, Gloria Gaggioli, and Jens David Ohlin (New York: Oxford University Press, 2020), 37–70; see also Physicians for Human Rights, *Break Them Down*.

78 United Nations, *Report of the Special Rapporteur*.

79 Central Intelligence Agency, *Human Resource Exploitation*; National Security Archive, n.d., *Prisoner Abuse: Patterns from the Past (Electronic Briefing Book No. 122)*, accessed May 5, 2022, https://nsarchive2.gwu.edu/NSAEBB/NSAEBB122/.

80 McCoy, *A Question of Torture*.

81 Slahi, *Guantanamo Diary*.

82 Ibid., 267.

83 Mansoor Adayfi, *Don't Forget Us Here: Lost and Found at Guantanamo* (New York: Hachette Books, 2021).

84 Ibid., 49, 106, 137, 62.

85 Other first-person accounts from former prisoners at Guantanamo include Sami Al-Hajj, *Prisoner 345: My Six Years in Guantanamo* (Al-Jazeera ebook, 2018); Moazzam Begg, *Enemy Combatant: My Imprisonment at Guantánamo, Bagram, and Kandahar* (New York: New Press, 2007); Lakhdar Boumediene and Mustafa Ait Idir, *Witnesses of the Unseen: Seven Years in Guantanamo* (Stanford, California: Redwood Press, 2017); Ahmed Errachidi, *The General: The Ordinary Man Who Challenged Guantanamo* (London: Chatto & Windus, 2013); David Hicks, *Guantanamo: My Journey* (North Sydney: Random House Australia, 2010); Murat Kurnaz, *Five Years of My Life: An Innocent Man in Guantanamo* (New York: Palgrave MacMacmillan, 2008).

86 Matt Apuzzo, Sherri Fink, and James Risen, "How U.S. Torture Left a Legacy of Damaged Minds," *New York Times*, October 8, 2016, https://www.nytimes.

com/2016/10/09/world/cia-torture-guantanamo-bay.html; see also Lauran
Neergaard, "Torture Can Affect the Brain, Leaving Long-Term Psychological
Scars," PBS *NewsHour,* December 23, 2014, https://www.pbs.org/newshour/
nation/torture-can-affect-brain-leaving-long-term-psychological-scars.

87 Mary R. Fabri, "Reconstructing Safety: Adjustments to the Therapeutic Frame in
the Treatment of Survivors of Political Torture," *Professional Psychology Research
and Practice* 32, no. 5 (2001): 453, https://doi.org/10.1037/0735-7028.32.5.452.

88 Physicians for Human Rights, *Break Them Down*; see also Nora Sveaass,
"Destroying Minds: Psychological Pain and the Crime of Torture," *New York
City Law Review* 11, no. 2 (2009): 303–24.

89 Ronnie Janoff-Bulman, *Shattered Assumptions: Towards a New Psychology of
Trauma* (New York: Free Press, 1992).

90 Several valuable films over the past two decades are directly relevant. The
docudrama *The Road to Guantanamo* (2006) from directors Mat Whitecross
and Michael Winterbottom recounts the experiences of three British Muslim
men incarcerated at Guantanamo and later released without charge. *Taxi to the
Dark Side* (2007), directed by Alex Gibney, focuses on the brutal death of an
Afghan taxi driver while in US custody. Director Rory Kennedy's documentary *Ghosts of Abu Ghraib* (2007) provides a close examination of the atrocities
committed by US forces at the infamous prison in Iraq. Dissident psychologist
Martha Davis created two informative documentaries – *Doctors of the Dark Side*
(2013) and *Expert Witness: Health Professionals on the Frontline Against Torture*
(2016) – about the involvement of health professionals in detainee abuse and in
the subsequent efforts to end it. Director Scott Z. Burns's *The Report* (2019) portrays the investigative work of Daniel Jones on behalf of the Senate Intelligence
Committee, and the obstacles he faced in researching CIA black-site torture.
Director Stephen Bennett's documentary *Eminent Monsters* (2020) illuminates
the role of health professionals in the development of modern torture techniques
before the 9/11 attacks, and their later applications in the "war on terror." In *The
Mauritanian* (2021), director Kevin Macdonald recounts the unjust imprisonment of Guantanamo detainee Mohamedou Ould Slahi – who was held for fourteen years without charge – and the legal efforts that led to his eventual release.
Most recently, director Alex Gibney's *The Forever Prisoner* (2021) examines the
imprisonment and torture of Abu Zubaydah by the CIA.

91 Carrie H. Kennedy, Rosemary C. Malone, and Michael J. Franks, "Provision
of Mental Health Services at the Detention Hospital in Guantanamo Bay,"
Psychological Services 6, no. 1 (2009): 1–10, http://humanrights.ucdavis.edu/
projects/the-guantanamo-testimonials-project/testimonies/testimonies-of-
military-psychologists-index/kennedy_malone_franks.pdf.

92 Ghislaine Boulanger, "The American Psychological Association: From Impunity
to Shame," *International Journal of Applied Psychoanalytical Studies* 14, no. 2
(2017): 108–15.

93 Vincent Iacopino, and Stephen N. Xenakis, "Neglect of Medical Evidence of Torture in Guantanamo Bay: A Case Series," *PloS Medicine* 8, no. 4 (2011): e1001027, https://journals.plos.org/plosmedicine/article?id=10.1371/journal.pmed.1001027.

94 "Presidential News Conference," C-SPAN, September 15, 2006, https://www.c-span.org/video/?194320-1/presidential-news-conference%20%20%20; see also Jim Rutenberg and Sheryl Gay Stolberg, "Bush Says G.O.P. Rebels Are Putting Nation at Risk," *New York Times*, September 16, 2006, https://www.nytimes.com/2006/09/16/us/threats-and-responses-the-president-bush-says-gop-rebels-are-putting.html.

95 Jessica Wolfendale, "The Myth of 'Torture Lite,'" *Ethics & International Affairs* 23, no. 1 (2009): 58, https://www.cambridge.org/core/journals/ethics-and-international-affairs/article/abs/myth-of-torture-lite/E5AB20301F59BB31E4B11146C25B2461.

96 Ibid., 49.

97 For example, see Adam Goldman and Peyton Craighill, "New Poll Finds Majority of Americans Think Torture Was Justified after 9/11 Attacks," *Washington Post*, December 16, 2014, https://www.washingtonpost.com/world/national-security/new-poll-finds-majority-of-americans-believe-torture-justified-after-911-attacks/2014/12/16/f6ee1208-847c-11e4-9534-f79a23c40e6c_story.html; Richard Wike, "Global Opinion Varies Widely on Use of Torture Against Suspected Terrorists," *Pew Research Center*, February 9, 2016, https://www.pewresearch.org/fact-tank/2016/02/09/global-opinion-use-of-torture/; for additional international views on torture, see International Committee of the Red Cross, *People on War: Perspectives from 16 Countries*, December 2016, https://www.icrc.org/en/document/people-on-war; Kathie Malley-Morrison, Sherri McCarthy, and Denise Hines, eds., International Handbook of War, Torture, and Terrorism (New York: Springer, 2013).

98 Ronnie Janoff-Bulman, "Erroneous Assumptions: Popular Belief in the Effectiveness of Torture Interrogation," *Peace and Conflict: Journal of Peace Psychology* 13, no. 4 (2007): 429–35.

99 Roy Eidelson, "How Americans Think about Torture – and Why," *Common Dreams*, May 11, 2009, https://www.commondreams.org/views/2009/05/11/how-americans-think-about-torture-and-why.

100 Eyal Press, "In Torture We Trust?," *Nation*, March 13, 2003, https://www.thenation.com/article/archive/torture-we-trust/; for a broader discussion of how US society depends upon but shuns those whose work is morally compromised, see Eyal Press, *Dirty Work: Essential Jobs and the Hidden Toll of Inequality in America* (New York: Farrar, Straus and Giroux, 2021).

101 For further background, see the following: Spencer Ackerman, Dominic Rushe, and Julian Borger, "Senate Report on CIA Torture Claims Spy Agency Lied about 'Ineffective' Program," *The Guardian*, December 9, 2014, https://www.theguardian.com/us-news/2014/dec/09/cia-torture-report-released; Constitution Project, "Statement of Members of The Constitution Project Task

Force on Detainee Treatment," December 9, 2014, http://detaineetaskforce.
org/wp-content/uploads/2014/12/2014.12.09_CIATortureReport.pdf; Janoff-
Bulman, "Erroneous Assumptions"; Shane O'Mara, "Interrogating the Brain:
Torture and the Neuroscience of Humane Interrogation," in *Interrogation and
Torture: Integrating Efficacy with Law and Morality*, eds. Steven J. Barela, Mark
Fallon, Gloria Gaggioli, and Jens David Ohlin (New York: Oxford University
Press, 2020), 197–221; United States Senate, CIA *Detention and Interrogation
Program*; Albert Vrij, Christian A. Meissner, Ronald P. Fisher, Saul M. Kassin,
Charles A. Morgan III, and Steven M. Kleinman, "Psychological Perspectives on
Interrogation," *Perspectives on Psychological Science* 12, no. 6 (2017): 927–55.

102 *Military Commissions Act of 2006*, S3990, 109th Cong., 2nd sess., *Congressional
Record*, S10354-S10431, https://www.loc.gov/rr/frd/Military_Law/pdf/SCOR-
2006-09-28.pdf.

103 O'Mara, "Interrogating the Brain," 221.

104 Resources that provide in-depth discussion of moral injury, its consequences,
and its treatment include the following: Joseph M. Currier, Kent D. Drescher,
and Jason Nieuwsma, eds., *Addressing Moral Injury in Clinical Practice*
(Washington, DC: American Psychological Association, 2021), https://doi.
org/10.1037/0000204-000; Brandon J. Griffin, Natalie Purcell, Kristine Burkman,
Brett T. Litz, Craig J. Bryan, Martha Schmitz, Claudia Villierme, Jessica Walsh,
and Shira Maguen, "Moral Injury: An Integrative Review," *Journal of Traumatic
Stress* 32, no. 3 (2019): 350–62, https://doi.org/10.1002/jts.22362; Brett T. Litz,
Nathan Stein, Eileen Delaney, Leslie Lebowitz, William P. Nash, Caroline
Silva, and Shira Maguen, "Moral Injury and Moral Repair in War Veterans:
A Preliminary Model and Intervention Strategy," *Clinical Psychology Review* 29,
no. 8 (2009): 695–706, https://doi.org/10.1016/j.cpr.2009.07.003; Robert E.
Meagher and Douglas A. Pryer, eds., *War and Moral Injury: A Reader* (Eugene,
OR: Cascade Books, 2018); Nancy Sherman, *Afterwar: Healing the Moral
Wounds of Our Soldiers* (New York: Oxford University Press, 2015); Jonathan
Shay, *Achilles in Vietnam: Combat Trauma and the Undoing of Character*
(New York: Scribner, 1995).

105 Litz et al., "Moral Injury and Moral Repair," 700.

106 Phillips, *None of Us Were Like This Before*, 186.

107 Rebecca Gordon, *Mainstreaming Torture: Ethical Approaches in the Post-9/11
United States* (New York: Oxford University Press, 2014).

108 Richard Matthews, *The Absolute Violation: Why Torture Must Be Prohibited*
(Montreal: McGill-Queen's University Press, 2008); see also Jean Maria Arrigo,
"A Utilitarian Argument Against Torture Interrogation of Terrorists," *Science
and Engineering Ethics* 10, no. 3 (2004): 543–72; Vittorio Buffachi and Jean Maria
Arrigo, "Torture, Terrorism and the State: A Refutation of the Ticking-Bomb
Argument," *Journal of Applied Philosophy* 23, no. 3 (2006): 355–73.

109 Rebecca Gordon, *American Nuremberg: The U.S. Officials Who Should Stand
Trial for Post-9/11 War Crimes* (New York: Hot Books, 2016).

110 Karen J. Greenberg, "The Achilles Heel of Torture: What the JAG Memos Tell Us," *Tom Dispatch*, August 25, 2005, https://tomdispatch.com/greenberg-on-why-u-s-military-lawyers-opposed-torture/.

Chapter Three

1 For further background, see Rebecca Leung, "Abuse of Iraqi POWs by GIS Probed," *60 Minutes II*, April 27, 2004, https://www.cbsnews.com/news/abuse-of-iraqi-pows-by-gis-probed/; Seymour Hersh, "Torture at Abu Ghraib," *New Yorker*, May 10, 2004, https://www.newyorker.com/magazine/2004/05/10/torture-at-abu-ghraib; Antonio M. Taguba, *Article 15-6 Investigation of the 800th Military Police Brigade*, 2004, https://www.thetorturedatabase.org/files/foia_subsite/pdfs/DODDOA000248.pdf.

2 Steven J. Breckler, "How Can the Science of Human Behavior Help Us Understand Abu Ghraib?," News Release, American Psychological Association, June 10, 2004, https://www.apa.org/topics/violence/abu-ghraib.

3 Ibid.

4 Ibid.

5 American Psychological Association, "Task Force to Examine Ethics and National Security," *Science Policy Insider News*, February 2005, http://www.apa.org/about/gr/science/spin/2005/02/ethics.aspx.

6 Stephen Soldz, Nathaniel Raymond, Steven Reisner, Scott A. Allen, Isaac L. Baker, and Allen S. Keller, *All the President's Psychologists: The American Psychological Association's Secret Complicity with the White House and US Intelligence Community in Support of the CIA's 'Enhanced' Interrogation Program*, April 2015, 38–9, https://s3.amazonaws.com/s3.documentcloud.org/documents/2069718/report.pdf.

7 M. Gregg Bloche, *The Hippocratic Myth: Why Doctors Are Under Pressure to Ration Care, Practice Politics, and Compromise Their Promise to Heal* (New York: Palgrave Macmillan, 2011).

8 United States Senate Select Committee on Intelligence, *Committee Study of the Central Intelligence Agency's Detention and Interrogation Program*, 2014, https://www.intelligence.senate.gov/sites/default/files/publications/CRPT-113srpt288.pdf.

9 American Psychological Association, "Science Policy Staff Meet with Psychologists in Counterintelligence," *Science Policy Insider News*, October 2004, https://web.archive.org/web/20140312223647/http://www.apa.org/about/gr/science/spin/2004/10/also-issue.aspx.

10 Mark Mazzetti, "Pentagon Is Expected to Close Intelligence Unit," *New York Times*, April 2, 2008, https://www.nytimes.com/2008/04/02/washington/02intel.html; Walter Pincus, "Pentagon Will Review Database on U.S. Citizens," *Washington Post*, December 15, 2005, https://www.washingtonpost.com/archive/

politics/2005/12/15/pentagon-will-review-database-on-us-citizens/06a11a7b-d441-400c-9590-cff2645b71e0/.

11 American Psychological Association, *Report to the Council of Representatives from Central Office*, July 2004–January 2005, 97.

12 Neil Lewis, "Red Cross Finds Detainee Abuse in Guantanamo," *New York Times*, November 30, 2004, https://www.nytimes.com/2004/11/30/politics/red-cross-finds-detainee-abuse-in-guantanamo.html; Neil Lewis, "Fresh Details Emerge on Harsh Methods at Guantanamo," *New York Times*, January 1, 2005, https://www.nytimes.com/2005/01/01/us/fresh-details-emerge-on-harsh-methods-at-guantanamo.html.

13 Carol Leonnig and Dana Priest, "Detainees Accuse Female Interrogators," *Washington Post*, February 10, 2005, https://www.washingtonpost.com/archive/politics/2005/02/10/detainees-accuse-female-interrogators/1e472805-5bf4-4144-ac5a-f46a1968c9dd/.

14 Tim Golden, "In U.S. Report, Brutal Details of 2 Afghan Inmates' Deaths," *New York Times*, May 20, 2005, https://www.nytimes.com/2005/05/20/world/asia/in-us-report-brutal-details-of-2-afghan-inmates-deaths.html.

15 Adam Zagorin and Michael Duffy, "Inside the Interrogation of Detainee 063," *Time*, June 20, 2005, https://time.com/3624326/inside-the-interrogation-of-detainee-063/.

16 M. Gregg Bloche and Jonathan H. Marks, "Doctors and Interrogators at Guantanamo Bay," *New England Journal of Medicine* 353 (2005): 7, https://www.nejm.org/doi/full/10.1056/NEJMp058145; see also M. Gregg Bloche and Jonathan H. Marks, "When Doctors Go to War," *New England Journal of Medicine* 352 (2005): 3–6, https://www.nejm.org/doi/full/10.1056/nejmp048346.

17 Bloche and Marks, "Doctors and Interrogators," 8.

18 Neil Lewis, "Interrogators Cite Doctors' Aid at Guantanamo," *New York Times*, June 24, 2005, https://www.nytimes.com/2005/06/24/us/interrogators-cite-doctors-aid-at-guantanamo.html.

19 M. Gregg Bloche, "Beyond Ethics on the Sly," in *Interrogation and Torture: Integrating Efficacy with Law and Morality*, eds. Steven J. Barela, Mark Fallon, Gloria Gaggioli, and Jens David Ohlin (New York: Oxford University Press, 2020), 290.

20 For brief background on the task force members, see Society for the Study of Peace, Conflict, and Violence, "American Psychological Association Presidential Task Force on Psychological Ethics and National Security," 2005, https://www2.clarku.edu/faculty/derivera/peacepsychology/tfpens.html; for a detailed review of the task force member selection process, see David H. Hoffman, Danielle J. Carter, Cara R. Viglucci Lopez, Heather L. Benzmiller, Ava X. Guo, S. Yasir Latifi, and Daniel C. Craig, *Report to the Special Committee of the Board of Directors of the American Psychological Association: Independent Review Relating to APA Ethics Guidelines, National Security Interrogations, and Torture*, rev. ed.

(Chicago: Sidley Austin LLP, 2015), 206–42, https://www.apa.org/independent-review/revised-report.pdf.

21 Larry James, *Fixing Hell: An Army Psychologist Confronts Abu Ghraib* (New York: Grand Central Publishing, 2008), 180.

22 Ibid., 50–1.

23 Cathy Scott-Clark and Adrian Levy, *The Forever Prisoner* (New York: Atlantic Monthly Press, 2022), 291.

24 United States Senate Committee on Armed Services, *Inquiry into the Treatment of Detainees in U.S. Custody*, 2008, 142, https://www.armed-services.senate.gov/imo/media/doc/Detainee-Report-Final_April-22-2009.pdf.

25 David G. Bolgiano and L. Morgan Banks, "Military Interrogation of Terror Suspects," *Military Review*, November–December 2010, 3, https://apps.dtic.mil/dtic/tr/fulltext/u2/a532757.pdf.

26 David H. Hoffman, Danielle J. Carter, Cara R. Viglucci Lopez, Heather L. Benzmiller, Ava X. Guo, S. Yasir Latifi, and Daniel C. Craig, *Report to the Special Committee of the Board of Directors of the American Psychological Association: Independent Review Relating to APA Ethics Guidelines, National Security Interrogations, and Torture, Binder 1* (Chicago, IL: Sidley Austin LLP, September 4, 2015): 675, https://www.apa.org/independent-review/binder-1.pdf.

27 National Public Radio, "Transcript: Military Psychologist Says Harsh Tactics Justified," May 4, 2009, http://www.npr.org/templates/transcript/transcript.php?storyId=103787285; Lefever has disputed NPR's account here: Bryce Lefever, "NPR's 'Report,'" March 2011, http://brycelefever.com/npr/.

28 Jane Mayer, *The Dark Side: The Inside Story of How the War on Terror Turned into a War on American Ideals* (New York: Doubleday, 2008); Katherine Eban, "Rorschach and Awe," *Vanity Fair*, July 17, 2007, https://www.vanityfair.com/news/2007/07/torture200707; Scott-Clark and Levy, *The Forever Prisoner*, 131; Scott Shane, "2 U.S. Architects of Harsh Tactics in 9/11's Wake," *New York Times*, August 11, 2009, https://www.nytimes.com/2009/08/12/us/12psychs.html.

29 American Psychological Association, "Science Policy Staff Meet with Psychologists in Counterintelligence," *Science Policy Insider News*, October 2004, https://web.archive.org/web/20140312223647/http://www.apa.org/about/gr/science/spin/2004/10/also-issue.aspx.

30 Charlie Savage, "Abuse Outraged Navy at Guantanamo Bay," *New York Times*, March 17, 2005, https://www.nytimes.com/2005/03/17/world/americas/abuse-outraged-navy-at-guantanamo-bay.html.

31 Charles P. Ewing and Michael G. Gelles, "Ethical Concerns in Forensic Consultation Regarding National Safety and Security," *Journal of Threat Assessment* 2, no. 3 (2003): 106.

32 American Psychological Association, *Report of the American Psychological Association Presidential Task Force on Psychological Ethics and National Security* (Washington, DC: American Psychological Association, 2005), 8, https://www.apa.org/pubs/reports/pens.pdf.

33 United States Department of Defense Joint Task Force-Guantanamo, *Behavioral Science Consultation Team Standard Operating Procedures*, March 28, 2005, http://humanrights.ucdavis.edu/projects/the-guantanamo-testimonials-project/testimonies/testimonies-of-standard-operating-procedures/bsct_sop_2005.pdf.

34 Kenneth S. Pope and Thomas G. Gutheil, "Psychologists Abandon the Nuremberg Ethic: Concerns for Detainee Interrogations," *International Journal of Law and Psychiatry* 32, no. 3 (2009): 161–6.

35 American Psychological Association, *Task Force on Psychological Ethics*, 3.

36 Ibid., 5.

37 Ibid., 5.

38 United States Department of Defense, Joint Chiefs of Staff, *Joint Publication 3-63: Joint Doctrine for Detainee Operations*, March 23, 2005, I–11, https://www.hrw.org/legacy/campaigns/torture/jointdoctrine/jointdoctrine040705.pdf.

39 Bloche, "Beyond Ethics on the Sly."

40 "Email Messages from the Listserv of the American Psychological Association's Presidential Task Force on Psychological Ethics and National Security: April 22, 2005 – June 26, 2006," 156, http://s3.amazonaws.com/propublica/assets/docs/pens_listserv.pdf.

41 Soldz et al., *All the President's Psychologists*.

42 Lewis, "Detainee Abuse in Guantanamo."

43 American Psychological Association, *Task Force on Psychological Ethics*, 8.

44 Nathaniel Raymond, Scott Allen, Vincent Iacopino, Allen Keller, Stephen Soldz, Steven Reisner, and John Bradshaw, *Experiments in Torture: Evidence of Human Subject Research and Experimentation in the 'Enhanced' Interrogation Program*, June 2010, https://phr.org/wp-content/uploads/2010/06/Experiments_in_Torture.pdf.

45 Nina Thomas subsequently wrote about her feelings of regret, betrayal, and gaslighting regarding the PENS Task Force here: Nina K. Thomas, "Gaslighting, Betrayal and the Boogeyman: Personal Reflections on the American Psychological Association, PENS and the Involvement of Psychologists in Torture," *International Journal of Applied Psychoanalytic Studies* 14, no. 2 (2017): 125–32, https://doi.org/10.1002/aps.1520.

46 For further background related to this task force dispute, see American Psychological Association, "Letter from Jean Maria Arrigo," *Monitor on Psychology* 37, no. 5 (2006): 4, http://www.apa.org/monitor/may06/letters.aspx; Democracy Now!, "'The Task Force Report Should Be Annulled' – Member of 2005 APA Task Force on Psychologist Participation in Military Interrogations Speaks Out," June 1, 2007, https://www.democracynow.org/2007/6/1/the_task_force_report_should_be; Democracy Now!, "Dissident Voices: Ex-Task Force Member Dr. Michael Wessells Speaks Out on Psychologists and Torture," August 20, 2007, https://www.democracynow.org/2007/8/20/dissident_voices_ex_task_force_member; "Email Messages from the Listserv: April 22, 2005 – June 26, 2006"; Thomas, "Gaslighting, Betrayal and the Boogeyman"; Michael Wessells,

Nora Sveaass, Donald Foster, and Andrew Dawes, "Do No Harm? How Psychologists Have Supported Torture and What to Do about It," in *Enlarging the Scope of Peace Psychology: African and World-Regional Contributions*, eds. Mohamed Seedat, Shahnaaz Suffla, and Daniel J. Christie (Springer International Publishing AG, 2017), 269–94, https://doi.org/10.1007/978-3-319-45289-0_14.

47 "Email Messages from the Listserv: April 22, 2005 – June 26, 2006," 160.

48 For further analysis on this point, see Derek Jinks and David Sloss, "Is the President Bound by International Law?," *Cornell Law Review* 90, no. 1 (2004): 97–202, https://scholarship.law.cornell.edu/cgi/viewcontent.cgi?article=2976&context=clr; Deborah Pearlstein, "Contra CIA, Non-Self-Executing Treaties Are Still the Supreme Law of the Land," *Opinio Juris*, October 28, 2015, http://opiniojuris.org/2015/10/28/contra-cia-non-self-executing-treaties-are-still-the-supreme-law-of-the-land/.

49 "Email Messages from the Listserv: April 22, 2005 – June 26, 2006," 23.

50 Ibid., 175.

51 David H. Hoffman, Danielle J. Carter, Cara R. Viglucci Lopez, Heather L. Benzmiller, Ava X. Guo, S. Yasir Latifi, and Daniel C. Craig, *Report to the Special Committee of the Board of Directors of the American Psychological Association: Independent Review Relating to APA Ethics Guidelines, National Security Interrogations, and Torture, Binder 1* (Chicago, IL: Sidley Austin LLP, September 4, 2015): 1009, https://www.apa.org/independent-review/binder-1.pdf.

52 Jean Maria Arrigo, "A Counterintelligence Perspective on APA PENS Task Force Process," August 17, 2007, 3, https://www.ethicalpsychology.org/materials/Arrigo-PENS-Process-APA07.pdf.

53 Hoffman et al., *Independent Review-Binder-1*, 908.

54 Mark Benjamin, "Psychologists Group Still Rocked by Torture Debate," *Salon*, August 4, 2006, https://www.salon.com/2006/08/04/apa/.

55 "Email Messages from the Listserv: April 22, 2005 – June 26, 2006," 169.

56 Mark Benjamin, "Psychological Warfare," *Salon*, July 26, 2006, https://www.salon.com/2006/07/26/interrogation_3/; the names of the task force members had previously been published on the website of the APA's Division 48 (Society for the Study of Peace, Conflict and Violence), but *not* on the APA's website.

57 These paragraphs reflect personal communications between Jean Maria Arrigo and the author over various dates, most recently August 8, 2022; see also Arrigo, "A Counterintelligence Perspective," 3.

58 "Email Messages from the Listserv: April 22, 2005 – June 26, 2006."

59 For other excellent discussions of the PENS process and report, see Bloche, *The Hippocratic Myth*; Brad Olson, Stephen Soldz, and Martha Davis, "The Ethics of Interrogation and the American Psychological Association: A Critique of Policy and Process," *Philosophy, Ethics, and Humanities in Medicine* 3, no. 3 (2008), https://peh-med.biomedcentral.com/articles/10.1186/1747-5341-3-3; Wessells et al., "Do No Harm?"

60 "Email Messages from the Listserv: April 22, 2005 – June 26, 2006," 167.
61 Jane Mayer, "The Experiment," *New Yorker*, July 3, 2005, https://www.newyorker.com/magazine/2005/07/11/the-experiment-3.
62 Ibid.
63 See the following: Mark Benjamin, "The CIA's Torture Teachers," *Salon*, June 21, 2007, https://www.salon.com/2007/06/21/cia_sere/; Eban, "Rorschach and Awe"; Jane Mayer, "The Black Sites," *New Yorker*, August 5, 2007, https://www.newyorker.com/magazine/2007/08/13/the-black-sites.
64 Stephen Behnke, "Psychological Ethics and National Security: The Position of the American Psychological Association," *European Psychologist* 11, no. 2 (2016): 153–6, https://econtent.hogrefe.com/doi/full/10.1027/1016-9040.11.2.153.
65 Democracy Now!, "Psychological Warfare?"
66 Ibid.
67 "Email Messages from the Listserv: April 22, 2005 – June 26, 2006," 13.
68 Gerald P. Koocher, "Speaking against Torture," *Monitor on Psychology* 37, no. 2 (2006): 5, http://www.apa.org/monitor/feb06/pc.aspx.
69 Gerald P. Koocher, "Varied and Valued Roles," *Monitor on Psychology* 37, no. 7 (2006): 5, https://www.apa.org/monitor/julaug06/pc.
70 Kenneth S. Pope and Thomas G. Gutheil, "Contrasting Ethical Policies of Physicians and Psychologists Concerning Interrogation of Detainees," *British Medical Journal* 338, b1653 (2009).
71 American Psychiatric Association, "Position Statement on Psychiatric Participation in Interrogation of Detainees," May 2006, https://www.psychiatry.org/File%20Library/About-APA/Organization-Documents-Policies/Policies/Position-Psychiatric-Participation-in-Interrogation-of-Detainees.pdf.
72 American Medical Association, "New AMA Ethical Policy Opposes Direct Physician Participation in Interrogation," June 12, 2006, https://web.archive.org/web/20060617230050/http://www.ama-assn.org/ama/pub/category/16446.html.
73 Neil Lewis, "Military Alters the Makeup of Interrogation Advisers," *New York Times*, June 7, 2006, https://www.nytimes.com/2006/06/07/washington/07detain.html.
74 Stephen Soldz, "Petition: Against Psychologists' Participation in Interrogation of 'Enemy Combatants,'" accessed May 3, 2022, https://www.thepetitionsite.com/takeaction/483/607/021/.
75 Neil Lewis, "Psychologists Preferred for Detainees," *New York Times*, June 7, 2006, https://www.nytimes.com/2006/06/07/us/national-briefing-washington-psychologists-preferred-for-detainees.html.
76 Stephen Behnke, "Ethics and Interrogations: Comparing and Contrasting the American Psychological, American Medical and American Psychiatric Association Positions," *Monitor on Psychology* 37, no. 7 (2006): 66, https://www.apa.org/monitor/julaug06/interrogations.
77 Olson, Soldz, and Davis, "The Ethics of Interrogation."

78 Gregory Hooks and Clayton Mosher, "Outrages against Personal Dignity: Rationalizing Abuse and Torture in the War on Terror," *Social Forces* 83, no. 4 (June 2005): 1628, https://doi.org/10.1353/sof.2005.0068.

79 Jeffrey Kaye, "APA Ethics Director Consulted on Development of BSCT Training Program," *Shadowproof*, May 2, 2015, https://shadowproof.com/2015/05/02/apa-ethics-director-consulted-on-development-of-bsct-training-program/; for further background, see Hoffman et al., *Independent Review*, 358–61.

80 David H. Hoffman, Danielle J. Carter, Cara R. Viglucci Lopez, Heather L. Benzmiller, Ava X. Guo, S. Yasir Latifi, and Daniel C. Craig, *Report to the Special Committee of the Board of Directors of the American Psychological Association: Independent Review Relating to APA Ethics Guidelines, National Security Interrogations, and Torture, Binder 2* (Chicago: Sidley Austin LLP, 2015), 27, https://www.apa.org/independent-review/binder-2.pdf.

81 Ibid., 28.

82 Ibid., 1435.

83 Arthur Levine, "Collective Unconscionable," *Washington Monthly*, January 1, 2007, https://washingtonmonthly.com/2007/01/01/collective-unconscionable/.

84 Benjamin, "Psychologists Group Still Rocked."

85 Personal communications between Steven Reisner and the author over various dates, most recently February 25, 2022.

86 Christopher Munsey and Laurie Meyers, "Debating Psychologists' Wartime Roles," *Monitor on Psychology* 37, no. 9 (2006): 28, https://www.apa.org/monitor/oct06/wartime; see also Joan H. Liem and Brinton Lykes, "Martín-Baró's Legacy, Guantánamo, and a Challenge to Psychologists," *The Just Word*, Spring 2006, http://martinbarofund.org/wp-content/uploads/2018/08/spring06.pdf.

87 Eban, "Rorschach and Awe."

88 This email exchange did not become publicly available until 2015, in Soldz et al., *All the President's Psychologists*, 42–8.

89 Stephen H. Behnke and Gerald P. Koocher, "Commentary on 'Psychologists and the Use of Torture in Interrogations,'" *Analyses of Social Issues and Public Policy* 7, no. 1 (2007): 25; the Behnke and Koocher commentary was written in response to Mark Costanzo, Ellen Gerrity, and M. Brinton Lykes, "Psychologists and the Use of Torture in Interrogations," *Analyses of Social Issues and Public Policy* 7, no. 1 (2007): 7–20.

90 Hoffman et al., *Independent Review*; see also Roy J. Eidelson, "'No Cause for Action': Revisiting the Ethics Case of Dr. John Leso," *Journal of Social and Political Psychology* 3, no. 1 (2015): 198–212, https://jspp.psychopen.eu/index.php/jspp/article/view/4849/4849.pdf.

91 Gerald P. Koocher, "Letter from Gerald P. Koocher to Amy Goodman at Democracy Now!," September 2007, https://web.archive.org/web/20071012123737/http://psychoanalystsopposewar.org/blog/wp-content/uploads/2007/09/koocher_open_letter_to_amy_goodman.pdf.

92 Spencer Ackerman, "A 'National Hero': Psychologist Who Warned of Torture Collusion Gets Her Due," *The Guardian*, July 13, 2015, https://www.theguardian.com/law/2015/jul/13/psychologist-torture-doctors-collusion-jean-maria-arrigo.

Chapter Four

1 A collection of the Coalition's statements is available online at https://www.ethicalpsychology.org/resources/coalition.php; see also Peter Aldhous, "How Six Rebel Psychologists Fought a Decade-Long War on Torture – and Won," *Buzzfeed*, August 7, 2015, https://www.buzzfeednews.com/article/peteraldhous/the-dissidents.

2 Psychologists for an Ethical APA, "Steering Committee," n.d., accessed May 3, 2022, https://web.archive.org/web/20111107151439/http://www.ethicalapa.com/Steering_Committee.html.

3 Susan Opotow, "Subverting an Ethical Code: American Psychological Association and the Post-9/11 War on Terror," *Qualitative Psychology* (Advance online publication, March 28, 2022): 2, http://dx.doi.org/10.1037/qup0000223.

4 Ibid., 8.

5 Allen M. Omoto, "A Road to Human Rights, OR What Happened on the Way to a Moratorium?," *Society for the Psychological Study of Social Issues Newsletter* 233 (Fall 2007), https://www.spssi.org/_data/n_0001/resources/live/SPSSI%20Newsletter_Fall%202007.pdf; Society for the Study of Peace, Conflict, and Violence, "Call for an APA Moratorium Resolution," April 2007, https://www2.clarku.edu/faculty/derivera/peacepsychology/2007Moratorium/MoratoriumStatement07.html.

6 Military Commissions Act of 2006, Pub. L. No. 109-366, 120 Stat. 2600, https://www.loc.gov/rr/frd/Military_Law/pdf/PL-109-366.pdf; for further background, see American Civil Liberties Union, "Military Commissions Act," n.d., accessed May 3, 2022, https://www.aclu.org/files/pdfs/legpriorities2007p2.pdf; Center for Constitutional Rights, "Military Commissions Act of 2006: A Summary of the Law," October 17, 2006, https://ccrjustice.org/files/report_MCA.pdf; Michael C. Dorf, "The Orwellian Military Commissions Act of 2006," Cornell Law Faculty Publications, Paper 55, 2007, http://scholarship.law.cornell.edu/facpub/55; New York Times Editorial Board, "Rushing off a Cliff," *New York Times*, September 28, 2006, https://www.nytimes.com/2006/09/28/opinion/28thu1.html; John T. Parry, *Understanding Torture: Law, Violence, and Political Identity* (Ann Arbor: University of Michigan Press, 2010); Leila Nadya Sadat, "A Presumption of Guilt: The Unlawful Enemy Combatant and the U.S. War on Terror," *Denver Journal of International Law and Policy* 37, no. 4 (2009): 539–53, https://digitalcommons.du.edu/cgi/viewcontent.cgi?article=1241&context=djilp; Michael J.D. Sweeney, "Detention at Guantanamo Bay: A Linguistic Challenge to Law," *American Bar Association*, January 1, 2003, https://www.americanbar.org/groups/crsj/

publications/human_rights_magazine_home/human_rights_vol30_2003/
winter2003/irr_hr_winter03_detention/.

7   United Nations, *Universal Declaration of Human Rights* (December 10, 1948),
    https://www.un.org/en/about-us/universal-declaration-of-human-rights.

8   David H. Hoffman, Danielle J. Carter, Cara R. Viglucci Lopez, Heather L.
    Benzmiller, Ava X. Guo, S. Yasir Latifi, and Daniel C. Craig, *Report to the Special
    Committee of the Board of Directors of the American Psychological Association:
    Independent Review Relating to APA Ethics Guidelines, National Security
    Interrogations, and Torture, Binder 2* (Chicago: Sidley Austin LLP, 2015), 756,
    https://www.apa.org/independent-review/binder-2.pdf.

9   Ibid., 196, 251; for further background, see David H. Hoffman, Danielle J. Carter,
    Cara R. Viglucci Lopez, Heather L. Benzmiller, Ava X. Guo, S. Yasir Latifi, and
    Daniel C. Craig, *Report to the Special Committee of the Board of Directors of the
    American Psychological Association: Independent Review Relating to APA Ethics
    Guidelines, National Security Interrogations, and Torture*, rev. ed. (Chicago:
    Sidley Austin LLP, 2015), 404–13, https://www.apa.org/independent-review/
    revised-report.pdf.

10 This account of the meeting in Washington, DC, is based on the author's personal
    communication with Brad Olson, September 2, 2022.

11 Larry James, *Fixing Hell: An Army Psychologist Confronts Abu Ghraib* (New York:
    Grand Central Publishing, 2008), 251.

12 Robert Parker, "American Psychological Association Council Debate on
    Interrogations, August 2007," *Focus Reframed*, July 20, 2008, https://www.
    focusreframed.com/media/APACouncilFull.pdf.

13 Ibid.

14 Editorial Staff, "Human Wrongs / Psychologists Have No Place Assisting
    Interrogations at Places Such as Guantanamo Bay," *Houston Chronicle*, August
    23, 2007, https://web.archive.org/web/20081010160628/http:/www.chron.com:80/
    CDA/archives/archive.mpl?id=2007_4410052.

15 James, *Fixing Hell*.

16 Ibid., 180, 66.

17 Ibid., 162, 199.

18 Mark Fallon, *Unjustifiable Means: The Inside Story of How the CIA, Pentagon, and
    US Government Conspired to Torture* (New York: Regan Arts, 2017), 95–6, 183.

19 American Psychological Association, *Reaffirmation of the American
    Psychological Association Position Against Torture and Other Cruel, Inhuman, or
    Degrading Treatment or Punishment and Its Application to Individuals Defined
    in the United States Code as "Enemy Combatants"* (August 19, 2007), http://www.
    infocoponline.es/pdf/resolucion040907.pdf.

20 David H. Hoffman, Danielle J. Carter, Cara R. Viglucci Lopez, Heather L.
    Benzmiller, Ava X. Guo, S. Yasir Latifi, and Daniel C. Craig, *Report to the Special
    Committee of the Board of Directors of the American Psychological Association:
    Independent Review Relating to APA Ethics Guidelines, National Security*

Interrogations, and Torture, Binder 2 (Chicago: Sidley Austin LLP, 2015), 213–40, https://www.apa.org/independent-review/binder-2.pdf.

21 For further background, see Coalition for an Ethical Psychology, "Analysis of the American Psychological Association's Frequently Asked Questions Regarding APA's Policies and Positions on the Use of Torture or Cruel, Inhuman or Degrading Treatment during Interrogations," December 2007, https://ethical-psychology.org/materials/Coalition-FAQ-12-07.pdf; Jeffrey Kaye, "Post-Mortem: APA Torture Resolution Puzzle," *Invictus*, August 20, 2007, https://valtinsblog. blogspot.com/2007/08/postmortem-apa-torture-resolution.html; Linda Woolf, "A Sad Day for Psychologists, A Sadder Day for Human Rights," *OpEdNews*, December 1, 2007, https://www.opednews.com/populum/page.php?f=opedne_ linda_m__070901_a_sad_day_for_psycho.htm.

22 American Psychological Association, *Reaffirmation of the American Psychological Association Position Against Torture.*

23 For more information, see: Jamil Dakwar, "Guantanamo's Frequent Flyer Program," *American Civil Liberties Union*, June 20, 2008, https://www.aclu. org/blog/national-security/guantanamos-frequent-flyer-program; Office of the Inspector General United States Department of Justice, "Statement of Glenn A. Fine Inspector General, U.S. Department of Justice before the Senate Committee on the Judiciary concerning Detainee Interrogation Techniques," June 10, 2008, https://oig.justice.gov/node/733; Josh White, "Tactic Used after It Was Banned," *Washington Post*, August 8, 2008, https://www.washingtonpost.com/wp-dyn/ content/article/2008/08/07/AR2008080703004.html.

24 Coalition for an Ethical Psychology, "APA's Policies and Positions"; for the amended version of the resolution, see American Psychological Association, *Reaffirmation of the American Psychological Association Position Against Torture and Other Cruel, Inhuman, or Degrading Treatment or Punishment and Its Application to Individuals Defined in the United States Code as "Enemy Combatants,"* August 19, 2007, https://www.apa.org/about/policy/torture.

25 Democracy Now!, "APA Members Hold Fiery Town Hall Meeting on Interrogation, Torture," August 20, 2007, https://www.democracynow. org/2007/8/20/apa_members_hold_fiery_town_hall.

26 For a complete audio recording and transcript of the town hall meeting with the quotes I have provided, see Robert Parker, "American Psychological Association Town Hall on Interrogations, August 2007," *Focus Reframed*, July 20, 2008, https://focusreframed.com/?p=93.

27 Ibid.

28 Ibid.

29 Mary Pipher, "Why I Returned My Award to the American Psychological Association – Because It Sanctions Torture," *OpEdNews*, August 24, 2007, https://www.opednews.com/articles/opedne_mary_pip_070824_why_i_ve_ returned_my.htm; see also Democracy Now!, "Renowned Psychologist, Author Returns APA Award over Interrogation Policy," August 28, 2007, https://www.

democracynow.org/2007/8/28/renowned_psychologist_author_returns_apa_
award; Democracy Now!, "Psychologist, Author Mary Pipher Returns APA
Award over Interrogation Policy," August 29, 2007, https://www.democracynow.
org/2007/8/29/psychologist_author_mary_pipher_returns_apa.

30 David Glenn, "A Policy on Torture Roils Psychologists' Annual Meeting,"
Chronicle of Higher Education, September 7, 2007, https://www.chronicle.com/
article/a-policy-on-torture-roils-psychologists-annual-meeting/.

31 American Psychological Association, "2008 APA Petition Resolution Ballot," n.d.,
accessed May 3, 2022, https://www.apa.org/news/press/statements/work-
settings.

32 Hoffman et al., *Independent Review-Binder-2*, 333.

33 Ibid., 1001.

34 Ibid., 334–5.

35 Ibid., 1267.

36 Ibid., 1029–31.

37 Physicians for Human Rights, "Psychologists Prohibited from Abusive US
Detention Centers," News Release, September 17, 2008, https://phr.org/news/
psychologists-prohibited-from-abusive-us-detention-centers/.

38 Santiago Wills, "The Role of Health Professionals in Detainee Interrogation," *The
Atlantic*, November 11, 2012, https://www.theatlantic.com/health/archive/2012/11/
the-role-of-health-professionals-in-detainee-interrogation/263812/.

39 American Psychological Association, "Statement of the American Psychological
Association," news release, August 2008, https://www.apa.org/news/press/releases/
2008/08/apa-statement.

40 The descriptions of this episode are based on the author's personal communications with both Bryant Welch and Jean Maria Arrigo, August 20, 2022.

41 Benedict Carey, "Psychologists Vote to End Interrogation Consultations,"
New York Times, September 17, 2008, https://www.nytimes.com/2008/09/18/
us/18psych.html; through Psychologists for Social Responsibility, I contributed
a short video to the referendum campaign effort: https://www.youtube.com/
watch?v=-GDH4V8A_Qc.

42 American Psychological Association, *Report of the APA Presidential Advisory
Group on the Implementation of the Petition Resolution*, December 2008, https://
www.apa.org/ethics/advisory-group-final.pdf.

43 Hoffman et al., *Independent Review-Binder-2*, 1242.

44 Ibid., 1230–1.

45 United States Department of Defense, "Directive 3115.09 (DoD Intelligence
Interrogations, Detainee Debriefings, and Tactical Questioning)," October 11,
2012, https://fas.org/irp/doddir/dod/d3115_09.pdf.

46 Joint Task Force Guantanamo, "Guard Force," May 7, 2014, www.jtfgtmo.
southcom.mil.

47 American Psychological Association, "Continuing Education: Ethical Practice
in Operational Psychology: Military and National Intelligence Applications,"

2015, https://web.archive.org/web/20150419211024/http://www.apa.org/education/
ce/1360283.aspx.

48 American Psychological Association, "Annual Report: Proceedings of the American
Psychological Association for the Legislative Year 2005," *American Psychologist* 61,
· no. 5 (2006): 459, https://psycnet.apa.org/fulltext/2011-23524-004.html.

49 American Psychological Association, "APA Council Endorses Ethical Guidelines
for Psychologists Participating in National Security-Related Investigations and
Interrogations," news release, August 2005, https://www.apa.org/news/press/
releases/2005/08/security; Mark Benjamin, "Psychologists Group Still Rocked
by Torture Debate," *Salon*, August 4, 2006, https://www.salon.com/2006/08/04/
apa/; Ronald F. Levant, "Making Psychology a Household Word," *American
Psychologist* 61, no. 5 (2006): 383–95; Geoff Mumford, "When Legislative
Objectives Are in Conflict," *Monitor on Psychology* 37, no. 8 (2006): 68, https://
www.apa.org/monitor/mar06/ppup; Kenneth S. Pope, "Are the American
Psychological Association's Detainee Interrogation Policies Ethical and
Effective?," *Zeitschrift fur Psychologie / Journal of Psychology* 219, no. 3 (2011):
https://econtent.hogrefe.com/doi/10.1027/2151-2604/a000062.

50 American Psychological Association, *Report of the American Psychological
Association Presidential Task Force on Psychological Ethics and National Security*
(Washington, DC: American Psychological Association, 2005), https://www.apa.
org/pubs/reports/pens.pdf.

51 Kenneth S. Pope, "The Code Not Taken: The Path from Guild Ethics to Torture
and Our Continuing Choices," *Canadian Psychology/Psychologie Canadienne* 57,
no. 1 (2016): 51–9, https://kspope.com/PsychologyEthics.php.

52 Kenneth S. Pope, "Why I Resigned from the American Psychological
Association," February 6, 2008, https://kspope.com/apa/.

53 Psychologists for an Ethical APA, "Some History and Information about
'WithholdAPADues,'" n.d., accessed May 3, 2022, https://web.archive.org/
web/20111107153433/http://www.ethicalapa.com/Join_Withhold.html.

54 Hoffman et al., *Independent Review-Binder-2*, 1280–1.

55 American Psychological Association, "Public Comment Solicitation Website
for Ethical Standard 1.02," December 2008, https://www.apa.org/ethics/code/
responses-dec-2008.pdf.

56 American Psychological Association, "Annual Report: Proceedings of the
American Psychological Association for the Legislative Year 2009," *American
Psychologist* 65, no. 5 (2010): 444–5, https://psycnet.apa.org/record/2010-
14198-008.

57 American Psychological Association, "Annual Report: Proceedings of the
American Psychological Association for the Legislative Year 2010," *American
Psychologist* 66, no. 5, (2011): 363–80, https://psycnet.apa.org/record/2011-
14747-008; American Psychological Association, *Ethical Principles of
Psychologists and Code of Conduct* (Washington, DC: American Psychological
Association, 2017), https://www.apa.org/ethics/code/ethics-code-2017.pdf.

58 Coalition for an Ethical Psychology, "A Call for Annulment of the APA's PENS Report," 2011, http://www.ethicalpsychology.org/pens/.

59 Coalition for an Ethical Psychology, "Signers to the Call for Annulment of the APA's PENS Report," 2011, http://www.ethicalpsychology.org/pens/signers.php.

60 Jeffrey Younggren, "Open Letter from Division 42 President Jeffrey Younggren to the Coalition for an Ethical Psychology," October 26, 2012, https://www.ethical-psychology.org/materials/Div42-Response-to-Coalition-10-26-2012.pdf.

61 Coalition for an Ethical Psychology, "Open Letter from the Coalition to the Division 42 Board," October 31, 2012, https://www.ethicalpsychology.org/materials/Coalition-Response-to-Div42-Board.pdf.

62 "APA Member-Initiated Task Force to Reconcile Policies Related to Psychologists' Involvement in National Security Settings," February 2012, http://faculty.webster.edu/woolflm/MemberInitiatedTaskForce/MissionStatement.html.

63 American Psychological Association, Division 19 E-Newsletter, "President's Message," *Military Psychologist* 26, no. 1 (2010): 1.

64 "APA Member-Initiated Task Force to Reconcile Policies."

65 Roy Eidelson, "Protecting Psychologists Who Harm," *Counterpunch*, March 12, 2012, https://www.counterpunch.org/2012/03/12/protecting-psychologists-who-harm/.

66 For further background, see Coalition for an Ethical Psychology, "Coalition Declines Invitation from APA's 'PENS II' Task Force," July 1, 2012, http://www.ethicalpsychology.org/pens/Coalition_Declines_PENS_II_Invitation.pdf; Coalition for an Ethical Psychology, "A Resolution to Annul the APA's PENS Report," July 26, 2012, http://www.ethicalpsychology.org/pens/A-Resolution-to-Annul-the-APA-PENS-Report.pdf; Coalition for an Ethical Psychology, "Letter to APA Board and Council of Representatives," February 18, 2013, https://www.ethicalpsychology.org/materials/Coalition-Letter-APA-Council-2-18-13.pdf.

67 American Psychological Association, *Policy Related to Psychologists' Work in National Security Settings and Reaffirmation of the APA Position Against Torture and Other Cruel, Inhuman, or Degrading Treatment or Punishment* (Washington, DC: American Psychological Association, 2013), https://www.apa.org/about/policy/national-security; American Psychological Association, *Report of the Member-Initiated Task Force to Reconcile APA Policies Related to Psychologists' Work in National Security Settings* (Washington, DC: American Psychological Association, 2013), https://www.apa.org/about/policy/psychologists-national-security.pdf.

68 American Psychological Association, *Task Force on Psychological Ethics.*

69 For a detailed summary of the investigation, see: David H. Hoffman, Danielle J. Carter, Cara R. Viglucci Lopez, Heather L. Benzmiller, Ava X. Guo, S. Yasir Latifi, and Daniel C. Craig, *Report to the Special Committee of the Board of Directors of the American Psychological Association: Independent Review Relating to APA Ethics Guidelines, National Security Interrogations, and Torture*, rev. ed. (Chicago: Sidley Austin LLP, 2015), 493–518, https://www.apa.org/independent-review/revised-report.pdf; see also Trudy Bond, "If Not Now, When?," *Counterpunch*, May 19, 2008, https://www.counterpunch.org/2008/05/19/

if-not-now-when-2/; Roy J. Eidelson, "'No Cause for Action': Revisiting the Ethics Case of Dr. John Leso," *Journal of Social and Political Psychology* 3, no. 1 (2015): 198–212, https://jspp.psychopen.eu/index.php/jspp/article/view/4849/4849.pdf.

70 United States Senate Committee on Armed Services. *Inquiry into the Treatment of Detainees in U.S. Custody*, 2008, 50–3, https://www.armed-services.senate.gov/imo/media/doc/Detainee-Report-Final_April-22-2009.pdf.

71 Ibid.

72 For further background, see: Adam Zagorin and Michael Duffy, "Inside the Interrogation of Detainee 063," *Time*, June 20, 2005, https://time.com/3624326/inside-the-interrogation-of-detainee-063/; "Interrogation Log, Detainee 063," *Time*, n.d., accessed May 3, 2022, https://content.time.com/time/2006/log/log.pdf; Bob Woodward, "Guantanamo Detainee Was Tortured, Says Official Overseeing Military Trials," *Washington Post*, January 14, 2009, https://www.washingtonpost.com/wp-dyn/content/article/2009/01/13/AR2009011303372.html.

73 For example, see: International Committee of the Red Cross, *Basic Rules of the Geneva Conventions and Their Additional Protocols* (Geneva: International Committee of the Red Cross, 1983); United Nations General Assembly, *Convention against Torture and Other Cruel, Inhuman or Degrading Treatment or Punishment*, December 10, 1984, https://www.ohchr.org/en/professionalinterest/pages/cat.aspx; International Committee of the Red Cross, *Rule 90. Torture and Cruel, Inhuman or Degrading Treatment* (Geneva: International Committee of the Red Cross, n.d.), https://www.icrc.org/customary-ihl/eng/docs/v1_rul_rule90.

74 David H. Hoffman, Danielle J. Carter, Cara R. Viglucci Lopez, Heather L. Benzmiller, Ava X. Guo, S. Yasir Latifi, and Daniel C. Craig, *Report to the Special Committee of the Board of Directors of the American Psychological Association: Independent Review Relating to APA Ethics Guidelines, National Security Interrogations, and Torture (Revised) – Binder 4* (Chicago, IL: Sidley Austin LLP, September 4, 2015), 525–8, https://www.apa.org/independent-review/binder-4.pdf.

75 American Psychological Association, "Ethics Office Letter to Dr. Trudy Bond," December 31, 2013, http://www.theguardian.com/world/interactive/2014/jan/22/american-psychological-association-leso-letter.

76 Ibid.

77 Ibid.

78 Ibid.

79 American Psychological Association, "APA Response to *Forbes* Magazine Opinion Pieces by Todd Essig," news release, March 15, 2014, http://www.apa.org/news/press/response/forbes-response.aspx.

80 American Psychological Association, *Task Force on Psychological Ethics*.

81 American Psychological Association, "Letter to Dr. Trudy Bond."

82 Army Surgeon General Eric Schoomaker, "Letter to Ethics Office of the American Psychological Association," March 25, 2008; for the full letter, see Hoffman et al., *Independent Review-Binder-4*, 564–5, https://www.apa.org/independent-review/binder-4.pdf.

83 For the Hoffman Report's brief summary of the APA Ethics Office response to the complaint, see Hoffman et al., *Independent Review*, 520–2, https://www.apa.org/independent-review/revised-report.pdf.

84 For summaries of these cases, see Institute on Medicine as a Profession, *Ethics Abandoned: Medical Professionalism and Detainee Abuse in the War on Terror* (New York: The Institute, 2013), 204–13, https://hrp.law.harvard.edu/wp-content/uploads/2013/11/IMAP-EthicsTextFinal2.pdf.

85 Harvard Law School International Human Rights Clinic, "Dr. Trudy Bond et al. v. Larry James (Ohio, 2010)," n.d., accessed August 31, 2022, https://hrp.law.harvard.edu/areas-of-focus/previous-areas-of-focus/counterterrorism-human-rights/professional-misconduct-complaint-larry-james/.

86 Deborah Popowski, "Beyond the APA: The Role of Psychology Boards and State Courts in Propping up Torture," *Just Security*, August 24, 2015, https://www.just-security.org/25378/apa-role-psychology-boards-state-courts-propping-torture/.

87 Ibid.

88 Letter from the Ohio State Board of Psychology, January 26, 2011, http://hrp.law.harvard.edu/wp-content/uploads/2013/06/james-letter31.pdf.

89 Trudy Bond, personal communication with the author, August 31, 2022.

90 See Danny Robbins, "Texas Board Won't Discipline CIA Psychologist," *Victoria Advocate*, February 25, 2011, https://www.victoriaadvocate.com/news/2011/feb/25/bc-tx-psychologist-waterboarding/; among the media reports of Mitchell's activities that were available to the licensing board were the following: Katherine Eban, "Rorschach and Awe," *Vanity Fair*, July 17, 2007, https://www.vanityfair.com/news/2007/07/torture200707; Jane Mayer, *The Dark Side: The Inside Story of How the War on Terror Turned into a War on American Ideals* (New York: Doubleday, 2008); Scott Shane, "2 U.S. Architects of Harsh Tactics in 9/11's Wake," *New York Times*, August 11, 2009, https://www.nytimes.com/2009/08/12/us/12psychs.html.

91 Norine Johnson, "We, the People," *Monitor on Psychology* 32, no. 10 (2001): 5, https://www.apa.org/monitor/nov01/pc.

92 Carol Goodheart, "APA in the Age of Outrage," *Monitor on Psychology* 41, no. 1 (2010): 5, https://www.apa.org/monitor/2010/01/pc; see also Trudy Bond, "Psychologists in an Age of Torture," *Counterpunch*, January 13, 2010, https://www.counterpunch.org/2010/01/13/psychologists-in-an-age-of-torture/.

Chapter Five

1 James Risen, *Pay Any Price: Greed, Power, and Endless War* (New York: Houghton Mifflin Harcourt, 2014).

2 Cora Currier, "Blowing the Whistle on CIA Torture from Beyond the Grave," *The Intercept*, October 17, 2014, https://theintercept.com/2014/10/17/blowing-whistle-cia-torture-beyond-grave/.

3 For further background, see: M. Gregg Bloche, *The Hippocratic Myth: Why Doctors Are Under Pressure to Ration Care, Practice Politics, and Compromise Their Promise to Heal* (New York: Palgrave Macmillan, 2011); Jane Mayer, *The Dark Side: The Inside Story of How the War on Terror Turned into a War on American Ideals* (New York: Doubleday, 2008).

4 Kirk M. Hubbard, "Psychologists and Interrogations: What's Torture Got to Do with It?," *Analyses of Social Issues and Public Policy* 7, no. 1 (2007): 30, http://www.scra27.org/files/4014/3777/4629/Hubbard-2007-Analyses_of_Social_Issues_and_Public_Policy.pdf.

5 Stephen Soldz, Nathaniel Raymond, Steven Reisner, Scott A. Allen, Isaac L. Baker, and Allen S. Keller, *All the President's Psychologists: The American Psychological Association's Secret Complicity with the White House and US Intelligence Community in Support of the* CIA's *'Enhanced' Interrogation Program*, April 2015, 37, https://s3.amazonaws.com/s3.documentcloud.org/documents/2069718/report.pdf.

6 American Psychological Association, "APA Response to Risen Book and Allegations of Support for Torture," News Release, October 2014, https://www.apa.org/news/press/response/risen-book.

7 Coalition for an Ethical Psychology, "Questions for the APA Board Regarding Claims in James Risen's Book *Pay Any Price*," October 19, 2014, http://www.ethicalpsychology.org/materials/Coalition-Questions-for-APA-Board.pdf.

8 Colleen Flaherty, "'Pay Any Price,'" *Inside Higher Ed*, October 21, 2014, https://www.insidehighered.com/news/2014/10/21/psychology-group-objects-books-portrayal-its-role-post-911-torture.

9 Physicians for Human Rights, "PHR Calls for Federal Probe into American Psychological Association's Role in CIA Torture Program," news release, October 16, 2014, https://phr.org/news/phr-calls-for-federal-probe-into-american-psychological-associations-role-in-cia-torture-program/.

10 American Psychological Association, "APA Board of Directors Resolution Regarding Independent Review," November 2014, https://www.apa.org/about/governance/board/independent-review; American Psychological Association, "Statement of APA Board of Directors: Outside Counsel to Conduct Independent Review of Allegations of Support for Torture," news release, November 2014, https://www.apa.org/news/press/releases/2014/11/risen-allegations.

11 United States Senate Select Committee on Intelligence, *Committee Study of the Central Intelligence Agency's Detention and Interrogation Program*, 2014, https://www.intelligence.senate.gov/sites/default/files/publications/CRPT-113srpt288.pdf.

12 Physicians for Human Rights, "CIA Torture Report Highlights Unnecessary Medical Procedure: Rectal Hydration and Rectal Feeding Is Not Medically Justified," Press Release, December 10, 2014, https://phr.org/news/cia-torture-report-highlights-unnecessary-medical-procedure/.

13 United States Senate, CIA *Detention and Interrogation Program*.

14 Physicians for Human Rights, *Doing Harm: Health Professionals' Central Role in the CIA Torture Program*, December 2014, 5, https://phr.org/wp-content/uploads/2014/12/doing-harm-health-professionals-central-role-in-the-cia-torture-program.pdf. Coalition members Steven Reisner and Stephen Soldz contributed to this report.

15 For further background, see: Bill Chappell, "Psychologists behind CIA 'Enhanced Interrogation' Program Settle Detainees' Lawsuit," National Public Radio, August 17, 2017, https://www.npr.org/sections/thetwo-way/2017/08/17/544183178/psychologists-behind-cia-enhanced-interrogation-program-settle-detainees-lawsuit; Sherri Fink, "Settlement Reached in C.I.A. Torture Case," *New York Times*, August 17, 2017, https://www.nytimes.com/2017/08/17/us/cia-torture-lawsuit-settlement.html.

16 American Psychological Association, "APA Applauds Release of Senate Intelligence Committee Report Summary," News Release, December 9, 2014, https://www.apa.org/news/press/releases/2014/12/senate-intelligence.

17 David H. Hoffman, Danielle J. Carter, Cara R. Viglucci Lopez, Heather L. Benzmiller, Ava X. Guo, S. Yasir Latifi, and Daniel C. Craig, *Report to the Special Committee of the Board of Directors of the American Psychological Association: Independent Review Relating to APA Ethics Guidelines, National Security Interrogations, and Torture*, rev. ed. (Chicago: Sidley Austin LLP, 2015), 485–96, https://www.apa.org/independent-review/revised-report.pdf.

18 Ibid. The report, first made public in July of 2015, was subsequently slightly revised in September of that year; my citations are drawn from the September version. Six "binders" of emails and other documents collected by the independent review team are available online: https://www.apa.org/independent-review/binder-1.pdf; https://www.apa.org/independent-review/binder-2.pdf; https://www.apa.org/independent-review/binder-3.pdf; https://www.apa.org/independent-review/binder-4.pdf; https://www.apa.org/independent-review/binder-5.pdf; https://www.apa.org/independent-review/binder-6.pdf. In light of ongoing efforts to discredit the Hoffman Report, the many emails in these binders are especially valuable because they represent primary source material not readily subject to alternative interpretation. I have cited several of them throughout *Doing Harm*.

19 Hoffman et al., *Independent Review*, 9.

20 Ibid., 72.

21 David H. Hoffman, Danielle J. Carter, Cara R. Viglucci Lopez, Heather L. Benzmiller, Ava X. Guo, S. Yasir Latifi, and Daniel C. Craig, *Report to the Special Committee of the Board of Directors of the American Psychological Association: Independent Review Relating to APA Ethics Guidelines, National Security Interrogations, and Torture, Binder 1* (Chicago, IL: Sidley Austin LLP, September 4, 2015): 908, https://www.apa.org/independent-review/binder-1.pdf.

22 David H. Hoffman, Danielle J. Carter, Cara R. Viglucci Lopez, Heather L. Benzmiller, Ava X. Guo, S. Yasir Latifi, and Daniel C. Craig, *Report to the Special*

Committee of the Board of Directors of the American Psychological Association: Independent Review Relating to APA Ethics Guidelines, National Security Interrogations, and Torture, Binder 2 (Chicago: Sidley Austin LLP, 2015), 135, https://www.apa.org/independent-review/binder-2.pdf.

23 Hoffman et al., *Independent Review*, 47.

24 Ibid., 46.

25 Jean Maria Arrigo, Lawrence P. Rockwood, Jack O'Brien, Dutch Franz, David DeBatto, and John Kiriakou, "A Military/Intelligence Operational Perspective on the Weaponization of Psychology by the American Psychological Association," *History of the Human Sciences* (in press).

26 Soldz et al., *All the President's Psychologists*; see also Trudy Bond and Roy Eidelson, "The APA Relied on the CIA for Ethical Guidance," *Truthout*, May 4, 2015, https://truthout.org/articles/the-apa-relied-on-the-cia-for-ethical-guidance/; James Risen, "American Psychological Association Bolstered C.I.A. Torture Program, Report Says," *New York Times*, April 30, 2015, https://www.nytimes.com/2015/05/01/us/report-says-american-psychological-association-collaborated-on-torture-justification.html.

27 Soldz et al., *All the President's Psychologists*, 37.

28 Ibid., 32.

29 American Psychological Association, "Press Release and Recommended Actions: Independent Review Cites Collusion among APA Individuals and Defense Department Officials in Policy on Interrogation Techniques," news release, July 10, 2015, https://www.apa.org/news/press/releases/2015/07/independent-review-release.

30 Ibid.

31 American Psychological Association, "APA Announces Retirements and Resignation of Senior Leaders," news release, July 14, 2015, https://www.apa.org/news/press/releases/2015/07/retirements-resignation; see also Spencer Ackerman, "Three Senior Officials Lose Their Jobs at APA after US Torture Scandal," *The Guardian*, July 14, 2015, https://www.theguardian.com/us-news/2015/jul/14/apa-senior-officials-torture-report-cia.

32 Spencer Ackerman, "Psychologist Accused of Enabling US Torture Backed by Former FBI Chief," *The Guardian*, July 12, 2015, https://www.theguardian.com/law/2015/jul/12/apa-torture-report-louis-freeh-stephen-behnke.

33 Special Psychological Applications, Inc., "Our People," 2016, accessed May 3, 2022, http://spasupportinc.com/our-people/.

34 For example, see: Greg Miller, "Inquiry: Psychologists Group Colluded with Pentagon, CIA on Interrogations," *Washington Post*, July 10, 2015, https://www.washingtonpost.com/world/national-security/report-american-psychological-association-colluded-with-us-interrogation-programs/2015/07/10/42b0cbec-2741-11e5-b72c-2b7d516e1e0e_story.html; New York Times Editorial Board, "Psychologists Who Greenlighted Torture," *New York Times*, July 10, 2015, https://www.nytimes.com/2015/07/11/opinion/psychologists-who-greenlighted-

torture.html; James Risen, "Outside Psychologists Shielded U.S. Torture Program, Report Finds," *New York Times*, July 10, 2015, https://www.nytimes.com/2015/07/11/us/psychologists-shielded-us-torture-program-report-finds.html.

35 Physicians for Human Rights, "U.S. Justice Department Must Investigate American Psychological Association's Role in U.S. Torture Program," news release, July 10, 2015, https://phr.org/news/u-s-justice-department-must-investigate-american-psychological-associations-role-in-u-s-torture-program/.

36 Dror Ladin and Steven M. Watt, "The Psychologists Who Enabled Torture," *American Civil Liberties Union*, July 16, 2015, https://www.aclu.org/blog/national-security/torture/psychologists-who-enabled-torture.

37 Psychologists for Social Responsibility, "PsySR Responds to Hoffman Report about APA Collusion," news release, July 13, 2015, https://web.archive.org/web/20150905085028/http://www.psysr.org/about/statements/PsySR_Statement-Hoffman_Report.pdf.

38 Barry Anton, "Email to APA Council of Representatives: Statement Regarding the Independent Review," July 31, 2015, https://www.opa.org/assets/docs/APA/anton%20response.pdf; Gerald Koocher, "Open Letter: My Regrets and Apologies," July 26, 2015, https://scra27.org/files/6814/3845/5779/Koocher._Response.pdf; Ronald F. Levant, "Email to APA Division Officers: Message from Ron Levant," July 31, 2015.

39 L. Morgan Banks, Debra Dunivin, Larry C. James, and Russ Newman, "A Response to the Hoffman Report," August 1, 2015, 1–3, https://web.archive.org/web/20210306142431/http://www.division19students.org/uploads/2/5/7/7/25774008/final_release-newman-banks-dunivin-james-1aug2015.pdf.

40 Ibid., 1.

41 United States Army, *Human Intelligence Collector Operations*, FM-2-22.3 (FM 34-52), September 2006, https://fas.org/irp/doddir/army/fm2-22-3.pdf; see also Beth Van Schaack, "The Torture Convention & Appendix M of the Army Field Manual on Interrogations," *Just Security*, December 5, 2014, https://www.justsecurity.org/18043/torture-convention-appendix-army-field-manual-interrogations/.

42 Thomas Williams, "Letter to Nadine Kaslow and Susan McDaniel," July 29, 2015, http://psychcoalition.org/5/post/2015/07/mil-letter-to-apa.html.

43 Merriam-Webster Dictionary, accessed May 3, 2022, https://www.merriam-webster.com/dictionary/collusion.

44 Williams, Letter to Nadine Kaslow and Susan McDaniel.

45 Democracy Now!, "Gitmo Is a 'Rights-Free Zone': Dissident Psychologists Speak Out on APA Role in CIA-Pentagon Torture," August 7, 2015, https://www.democracynow.org/2015/8/7/gitmo_is_a_rights_free_zone.

46 Descriptions here are based on the author's personal communications with Naomi Podber and Susan Opotow, August 29, 2022.

47 Naomi Podber, "Building Connections While Maintaining the Band: The Challenging Politics of Inclusion in Activist Work," in *HONK! A Street Band*

Renaissance of Music and Activism, eds. Reebee Garofalo, Erin T. Allen, and Andrew Snyder (New York: Routledge, 2020), 131–44.

48 Podber's collaborators included librarian Melissa Morrone and fellow students Patrick Sweeney and Wen Liu.

49 Democracy Now!, "No More Torture: World's Largest Group of Psychologists Bans Role in National Security Interrogations," August 10, 2015, https://www.democracynow.org/2015/8/10/no_more_torture_world_s_largest.

50 Ibid.

51 American Psychological Association, *Resolution to Amend the 2006 and 2013 Council Resolutions to Clarify the Roles of Psychologists Related to Interrogation and Detainee Welfare in National Security Settings, to Further Implement the 2008 Petition Resolution, and to Safeguard against Acts of Torture and Cruel, Inhuman, or Degrading Treatment or Punishment in All Settings*, 2015, https://www.apa.org/independent-review/psychologists-interrogation.pdf.

52 American Psychological Association, *Resolution to Amend the 2006 and 2013 Council Resolutions*.

53 United Nations General Assembly, *Convention against Torture and Other Cruel, Inhuman or Degrading Treatment or Punishment*, December 10, 1984, https://www.ohchr.org/en/professionalinterest/pages/cat.aspx.

54 American Psychological Association, *Resolution to Amend the 2006 and 2013 Council Resolutions*.

55 American Psychological Association, "APA Members Approve Petition Resolution on Detainee Settings," news release, September 2008, https://www.apa.org/news/press/releases/2008/09/detainee-petition.

56 American Psychological Association, *Resolution to Amend the 2006 and 2013 Council Resolutions*; for further background on the resolution and its adoption, see: Democracy Now!, "No More Torture"; Deborah Popowski, "The APA's Watershed Move to Ban Psychologists' Complicity in Torture," *Just Security*, August 11, 2015, https://www.justsecurity.org/25336/apas-watershed-move-ban-psychologists-complicity-torture/; James Risen, "Psychologists Approve Ban on Role in National Security Interrogations," *New York Times*, August 7, 2015, https://www.nytimes.com/2015/08/08/us/politics/psychologists-approve-ban-on-role-in-national-security-interrogations.html.

57 Democracy Now!, "No More Torture."

58 Ibid.

59 Joint Task Force-Guantanamo, "Camp Delta Standard Operating Procedures (SOP)," March 28, 2003, https://ccrjustice.org/sites/default/files/assets/Camp%20Delta%20Operating%20Procedures.pdf; see also William Glaberson, "Red Cross Monitors Barred from Guantanamo," *New York Times*, November 16, 2007, https://www.nytimes.com/2007/11/16/washington/16gitmo.html.

60 Shankar Vedantam, "APA Rules on Interrogation Abuse," *Washington Post*, August 20, 2007, https://www.washingtonpost.com/wp-dyn/content/article/2007/08/19/AR2007081901513.html.

61 Democracy Now!, "No More Torture."

62 This quote is taken from a transcript of the APA town hall meeting on August 8, 2015.

63 Hoffman et al., *Independent Review*.

64 These quotes are taken from a transcript of the APA town hall meeting on August 8, 2015.

65 I regret that the transcript of the event does not identify this student by name.

66 For background, see Maha Hilal, "When Life Is Disposable: Muslim Bodies as Precarious in the War on Terror," *Amnesty International*, February 1, 2016, https://www.amnestyusa.org/when-life-is-disposable-muslim-bodies-as-precarious-in-the-war-on-terror/; Maha Hilal, "The War on Terror Has Targeted Muslims Almost Exclusively," *Foreign Policy in Focus*, September 11, 2017, https://fpif.org/the-war-on-terror-has-targeted-muslims-almost-exclusively/.

67 American Middle Eastern/North African (MENA) Psychological Network, "Open Letter to the American Psychological Association & the Psychological Community," August 14, 2015, https://www.apa.org/independent-review/open-letter-mena.pdf; for information about the current work of the American Arab, Middle Eastern, and North African Psychological Association, see https://www.amenapsy.org.

68 Richard Matthews, *The Absolute Violation: Why Torture Must Be Prohibited* (Montreal: McGill-Queen's University Press, 2008), 58.

69 These quotes are taken from a transcript of the APA town hall meeting on August 8, 2015.

70 Ibid.

71 David G. Bolgiano and John Taylor, "Honi Soit Qui Mal y Pense: Evil Goings On behind the American Psychological Association Report on Interrogation," August 7, 2015, http://psychcoalition.org/hoffman-report-articles/honi-soit-qui-mal-y-pense.

72 PsychCoalition, "Purpose," n.d., accessed May 3, 2022, http://psychcoalition.org/index.html.

Chapter Six

1 For further background, see Kenneth S. Pope, "The Code Not Taken: The Path from Guild Ethics to Torture and Our Continuing Choices," *Canadian Psychology/Psychologie Canadienne* 57, no. 1 (2016): 51–9, https://kspope.com/PsychologyEthics.php; Frank Summers, "Counter Revolution," *International Journal of Applied Psychoanalytic Studies* 14, no. 2 (2017): 152–60, https://doi.org/10.1002/aps.1523.

2 L. Morgan Banks, Debra Dunivin, Larry C. James, and Russ Newman, "Hoffman's Key Conclusion Demonstrably False: The Omission of Key Documents," October 2015, http://www.hoffmanreportapa.com/resources/RESPONSETODAVIDHOFFMAN1026.pdf; Society for Military Psychology

(APA Division 19) Presidential Task Force, "Response to the Hoffman Independent Review," November 2015, http://www.hoffmanreportapa.com/resources/TF19%20Response%20to%20the%20Hoffman%20Report.pdf.

3 Sally Harvey, "The Hoffman Report: The Story Behind the Headlines. Presentation at APA Division 19 Symposium on Collaboration in Military Psychology Research," May 30, 2019; United States Army, "Warrior Ethos," n.d., accessed May 3, 2022, https://www.army.mil/values/warrior.html.

4 Stephen Soldz and Steven Reisner, "Attacks on Hoffman Report from Military Psychologists Obfuscate Detainee Abuse," *Counterpunch*, January 5, 2016, https://www.counterpunch.org/2016/01/05/attacks-on-hoffman-report-from-military-psychologists-obfuscate-detainee-abuse/.

5 Ibid. See also Roy Eidelson, "When Psychologists Deny Guantanamo Abuses," *Psychology Today*, December 1, 2015, https://www.psychologytoday.com/us/blog/dangerous-ideas/201512/when-psychologists-deny-guantanamo-s-abuses.

6 Banks et al., "Hoffman's Key Conclusion Demonstrably False."

7 David H. Hoffman, Danielle J. Carter, Cara R. Viglucci Lopez, Heather L. Benzmiller, Ava X. Guo, S. Yasir Latifi, and Daniel C. Craig, *Report to the Special Committee of the Board of Directors of the American Psychological Association: Independent Review Relating to APA Ethics Guidelines, National Security Interrogations, and Torture*, rev. ed. (Chicago: Sidley Austin LLP, 2015), 11, https://www.apa.org/independent-review/revised-report.pdf.

8 For example, see Center for Constitutional Rights, "Report on Torture and Cruel, Inhuman, and Degrading Treatment of Prisoners at Guantanamo Bay, Cuba," July 2006, https://ccrjustice.org/files/Report_ReportOnTorture.pdf; Inter-American Commission on Human Rights, "Report No. 29/20. Case 12.865. Merits (Publication). Djamel Ameziane. United States," April 22, 2020, https://ccrjustice.org/sites/default/files/attach/2020/05/Ameziane_IACHR_Merits_Decision-2020.pdf.

9 For example, see Dana Priest, "CIA Holds Terror Suspects in Secret Prisons," *Washington Post*, November 2, 2005, https://www.washingtonpost.com/archive/politics/2005/11/02/cia-holds-terror-suspects-in-secret-prisons/767f0160-cde4-41f2-a691-ba989990039c/; R. Jeffrey Smith and Josh White, "Cheney Plan Exempts CIA From Bill Barring Abuse of Detainees," *Washington Post*, October 25, 2005, https://www.washingtonpost.com/archive/politics/2005/10/25/cheney-plan-exempts-cia-from-bill-barring-abuse-of-detainees/dec08b17-f3f8-4587-b328-c98ef43a1ce7/.

10 United States Department of the Army Inspector General, "Detainee Operations Inspection," July 21, 2004, iv, http://hrlibrary.umn.edu/OathBetrayed/Mikolashek%20Report.pdf; see also Soldz and Reisner, "Attacks on Hoffman Report."

11 For example, see Mark Denbeaux and Joshua Denbeaux, "Torture: Who Knew? An Analysis of the FBI and Department of Defense Reactions to Harsh Interrogation

Methods at Guantanamo," *Seton Hall Law Review* 41, no. 4 (2011): 1319–37, https://scholarship.shu.edu/cgi/viewcontent.cgi?article=1404&context=shlr.

12 For further background, see Antonio M. Taguba, *Article 15-6 Investigation of the 800th Military Police Brigade*, 2004, https://www.thetorturedatabase.org/files/foia_subsite/pdfs/DODDOA000248.pdf; David Cloud, "General Says Prison Inquiry Led to His Forced Retirement," *New York Times*, June 17, 2007, https://www.nytimes.com/2007/06/17/washington/17ghraib.html; Seymour Hersh, "The General's Report," *New Yorker*, June 18, 2007, https://www.newyorker.com/magazine/2007/06/25/the-generals-report.

13 Keith Rohman, "Diagnosing and Analyzing Flawed Investigations: Abu Ghraib as a Case Study," *Penn State International Law Review* 28, no. 1 (2009): 36, https://elibrary.law.psu.edu/psilr/vol28/iss1/2/.

14 Ibid., 44.

15 David Frakt, "Closing Argument at Guantanamo: The Torture of Mohammed Jawad," *Harvard Human Rights Journal* 22, no. 1 (2009): 1–24, https://papers.ssrn.com/sol3/papers.cfm?abstract_id=2103825; David Frakt, "Military Accountability (or the Lack Thereof) for Detainee Abuse: The Instructive Case of Mohammed Jawad," *University of San Francisco Law Review* 45, no. 4 (2011): 873–910, https://papers.ssrn.com/sol3/papers.cfm?abstract_id=2103936.

16 Frakt, "Military Accountability (or the Lack Thereof)," 889.

17 George Orwell, "Politics and the English Language," *Horizon* (1946), https://www.orwellfoundation.com/the-orwell-foundation/orwell/essays-and-other-works/politics-and-the-english-language/.

18 Clive Stafford Smith, *Eight O'Clock Ferry to the Windward Side* (New York: Nation Books, 2007).

19 United States Army, *Human Intelligence Collector Operations, FM-2-22.3 (FM 34-52)*, September 2006, https://fas.org/irp/doddir/army/fm2-22-3.pdf.

20 For further background, see: Claire Finkelstein and Stephen N. Xenakis, "Repairing the Damage from Illegal Acts of State: The Costs of Failed Accountability for Torture," in *Interrogation and Torture: Integrating Efficacy with Law and Morality*, eds. Steven J. Barela, Mark Fallon, Gloria Gaggioli, and Jens David Ohlin (New York: Oxford University Press, 2020), 493–517; Human Rights and Security Coalition, "Letter to U.S. Secretary of Defense, Director of National Intelligence, Attorney General, and Director of the Federal Bureau of Investigation," May 20, 2021, https://s3.amazonaws.com/static.militarytimes.com/assets/pdfs/1621894483.pdf; Jeffrey Kaye, "UN Review Cites Torture & 'Ill Treatment' in US Army Field Manual's Appendix M," *Shadowproof*, November 28, 2014, https://shadowproof.com/2014/11/28/un-review-cites-torture-ill-treatment-in-u-s-army-field-manuals-appendix-m/; United Nations Committee against Torture, *Concluding Observations on the Third to Fifth Periodic Reports of United States of America*, November 2014, https://www.justsecurity.org/wp-content/uploads/2014/11/UN-Committee-Against-Torture-Concluding-Observations-United-States.pdf; Beth Van Schaack, "The Torture Convention

& Appendix M of the Army Field Manual on Interrogations," *Just Security*, December 5, 2014, https://www.justsecurity.org/18043/torture-convention-appendix-army-field-manual-interrogations/.

21 Examples include Matthew Alexander, "Torture's Loopholes," *New York Times*, January 20, 2010, https://www.nytimes.com/2010/01/21/opinion/21alexander.html; Susan Brandon and Mark Fallon, "The Mendez Principles: The Need to Update the Army Field Manual on Interrogation for the 21st Century," *Just Security*, June 11, 2021, https://www.justsecurity.org/76863/the-mendez-principles-the-need-to-update-the-army-field-manual-on-interrogation-for-the-21st-century/; Human Rights First, "Open Letter to Secretary of Defense Robert M Gates Re: Appendix M of the Army Field Manual on Interrogations," November 16, 2010, https://www.humanrightsfirst.org/sites/default/files/Interrogator-Appendix-M-Letter-to-Gates.pdf.

22 John T. Parry, *Understanding Torture: Law, Violence, and Political Identity* (Ann Arbor: University of Michigan Press, 2010), 200.

23 American Psychological Association, *Resolution to Amend the 2006 and 2013 Council Resolutions to Clarify the Roles of Psychologists Related to Interrogation and Detainee Welfare in National Security Settings, to Further Implement the 2008 Petition Resolution, and to Safeguard against Acts of Torture and Cruel, Inhuman, or Degrading Treatment or Punishment in All Settings*, 2015, https://www.apa.org/independent-review/psychologists-interrogation.pdf.

24 United States Army, "OTSG/MEDCOM Policy Memo 06-029: Behavioral Science Consultation Policy," October 20, 2006, https://humanrights.ucdavis.edu/projects/the-guantanamo-testimonials-project/testimonies/testimonies-of-standard-operating-procedures/behavioral_science_consultation_policy_memo_2006.pdf.

25 Ibid., 10.

26 Ibid.

27 United States Senate Committee on Armed Services, *Inquiry into the Treatment of Detainees in U.S. Custody*, 2008, 50–2, https://www.armed-services.senate.gov/imo/media/doc/Detainee-Report-Final_April-22-2009.pdf.

28 Amnesty International, "Public Statement: New Amnesty International Report Condemns Conditions in Guantanamo," April 5, 2007, https://www.amnesty.org/download/Documents/60000/amr510602007en.pdf.

29 Ibid.

30 Center for Constitutional Rights, "Current Conditions of Confinement at Guantanamo: Still in Violation of the Law," February 23, 2009, 4–5, https://ccrjustice.org/sites/default/files/assets/CCR_Report_Conditions_At_Guantanamo.pdf.

31 Center for Constitutional Rights, "The Guantanamo Prisoner Hunger Strikes & Protests: February 2002 – August 2005," 2005, https://ccrjustice.org/files/Final%20Hunger%20Strike%20Report%20Sept%202005.pdf; Paul Harris, "Guantanamo Bay Hunger Strike: Quarter of Inmates Now Being Force-Fed,"

The Guardian, June 6, 2013, https://www.theguardian.com/world/2013/jun/06/guantanamo-bay-hunger-strike-quarter-force-fed.

32 Spencer Ackerman, "Guantanamo Bay Psychologists to Remain Despite APA Torture Fallout," *The Guardian*, July 15, 2015, https://www.theguardian.com/us-news/2015/jul/15/psychologists-remain-guantanamo-bay-apa-torture.

33 Associated Press, "Guantanamo Detainees' Hunger Strikes Will No Longer Be Disclosed by U.S. Military," *Washington Post*, December 4, 2013, https://www.washingtonpost.com/world/national-security/guantanamo-detainees-hunger-strikes-will-no-longer-be-disclosed-by-us-military/2013/12/04/f6b1aa96-5d24-11e3-bc56-c6ca94801fac_story.html.

34 For further background, see American Association for the Advancement of Science, "Medical Professionals Condemn Force-Feeding at Guantanamo Bay," October 2, 2014, https://www.aaas.org/news/medical-professionals-condemn-force-feeding-guantanamo-bay; George J. Annas, "Hunger Strikes at Guantanamo – Medical Ethics and Human Rights in a 'Legal Black Hole,'" *New England Journal of Medicine* 355 (2006): 1377–82, https://www.nejm.org/doi/full/10.1056/NEJMhle062316; George J. Annas, Sondra S. Crosby, and Leonard H. Glantz, "Guantanamo Bay: A Medical Ethics-Free Zone?," *New England Journal of Medicine* 369 (2013): 101–3, https://www.nejm.org/doi/10.1056/NEJMp1306065; Sarah M. Dougherty, Jennifer Leaning, P. Gregg Greenough, and Frederick M. Burkle, Jr, "Hunger Strikers: Ethical and Legal Dimensions of Medical Complicity in Torture at Guantanamo Bay," *Prehospital and Disaster Medicine* 28 (2013): 1–9, https://www.cambridge.org/core/journals/prehospital-and-disaster-medicine/article/abs/hunger-strikers-ethical-and-legal-dimensions-of-medical-complicity-in-torture-at-guantanamo-bay/1FA37478EE58D78A37ABA1E01D677FE8; Samir Naji al Hasan Moqbel, "Gitmo Is Killing Me," *New York Times*, April 14, 2013, https://www.nytimes.com/2013/04/15/opinion/hunger-striking-at-guantanamo-bay.html; World Medical Association, "WMA Condemns All Forced Feeding," press release, October 16, 2006, https://www.wma.net/news-post/wma-condemns-all-forced-feeding/.

35 Jason Leopold, "Revised Guantanamo Force-Feed Policy Exposed," *Al Jazeera*, May 13, 2013, https://www.aljazeera.com/news/2013/5/13/revised-guantanamo-force-feed-policy-exposed.

36 Joe Nocera, "Is Force-Feeding Torture?," *New York Times*, May 31, 2013, https://www.nytimes.com/2013/06/01/opinion/nocera-is-force-feeding-torture.html.

37 Curt Goering, "Testimony to the Senate Judiciary Subcommittee on the Constitution, Civil Rights, and Human Rights: Closing Guantanamo: The National Security, Fiscal, and Human Rights Implications," July 24, 2013, 1, https://www.cvt.org/sites/default/files/CVT%20Testimony%20to%20the%20Senate%20Judiciary%20Subcommittee%20Hearing%20on%20Closing%20Guantanamo.pdf.

38 Ibid.

39 United Nations Committee against Torture, *Concluding Observations*; United Nations, "Close 'Disgraceful' Guantanamo Camp – UN Experts Urge Incoming US Administration," January 11, 2021, https://news.un.org/en/story/2021/01/1081842.

40 American Psychological Association, "An Open Letter to the APA Board of Directors from Former Chairs of the APA Ethics Committee," news release, February 16, 2016, https://www.apa.org/news/press/statements/ethics-chairs-letter01.pdf.

41 See the following: American Psychological Association, "Ethics Committee's Response to the Council of Representatives' Directive to Review a Discrepancy Between the Aspirational and Enforceable Sections of the *Ethical Principles of Psychologists and Code of Conduct* (2002) Related to Conflicts Between Ethics and Law and Conflicts between Ethics and Organizational Demands," 2009, https://www.apa.org/ethics/code/council-recommendation.pdf; Eidelson, "Dr. John Leso"; Hoffman et al., *Independent Review*, 485–96.

42 American Psychological Association, "Open Letter to the Board of Directors, Council of Representatives, Divisions and Staff," news release, June 11, 2016, https://www.apa.org/news/press/statements/past-presidents-letter.pdf.

43 Bryant Welch, "Torture, Psychology, and Daniel Inouye: The True Story behind Psychology's Role in Torture," *Huffington Post*, July 17, 2009, https://www.huffpost.com/entry/torture-psychology-and-da_b_215612.

44 M. Gregg Bloche, *The Hippocratic Myth: Why Doctors Are under Pressure to Ration Care, Practice Politics, and Compromise Their Promise to Heal* (New York: Palgrave Macmillan, 2011).

45 Martin E.P. Seligman, *The Hope Circuit: A Psychologist's Journey from Helplessness to Optimism* (New York: PublicAffairs, 2018).

46 Jeff Manning, "Joseph Matarazzo, OHSU Professor Emeritus, Says Reports of Role in CIA Torture Program Untrue," *The Oregonian/OregonLive*, December 16, 2014, https://www.oregonlive.com/watchdog/2014/12/joseph_matarazzo_ohsu_professo.html; Hunter Walker, "These 7 Men Owned the Company Linked to CIA Torture," *Business Insider*, December 11, 2014, https://www.businessinsider.com/the-company-behind-cia-torture-2014-12; Joseph D. Matarazzo, "The American Psychological Association's Hoffman Report Allegations of My Association with the 'CIA Torture' Program," *Health Psychology Open* (July–December 2018): 1–8, https://www.ncbi.nlm.nih.gov/pmc/articles/PMC6122255/.

47 Hoffman et al., *Independent Review*, 485–96.

48 Psychologists in Independent Practice (APA Division 42), "Letter to APA Board of Directors, Staff, Council of Representatives and Division Leaders," June 8, 2016, http://psychcoalition.org/hoffman-report-articles/division-42-resolution-of-no-confidence-in-apa-board-of-directors.

49 Jeffrey Younggren, "Open Letter from Division 42 President Jeffrey Younggren to the Coalition for an Ethical Psychology," October 26, 2012, https://www.ethicalpsychology.org/materials/Div42-Response-to-Coalition-10-26-2012.pdf;

see also Coalition for an Ethical Psychology, "Open Letter from the Coalition to the Division 42 Board," October 31, 2012, https://www.ethicalpsychology.org/materials/Coalition-Response-to-Div42-Board.pdf.

50 Daniel Engber, "The Bush Torture Scandal Isn't Over," *Slate*, September 5, 2017, https://slate.com/technology/2017/09/should-psycholo-gists-take-the-blame-for-greenlighting-bush-era-enhanced-interrogations.html.

51 James Risen, "Pentagon Curbs Use of Psychologists with Guantanamo Detainees," *New York Times*, December 31, 2015, https://www.nytimes.com/2016/01/01/us/pentagon-curbs-use-of-psychologists-with-guantanamo-detainees.html.

52 Office of the Under Secretary of Defense, "Letter to APA President and CEO," January 8, 2016, https://www.apa.org/news/press/releases/2016/01/dod-response-letter.pdf; for a response to the letter, see Coalition for an Ethical Psychology, "Preserve Do-No-Harm for Military Psychologists: Coalition Responds to Department of Defense Letter to the APA," February 8, 2016, https://www.ethicalpsychology.org/materials/Coalition-Responds-to-DoD-Letter-to-APA.pdf.

53 American Psychological Association, *Ethical Principles of Psychologists and Code of Conduct* (Washington, DC: American Psychological Association, 2017), 3, https://www.apa.org/ethics/code/ethics-code-2017.pdf.

54 United States Department of Defense, "Medical Program Support for Detainee Operations, Instruction 2310.08E," June 6, 2006, http://hrlibrary.umn.edu/OathBetrayed/Winkenwerder%206-6-2006.pdf.

55 Parry, *Understanding Torture*.

56 Office of the Under Secretary of Defense, "Letter to APA President and CEO."

57 Constitution Project, *The Report of the Constitution Project's Task Force on Detainee Treatment*, 2013, https://detaineetaskforce.org/pdf/Chapter-6_Role-of-Medical-Professionals.pdf; Institute on Medicine as a Profession, *Ethics Abandoned: Medical Professionalism and Detainee Abuse in the War on Terror* (New York: The Institute, 2013), https://hrp.law.harvard.edu/wp-content/uploads/2013/11/IMAP-EthicsTextFinal2.pdf; Physicians for Human Rights, *Broken Laws, Broken Lives: Medical Evidence of Torture by U.S. Personnel and Its Impact,* June 2008, https://s3.amazonaws.com/PHR_Reports/BrokenLaws_14.pdf; United States Senate, *Treatment of Detainees*.

58 United Nations Committee against Torture, *Concluding Observations*.

59 United States Army, Human Intelligence Collector Operations.

60 Juan E. Mendez, "Letter to APA Board of Directors and Council of Representatives," August 6, 2018, https://s3.amazonaws.com/PHR_other/APA_NB35_letter_Revised.pdf.

61 Ibid.

62 United Nations Committee Against Torture, *Concluding Observations*; United Nations, "Guantanamo Bay, 14 Years On – Rights Experts Urge the US to End Impunity and Close the Detention Facility," January 11, 2016, https://www.ohchr.org/EN/NewsEvents/Pages/DisplayNews.aspx?NewsID=16935&LangID=E.

63 Office of the Under Secretary of Defense, "Letter to APA President and CEO."

64 American Psychological Association, "Letter from APA President to Acting Assistant Secretary of Defense for Health Affairs," news release, September 21, 2018, https://www.apa.org/news/press/statements/detainee-policy-letter.pdf.

65 Ibid.

66 United States Department of Defense, "Behavioral Science Support (BSS) for Detainee Operations and Intelligence Interrogations: DoD Instruction 2310.09," September 5, 2019, 8, https://fas.org/irp/doddir/dod/i2310_09.pdf.

67 Stephen Soldz, "Is the American Psychological Association Undermining Its Own Policies on Guantanamo and Torture?," *Counterpunch*, March 23, 2021, https://www.counterpunch.org/2021/03/23/is-the-american-psychological-association-undermining-its-own-policies-on-guantanamo-and-torture/.

68 For further background, see Peter Aldhous, "Psychologists Are in a Nasty Fight about a Report on Torture," *Buzzfeed*, July 26, 2018, https://www.buzzfeednews.com/article/peteraldhous/psychology-torture-guantanamo-interrogation; American Psychological Association, *Resolution to Amend Council's 2009, 2013, and 2015 Resolutions to Clarify That Psychologists May Provide Treatment to Detainees or Military Personnel in National Security Settings (NBI #35b/ Aug 2017)*, August 2018, https://assets.documentcloud.org/documents/4618724/NBI-35B-Amend-Councils-Resolutions-Roles-of.pdf; Jeffrey Kaye, "Trump Ordered Guantanamo to Stay Open, Now APA to Vote on Overturning Ban on Psychologists at Guantanamo," *Medium*, July 19, 2018, https://jeff-kaye.medium.com/trump-ordered-guantanamo-to-stay-open-now-apa-to-vote-on-overturning-ban-on-psychologists-at-cd8dd905be12.

69 For further background, see Constitution Project, *Task Force on Detainee Treatment*; Sarah Dougherty, "The Human Cost of Guantanamo," *Physicians for Human Rights*, January 7, 2016, https://phr.org/our-work/resources/the-human-cost-of-guantnamo/; Vincent Iacopino and Stephen N. Xenakis, "Neglect of Medical Evidence of Torture in Guantanamo Bay: A Case Series," *PloS Medicine* 8, no. 4 (2011): e1001027, https://journals.plos.org/plosmedicine/article?id=10.1371/journal.pmed.1001027; Steven H. Miles, "Medical Ethics and the Interrogation of Guantanamo 063," *American Journal of Bioethics* 7, no. 4 (2007): 1–7; Kenneth S. Pope, "A Human Rights and Ethics Crisis Facing the World's Largest Organization of Psychologists," *European Psychologist* 24, no. 2 (2019): 180–94, https://psycnet.apa.org/fulltext/2018-62354-001.pdf.

70 Human Rights Watch, "Nine Rights Groups Tell APA Don't Undermine Independent Psychological Care at Guantanamo," August 6, 2018, https://www.hrw.org/news/2018/08/06/nine-rights-groups-tell-apa-dont-undermine-independent-psychological-care#.

71 American Psychological Association, "APA Rejects Proposal Expanding Role of Military Psychologists to Treat Detainees in All Settings," news release, August 8, 2018, https://www.apa.org/news/press/releases/2018/08/military-psychologists-detainees; see also Shilpa Jindia, "Psychologists Vote Not to

Return to Guantanamo amid Heated Debate over Torture Legacy," *The Intercept*, August 9, 2018, https://theintercept.com/2018/08/09/guantanamo-bay-psychology-torture/; Society for the Psychological Study of Social Issues, "SPSSI Reaffirms Its Longstanding Opposition to Torture and Longstanding Commitment to Human Rights," August 7, 2018, https://www.spssi.org/index.cfm?fuseaction=Page. ViewPage&PageID=2324.

72 *James et al. v. Hoffman et al. 2018-Ohio-2422* (Court of Appeals of Ohio, Second Appellate District, Montgomery County, Opinion Rendered on June 22, 2018); *Behnke et al. v. Hoffman et al.* #2017 CA 005989 B (Superior Court of the District of Columbia, filed August 28, 2017); *Behnke et al. v. Soldz et al.* #18–01968D (Commonwealth of Massachusetts Superior Court, filed June 25, 2018).

73 In the lawsuit that was dismissed by the Superior Court of the District of Columbia (*Behnke et al. v. Hoffman et al.* #2017 CA 005989 B), several individuals – including Barry Anton, Morgan Banks, Stephen Behnke, Debra Dunivin, Michael Gelles, Larry James, Bryce LeFever, Ronald Levant, Joseph Matarazzo, Russell Newman, and Scott Shumate – filed affidavits disputing various aspects of the accounts presented in the Hoffman Report. These affidavits are accessible via the court's online eAccess system (https://eaccess.dccourts.gov/eaccess/home.page) as part of the entry titled "Additional eFiling Document to Plaintiffs' Consolidated Opposition to Defendants' First Set of Contested Special Motions to Dismiss Filed October 13, 2017 under the District of Columbia Anti-SLAPP Act, D.C. Code 16-5502 Filed 11/18/2019." As former employees of the APA, both Behnke and Newman were subsequently compelled by the DC Court to pursue their claims via arbitration. A settlement was reached with Behnke in late 2020. Newman's motion went forward and was denied by the arbitrator, ending his case.

74 American Psychological Association, "Report of the Independent Reviewer and Related Materials," July 2015, https://www.apa.org/independent-review.

75 *Behnke et al. v. Hoffman et al.*, CA 005989 B (Superior Court of the District of Columbia, filed 12 March 2020), 28.

76 Ibid.

77 Ibid., 27.

78 Ibid., 24.

79 Ibid., 9.

80 Mitchell M. Handelsman, "A Teachable Ethics Scandal," *Teaching of Psychology* 44, no. 3 (2017): 278–84, https://psycnet.apa.org/record/2017-27867-014.

81 Daniel Engber, "The Bush Torture Scandal Isn't Over," *Slate*, September 5, 2017, https://slate.com/technology/2017/09/should-psychologists-take-the-blame-for-greenlighting-bush-era-enhanced-interrogations. html; Ian Hansen, "An Old Guard Psychologist Inspires a Chill on Academic Freedom," *OpEdNews*, August 21, 2017, https://www.opednews.com/articles/An-Old-Guard-Psychologist-by-Ian-Hansen-Academic-Freedom_Academics_Detainees_Ethics-170821-941.html.

82 For further background, see Ian Hansen, "Correspondence on an Academic Freedom Controversy," *OpEdNews*, August 23, 2017, https://www.opednews.com/articles/Correspondence-On-An-Acade-by-Ian-Hansen-Academic-Freedom_Ethics_Freedom_History-170823-551.html; Alice LoCicero, "What Keeps the APA from Healing?," *Psychology Today*, August 15, 2017, https://www.psychologytoday.com/us/blog/paradigm-shift/201708/what-keeps-the-apa-healing.

83 Victoria Stern, "Amid Legal Battle, Psych Journal Issuing Caution about Torture Paper," *Retraction Watch*, September 5, 2017, https://web.archive.org/web/20211106065128/https://retractionwatch.com/2017/09/05/amid-legal-battle-psych-journal-issuing-caution-torture-paper/.

84 Steven Reisner, "Letter to the Ethics Committee of the American Psychological Association," November 27, 2017, 1, https://s3.documentcloud.org/documents/4618723/REISNER-Response-to-Op-Psych-Ethics-Complaint.pdf.

85 Neil Lewis, "Red Cross Finds Detainee Abuse in Guantanamo," *New York Times*, November 30, 2004, https://www.nytimes.com/2004/11/30/politics/red-cross-finds-detainee-abuse-in-guantanamo.html.

86 Bob Woodward, "Guantanamo Detainee Was Tortured, Says Official Overseeing Military Trials," *Washington Post*, January 14, 2009, https://www.washington-post.com/wp-dyn/content/article/2009/01/13/AR2009011303372.html.

87 United Nations, "Close 'Disgraceful' Guantanamo Camp – UN Experts Urge Incoming US Administration," January 11, 2021, https://news.un.org/en/story/2021/01/1081842.

88 Hoffman et al., *Independent Review*.

89 American Psychological Association, *Resolution to Amend the 2006 and 2013 Council Resolutions to Clarify the Roles of Psychologists Related to Interrogation and Detainee Welfare in National Security Settings, to Further Implement the 2008 Petition Resolution, and to Safeguard against Acts of Torture and Cruel, Inhuman, or Degrading Treatment or Punishment in All Settings*, 2015, https://www.apa.org/independent-review/psychologists-interrogation.pdf.

Chapter Seven

1 American Psychological Association, *Ethical Principles of Psychologists and Code of Conduct* (Washington, DC: American Psychological Association, 2017), 3, https://www.apa.org/ethics/code/ethics-code-2017.pdf.

2 Ibid.

3 Carrie H. Kennedy and Thomas J. Williams, "Operational Psychology Ethics: Addressing Evolving Dilemmas," in *Ethical Practice in Operational Psychology: Military and National Intelligence Applications*, eds. Carrie H. Kennedy and Thomas J. Williams (Washington, DC: American Psychological Association, 2011), 16.

4 For detailed discussions of issues related to dual loyalty, see Peter A. Clark, "Medical Ethics at Guantanamo Bay and Abu Ghraib: The Problem of Dual Loyalty," *Journal of Law, Medicine & Ethics* 34, no. 3 (2006): 570–80, https://www.cambridge.org/core/journals/journal-of-law-medicine-and-ethics/article/abs/medical-ethics-at-guantanamo-bay-and-abu-ghraib-the-problem-of-dual-loyalty/9F7B2902F39EA0FA9FF7D7A4784951F5; Michael L. Gross, *Bioethics and Armed Conflict: Moral Dilemmas of Medicine and War* (Cambridge, MA: MIT Press, 2006); Michael L. Gross, *Military Medical Ethics in Contemporary Armed Conflict: Mobilizing Medicine in the Pursuit of Just War* (New York: Oxford University Press, 2021); Carrie H. Kennedy and W. Brad Johnson, "Mixed Agency in Military Psychology: Applying the American Psychological Association Ethics Code," *Psychological Services* 6, no. 1 (2009): 22–31, https://psycnet.apa.org/record/2009-01792-003; Physicians for Human Rights and School of Public Health and Primary Health Care, University of Cape Town, "Dual Loyalty & Human Rights," 2002, https://phr.org/wp-content/uploads/2003/03/dualloyalties-2002-report.pdf; Jerome A. Singh, "American Physicians and Dual Loyalty Obligations in the 'War on Terror,'" *BMC Medical Ethics* 4, no. 4 (2003), https://doi.org/10.1186/1472-6939-4-4.

5 For example, see Zackary Berger, Leonard S Rubenstein, and Matthew DeCamp, "Clinical Care and Complicity with Torture," *BMJ* 360 (2018), https://www.bmj.com/content/360/bmj.k449; United States Senate Select Committee on Intelligence, *Committee Study of the Central Intelligence Agency's Detention and Interrogation Program*, 2014, https://www.intelligence.senate.gov/sites/default/files/publications/CRPT-113srpt288.pdf.

6 American Psychological Association, *Report of the American Psychological Association Presidential Task Force on Psychological Ethics and National Security* (Washington, DC: American Psychological Association, 2005), 3, https://www.apa.org/pubs/reports/pens.pdf.

7 For example, see Kirk Kennedy, Randy Borum, and Robert Fein, "Ethical Dilemmas in Psychological Consultation to Counterintelligence and Counterterrorism Activities," in *Ethical Practice in Operational Psychology: Military and National Intelligence Applications*, eds. Carrie H. Kennedy and Thomas J. Williams (Washington, DC: American Psychological Association, 2011), 69–83; Thomas J. Williams and Carrie H. Kennedy, "Operational Psychology: Proactive Ethics in a Challenging World," in *Ethical Practice in Operational Psychology: Military and National Intelligence Applications*, eds. Carrie H. Kennedy and Thomas J. Williams (Washington, DC: American Psychological Association, 2011), 125–40.

8 Williams and Kennedy, "Operational Psychology: Proactive Ethics."

9 Charles P. Ewing and Michael G. Gelles, "Ethical Concerns in Forensic Consultation Regarding National Safety and Security," *Journal of Threat Assessment* 2, no. 3 (2003): 106.

10 Mark A. Staal, "Lies, Statistics, and Brookline: A Response to Soldz, Arrigo, Frakt, & Olson," *Peace and Conflict: Journal of Peace Psychology* 24 (2018): 458, https://doi.org/10.1037/pac0000332.

11 "Email Messages from the Listserv of the American Psychological Association's Presidential Task Force on Psychological Ethics and National Security: April 22, 2005 – June 26, 2006," 13, http://s3.amazonaws.com/propublica/assets/docs/pens_listserv.pdf.

12 Michael D. Matthews, *Head Strong: How Psychology Is Revolutionizing War* (New York: Oxford University Press, 2014), 183–7.

13 William O'Donohue, Cassandra Snipes, Georgia Dalto, Cyndy Soto, Alexandros Maragakis, and Sungjin Im, "The Ethics of Enhanced Interrogations and Torture: A Reappraisal of the Argument," *Ethics & Behavior* 24, no. 2 (2014): 109–25, https://www.tandfonline.com/doi/abs/10.1080/10508422.2013.814088.

14 Jean Maria Arrigo, David DeBatto, Lawrence Rockwood, and Timothy G. Mawe, "The 'Good' Psychologist, 'Good' Torture, and 'Good' Reputation – Response to O'Donohue, Snipes, Dalto, Soto, Maragakis, and Im (2014) 'The Ethics of Enhanced Interrogations and Torture,'" *Ethics & Behavior* 25, no. 5 (2015): 361–72, https://doi.org/10.1080/10508422.2015.1007996; For further thoughtful discussion of ethics related to torture, see Jean Maria Arrigo, "A Utilitarian Argument Against Torture Interrogation of Terrorists," *Science and Engineering Ethics* 10, no. 3 (2004): 543–72; Vittorio Buffachi and Jean Maria Arrigo, "Torture, Terrorism and the State: A Refutation of the Ticking-Bomb Argument," *Journal of Applied Philosophy* 23, no. 3 (2006): 355–73; Gordon, *Mainstreaming Torture*; Michael L. Gross, *Bioethics and Armed Conflict: Moral Dilemmas of Medicine and War* (Cambridge, MA: MIT Press, 2006), 211–43; Michael Ignatieff, *The Lesser Evil: Political Ethics in an Age of Terror* (Princeton, NJ: Princeton University Press, 2004), 136–44; Sanford Levinson, ed., *Torture: A Collection* (New York: Oxford University Press, 2004); Richard Matthews, *The Absolute Violation: Why Torture Must Be Prohibited* (Montreal: McGill-Queen's University Press, 2008).

15 American Psychological Association, *Ethical Principles*, 4.

16 For further background, see Jean Maria Arrigo, Roy J. Eidelson, and Ray Bennett, "Psychology under Fire: Adversarial Operational Psychology and Psychological Ethics," *Peace and Conflict: Journal of Peace Psychology* 18, no. 4 (2012): 384–400, http://dx.doi.org/ 10.1037/a0030323; Coalition for an Ethical Psychology, "Adversarial Operational Psychology Is Unethical for Psychologists," July 26, 2012, http://www.ethicalpsychology.org/pens/Adversarial-Operational-Psychology-Is-Unethical-for-Psychologists.pdf; Ethics of Operational Psychology Workshop, "The Brookline Principles on the Ethical Practice of Operational Psychology," September 20, 2015, http://www.ethicalpsychology.org/materials/Brookline-Principles-Ethical-Practice-of-Operational-Psychology.pdf; Stephen Soldz, Brad Olson, and Jean Maria Arrigo, "Interrogating the Ethics of Operational Psychology," *Journal of Community & Applied Social Psychology* 27, no. 4 (2017): 273–86, http://dx.doi.org/10.1002/casp.2321.

17 Arrigo, Eidelson, and Bennett, "Psychology under Fire."

18 Mark A. Staal and Carroll H. Greene III, "An Examination of 'Adversarial' Operational Psychology," *Peace and Conflict: Journal of Peace Psychology* 21, no. 2 (2015): 264–8, http://dx.doi.org/10.1037/pac0000095; Jean Maria Arrigo, Roy J. Eidelson, and Lawrence P. Rockwood, "Adversarial Operational Psychology Is Unethical Psychology: A Reply to Staal and Greene," *Peace and Conflict Journal of Peace Psychology* 21, no. 2 (2015): 269–78; Mark A. Staal and Carroll H. Greene III, "Operational Psychology: An Ethical Practice – A Reply to Arrigo, Eidelson, and Rockwood," Peace and Conflict: Journal of Peace Psychology 21, no. 2 (2015): 279–81; Jean Maria Arrigo, Roy J. Eidelson, and Lawrence P. Rockwood, "Adversarial Operational Psychology: Returning to the Foundational Issues," *Peace and Conflict: Journal of Peace Psychology* 21, no. 2 (2015): 282–4.

19 Ethics of Operational Psychology Workshop, "The Brookline Principles"; see also Stephen Soldz, Jean Maria Arrigo, and Brad Olson, "The Ethics of Operational Psychology Workshop: Report on Process, Findings, and Ethical Conundrums," *Coalition for an Ethical Psychology Working Paper Number 2*, July 2016, http://www.ethicalpsychology.org/Ethics-of-Operational-Psychology-Workshop-Report.pdf; Soldz, Olson, and Arrigo, "Interrogating the Ethics."

20 Mark A. Staal, "Applied Psychology under Attack: A Response to the Brookline Principles," *Peace and Conflict: Journal of Peace Psychology* 24, no. 4 (2018): 439–47, http://dx.doi.org/10.1037/pac0000333; Stephen Soldz, Jean Maria Arrigo, David Frakt, and Brad Olson, "Response to Staal: 'Psychological Ethics and Operational Psychology' – Fundamental Issues and Methods," *Peace and Conflict: Journal of Peace Psychology* 24, no. 4 (2018): 448–56, http://dx.doi.org/10.1037/pac0000330; Staal, "Lies, Statistics, and Brookline"; Stephen Soldz, Jean Maria Arrigo, David Frakt, and Brad Olson, "Second Response to Staal: Independent Moral Assessment, an Essential Requirement for Ethical Practice in Operational Psychology," *Peace and Conflict: Journal of Peace Psychology* 24, no. 4 (2018): 460–3, https://doi.org/10.1037/pac0000331.

21 American Psychological Association, *Ethical Principles*, 3.

22 For more information, see "The Nuremberg Code," bmj: *British Medical Journal* 313, no. 7070 (1947, 1996): 1448, https://media.tghn.org/medialibrary/2011/04/BMJ_No_7070_Volume_313_The_Nuremberg_Code.pdf; Evelyn Shuster, "Fifty Years Later: The Significance of The Nuremberg Code," *New England Journal of Medicine* 337 (1997): 1436–40, https://www.nejm.org/doi/full/10.1056/nejm199711133372006.

23 Nathaniel Raymond, Scott Allen, Vincent Iacopino, Allen Keller, Stephen Soldz, Steven Reisner, and John Bradshaw, *Experiments in Torture: Evidence of Human Subject Research and Experimentation in the 'Enhanced' Interrogation Program*, June 2010, https://phr.org/wp-content/uploads/2010/06/Experiments_in_Torture.pdf.

24 American Psychological Association, *Ethical Principles*, 4.

25 Tamsin Shaw, "The Psychologists Take Power," *New York Review of Books*, February 25, 2016, https://www.nybooks.com/articles/2016/02/25/the-psychologists-take-power/.

26 For further background, see Arrigo, Eidelson, and Bennett, "Psychology under Fire"; Tricia Bishop and the *Baltimore Sun*, "Universities Balance Secrecy and Academic Freedom in Classified Work," *Baltimore Sun*, September 13, 2013, https://www.baltimoresun.com/education/bs-md-higher-ed-intelligence-20130911-story.html; Henry A. Giroux, *The University in Chains: Confronting the Military-Industrial-Academic Complex* (Boulder, CO: Paradigm Publishers, 2007); David Malakoff, "Universities Review Policies for Onsite Classified Research," *Science* 295, no. 5559 (2002): 1438–9, https://www.science.org/doi/10.1126/science.295.5559.1438; Stephen Soldz, "Deception Detection and Torture: The American Psychological Association Serves the Intelligence Services," in *The CIA on Campus: Essays on Academic Freedom and the National Security State*, ed. Philip Zwerling (Jefferson, NC: McFarland Publishers, 2011), 113–46; Nick Turse, "The Military-Academic Complex: Who's the Real National Champion?," *Tom Dispatch*, April 27, 2004, https://tomdispatch.com/nick-turse-arm-wrestles-the-military-academic-complex/.

27 Martin E.P. Seligman, "What Are the Pressing Scientific Issues for the Nation and the World, and What Is Your Advice on How I Can Begin to Deal with Them? – GWB," *Edge*, 2003, https://www.edge.org/response-detail/11109.

28 See: Staal, "Applied Psychology under Attack"; Staal, "Lies, Statistics, and Brookline," 458.

29 Thomas J. Williams, "Foreword," in *Operational Psychology: A New Field to Support National Security and Public Safety*, eds. Mark A. Staal and Sally C. Harvey (Santa Barbara, CA: Praeger, 2019), 10.

30 Journal articles and exchanges among opposing sides in this debate include the following: Arrigo, Eidelson, and Bennett, "Psychology under Fire"; Arrigo, Eidelson, and Rockwood, "Returning to the Foundational Issues"; Arrigo, Eidelson, and Rockwood, "Adversarial Operational Psychology"; Soldz, Arrigo, Frakt, and Olson, "Response to Staal"; Soldz, Arrigo, and Olson, "The Ethics of Operational Psychology Workshop"; Soldz, Olson, and Arrigo, "Interrogating the Ethics"; Staal, "Applied Psychology under Attack"; Staal, "Lies, Statistics, and Brookline"; Staal and Greene, "An Examination of 'Adversarial' Operational Psychology."

31 For further background, see: Arrigo, Eidelson, and Bennett, "Psychology under Fire"; Defense Health Board, "Ethical Guidelines and Practices for U.S. Military Medical Professionals," March 3, 2015, https://www.health.mil/Reference-Center/Reports/2015/03/03/Ethical-Guidelines-and-Practices-for-US-Military-Medical-Professionals; Carrie H. Kennedy and Thomas J. Williams, eds., *Ethical Practice in Operational Psychology: Military and National Intelligence Applications* (Washington, DC: American Psychological Association, 2011).

32 For more information, see: Mark Benjamin, "Soufan: CIA Torture Actually Hindered Our Intelligence Gathering," *Salon*, May 14, 2009, https://www.salon.com/2009/05/14/torture_24/; Mark A. Costanzo and Ellen Gerrity, "The Effects and Effectiveness of Using Torture as an Interrogation Device: Using Research to Inform the Policy Debate," *Social Issues and Policy Review* 3, no. 1 (2009): 179–210; Lisa Hajjar, "Does Torture Work? A Socio-Legal Assessment of the Practice in Historical and Global Perspective," *Annual Review of Law and Social Science* 5 (2009): 311–45, https://papers.ssrn.com/sol3/papers.cfm?abstract_id=1599987; Darius Rejali, *Torture and Democracy* (Princeton, NJ: Princeton University Press, 2009); United States Senate, CIA *Detention and Interrogation Program.*

33 For example, see: Kennedy and Williams, "Operational Psychology Ethics"; Kennedy, Borum, and Fein, "Ethical Dilemmas in Psychological Consultation."

34 Kennedy and Williams, eds., *Ethical Practice in Operational Psychology.*

35 Stephen Behnke, "Psychological Ethics and National Security: The Position of the American Psychological Association," *European Psychologist* 11, no. 2 (2016): 154, https://econtent.hogrefe.com/doi/full/10.1027/1016-9040.11.2.153154.

36 Soldz, Arrigo, Frakt, and Olson, "Response to Staal."

37 Ibid. See also Mark Fallon, *Unjustifiable Means: The Inside Story of How the CIA, Pentagon, and US Government Conspired to Torture* (New York: Regan Arts, 2017); Claire Finkelstein and Harvey Rishikof, *Beyond Guantanamo: Restoring the Rule of Law to the Law of War* (Philadelphia, PA: Center for Ethics and the Rule of Law and Annenberg Public Policy Center, University of Pennsylvania, 2022), https://www.penncerl.org/wp-content/uploads/2022/09/Beyond-Guantanamo-Restoring-the-Rule-of-Law-to-the-Law-of-War.pdf; Douglas A. Johnson, Alberto Mora, and Averell Schmidt, "The Strategic Costs of Torture: How 'Enhanced Interrogation' Hurt America," *Foreign Affairs*, September/October 2016, https://www.foreignaffairs.com/articles/united-states/strategic-costs-torture.

38 National Public Radio, "Transcript: Military Psychologist Says Harsh Tactics Justified," May 4, 2009, http://www.npr.org/templates/transcript/transcript.php?storyId=103787285.

39 Operational Psychology Practice Guidelines Task Force, "Professional Practice Guidelines for Operational Psychology" (January 2022), https://apps.apa.org/CommentCentral2/attachments/Site85_Proposed%20Guidelines%20for%20Operational%20Psychology%20(DraftLined)%20(1).pdf; see also American Psychological Association, "Professional Practice Guidelines: Guidance for Developers and Users," *American Psychologist* 70, no. 9 (2015): 823–31, http://dx.doi.org/10.1037/a0039644.

40 Operational Psychology Practice Guidelines Task Force, "Professional Practice Guidelines," 2.

41 Ibid., 5.

42 See the following: Roy Eidelson, "The 'Operational Psychology Professional Practice Guidelines' Are Deeply Flawed – The American Psychological

Association Needs Your Comments," *royeidelson.com* (blog), January 24, 2022, https://www.royeidelson.com/the-operational-psychology-professional-practice-guidelines-are-deeply-flawed/; Stephen Soldz, "Operational Psychology, Professional Ethics, and Democracy: A Challenge for Our Time," *Torture Journal: Journal on Rehabilitation of Torture Victims and Prevention of Torture* 32, no. 1–2 (2022): 193–200.

43 Operational Psychology Practice Guidelines Task Force, "Professional Practice Guidelines," 10.
44 Ibid., 11.
45 Ibid., 15.
46 Ibid., 8.
47 Soldz, Arrigo, Frakt, and Olson, "Response to Staal."
48 Arthur Levine, "Collective Unconscionable," *Washington Monthly*, January 1, 2007, https://washingtonmonthly.com/2007/01/01/collective-unconscionable/.
49 For further background, see Coalition for an Ethical Psychology, "Adversarial Operational Psychology"; Soldz, Olson, and Arrigo, "Interrogating the Ethics"; Stephen Soldz and Steven Reisner, "Professional Standards in the Aftermath of Torture: The Struggles of the American Psychological Association," in *Interrogation and Torture: Integrating Efficacy with Law and Morality*, eds. Steven J. Barela, Mark Fallon, Gloria Gaggioli, and Jens David Ohlin (New York: Oxford University Press, 2020), 225–52.
50 Staal, "Applied Psychology under Attack," 439.
51 Arrigo, Eidelson, and Rockwood, "Adversarial Operational Psychology."
52 Soldz, Arrigo, and Olson, "The Ethics of Operational Psychology Workshop," 19.

Chapter Eight

1 For further reading about institutional betrayal, see: Jennifer M. Gómez, Carly P. Smith, Robyn L. Gobin, Shin S. Tang, and Jennifer J. Freyd, "Collusion, Torture, and Inequality: Understanding the Actions of the American Psychological Association as Institutional Betrayal," *Journal of Trauma & Dissociation* 17, no. 5 (2016): 527–44; Sarah J. Harsey, Eileen L. Zurbriggen, and Jennifer J. Freyd, "Perpetrator Responses to Victim Confrontation: DARVO and Victim Self-Blame," *Journal of Aggression, Maltreatment & Trauma* 26, no. 6 (2017): 644–63; Carly P. Smith and Jennifer J. Freyd, "Institutional Betrayal," *American Psychologist* 69, no. 6 (2014): 575–87.
2 For further background about DARVO, see Harsey, Zurbriggen, and Freyd, "DARVO and Victim Self-Blame."
3 For further information about betrayal blindness and betrayal trauma, see Jennifer J. Freyd, *Betrayal Trauma: The Logic of Forgetting Childhood Abuse* (Cambridge, MA: Harvard University Press, 1996); Jennifer J. Freyd, "What Is a Betrayal Trauma? What Is Betrayal Trauma Theory?," 2020, http://pages.

uoregon.edu/dynamic/jjf/defineBT.html; Jennifer Freyd and Pamela Birrell, *Blind to Betrayal: Why We Fool Ourselves We Aren't Being Fooled* (Hoboken, NJ: John Wiley & Sons, 2013).

4 Kimberly D. Elsbach, "Organizational Perception Management," *Research in Organizational Behavior* 25 (2003): 297–332, https://doi.org/10.1016/S0191-3085(03)25007-3.

5 Gómez et al., "Collusion, Torture, and Inequality."

6 Ryan Jaslow, "Big Tobacco Kept Cancer Risk in Cigarettes Secret: Study," CBS News, September 30, 2011, http://www.cbsnews.com/news/big-tobacco-kept-cancer-risk-in-cigarettes-secret-study/.

7 Bill Sells, "What Asbestos Taught Me about Managing Risk," *Harvard Business Review*, March–April 1994, https://hbr.org/1994/03/what-asbestos-taught-me-about-managing-risk.

8 For further background, see Tim Higgins and Nick Summers, "GM Recalls: How General Motors Silenced a Whistle-Blower," *Bloomberg Businessweek*, June 19, 2014, http://www.businessweek.com/articles/2014-06-18/gm-recalls-whistle-blower-was-ignored-mary-barra-faces-congress; Doron Levin, "Here Are Some of [the] Worst Car Scandals in History," *Fortune*, September 26, 2015, http://fortune.com/2015/09/26/auto-industry-scandals/.

9 Shannon Hall, "Exxon Knew about Climate Change Almost 40 Years Ago," *Scientific American*, October 26, 2015, https://www.scientificamerican.com/article/exxon-knew-about-climate-change-almost-40-years-ago/.

10 Investigative Staff of the Boston Globe, *Betrayal: The Crisis in the Catholic Church* (Boston: Little, Brown & Company, 2002); see also Elizabeth Bruenig, "The Catholic Sex Abuse Crisis Is Far from Over," *New York Times*, November 10, 2020, https://www.nytimes.com/2020/11/10/opinion/McCarrick-Catholic-sex-abuse.html.

11 For further background, see C. Todd Lopez, "Commission Begins 90-Day Look into Sexual Assault in Military," *Defense News*, March 24, 2021, https://www.defense.gov/Explore/News/Article/Article/2548632/commission-begins-90-day-look-into-sexual-assault-in-military/; Melinda Wenner Moyer, "'A Poison in the System': The Epidemic of Military Sexual Assault," *New York Times*, August 3, 2021, https://www.nytimes.com/2021/08/03/magazine/military-sexual-assault.html; Dave Philipps, "'This Is Unacceptable.' Military Reports a Surge of Sexual Assaults in the Ranks," *New York Times*, May 2, 2019, https://www.nytimes.com/2019/05/02/us/military-sexual-assault.html.

12 For example, see Michael Levenson, "Former Penn State President Will Serve 2 Months in Jail in Child Abuse Scandal," *New York Times*, May 26, 2021, https://www.nytimes.com/2021/05/26/sports/football/Graham-Spanier-Sentenced-Penn-State-Scandal.html; Richard Pérez-Peña, "In Report, Failures throughout Penn State," *New York Times*, July 12, 2012, https://www.nytimes.com/2012/07/13/sports/ncaafootball/in-freeh-report-on-sandusky-failures-throughout-penn-state.html; Mitch Smith and Anemona Hartocollis, "Michigan State's $500 Million

for Nassar Victims Dwarfs Other Settlements," *New York Times*, May 16, 2018, https://www.nytimes.com/2018/05/16/us/larry-nassar-michigan-state-settlement.html.

13 Gómez et al., "Collusion, Torture, and Inequality."

14 Kenneth S. Pope, "The Code Not Taken: The Path from Guild Ethics to Torture and Our Continuing Choices," *Canadian Psychology/Psychologie Canadienne* 57, no. 1 (2016): 51–9, https://kspope.com/PsychologyEthics.php.

15 Kenneth S. Pope, "A Human Rights and Ethics Crisis Facing the World's Largest Organization of Psychologists," *European Psychologist* 24, no. 2 (2019): 180–94, https://psycnet.apa.org/fulltext/2018-62354-001.pdf.

16 Ibid.

17 Marvin B. Scott and Stanford M. Lyman, "Accounts," *American Sociological Review* 33, no. 1 (1968): 46.

18 Ibid., 47.

19 Gresham M. Sykes and David Matza, "Techniques of Neutralization: A Theory of Delinquency," *American Sociological Review* 22, no. 6 (1957): 664–70.

20 Stanley Cohen, *States of Denial: Knowing about Atrocities and Suffering* (Malden, MA: Polity Press, 2001); see also Emily Bryant, Emily Brooke Schimke, Hollie Nyseth Brehm, and Christopher Uggen, "Techniques of Neutralization and Identity Work among Accused Genocide Perpetrators," *Social Problems* 65, no. 4 (2018): 584–602, https://doi.org/10.1093/socpro/spx026; Stanley Cohen, "Government Responses to Human Rights Reports: Claims, Denials, and Counterclaims," *Human Rights Quarterly* 18, no. 3 (1996): 517–43.

21 Cohen, *States of Denial*, 9.

22 Ibid., 114.

23 For example, see Kimberly D. Elsbach and Robert I. Sutton, "Acquiring Organizational Legitimacy through Illegitimate Actions: A Marriage of Institutional and Impression Management Theories," *Academy of Management Journal* 35, no. 4 (1992): 699–738, https://journals.aom.org/doi/abs/10.5465/256313; Isabel Schoultz and Janne Flyghed, "From 'We Didn't Do It' to 'We've Learned Our Lesson': Development of a Typology of Neutralizations of Corporate Crime," *Critical Criminology* 28 (2020): 739–57, https://doi.org/10.1007/s10612-019-09483-3; Mark C. Suchman, "Managing Legitimacy: Strategic and Institutional Approaches," *Academy of Management Review* 20, no. 3 (1995): 571–610; David Whyte, "It's Common Sense, Stupid! Corporate Crime and Techniques of Neutralization in the Automobile Industry," *Crime, Law and Social Change* 66, no. 2 (2016): 165–81, https://doi.org/10.1007/s10611-016-9616-8.

24 Suchman, "Managing Legitimacy," 574.

25 Elsbach and Sutton, "Acquiring Organizational Legitimacy."

26 American Psychological Association, "An Open Letter from the Board of Directors," June 18, 2009, https://www.apa.org/news/press/statements/open-letter-membership.pdf; for a response to this letter from a dozen human rights organizations, see Coalition for an Ethical Psychology et al., "Open Letter in

Response to the American Psychological Association Board," June 29, 2009, https://www.ethicalpsychology.org/materials/Letter-APA-Board-6-29-09.pdf.

27 Suchman, "Managing Legitimacy," 597.

28 Arthur Evans, Jr, "Letters to the Editor: Psychologists Strive to Do Good Work," *Washington Post*, October 22, 2017, https://www.washingtonpost.com/opinions/psychologists-strive-to-do-good-work/2017/10/22/cf3ef926-b4d4-11e7-9b93-b97043e57a22_story.html; for my original essay and my response to Evans, see Roy Eidelson, "Psychologists Are Facing Consequences for Helping with Torture. It's Not Enough," *Washington Post*, October 13, 2017, https://www.washington-post.com/outlook/psychologists-are-facing-consequences-for-helping-with-torture-its-not-enough/2017/10/13/2756b734-ad14-11e7-9e58-e6288544af98_story.html; Roy Eidelson, "Facing History: My Reply to APA CEO Arthur Evans," *Psychology Today*, October 25, 2017, https://www.psychologytoday.com/us/blog/dangerous-ideas/201710/facing-history-my-reply-apa-ceo-arthur-evans.

29 Gavin Crowell-Williamson, "Psychology and Poverty: An Interview with APA President Rosie Phillips Davis," *Mad in America*, January 22, 2020, https://www.madinamerica.com/2020/01/psychology-poverty-interview-apa-president-rosie-phillips-davis/.

30 Dan Aalbers and Thomas Teo, "The American Psychological Association and the Torture Complex: A Phenomenology of the Banality and Workings of Bureaucracy," *Journal fur Psychologie* 25, no. 1 (2017): 185.

31 Ibid., 185.

32 Ibid., 191.

33 Ibid., 192.

34 For further background about groupthink, see Irving L. Janis, *Groupthink*, 2nd ed. (Boston: Houghton Mifflin, 1982); Irving Janis, "Groupthink," in *A First Look at Communication Theory*, ed. Emory A. Griffin (New York: McGraw Hill, 1991), 235–46; Clark R. McCauley, "The Nature of Social Influence in Groupthink: Compliance and Internalization," *Journal of Personality and Social Psychology* 57, no. 2 (1989): 250–60; Cass R. Sunstein and Reid Hastie, *Wiser: Getting Beyond Groupthink to Make Groups Smarter* (Boston: Harvard Business Review Press, 2015). A related phenomenon is the culture of silence. For example, see Peter Verhezen, "Giving Voice in a Culture of Silence. From a Culture of Compliance to a Culture of Integrity," *Journal of Business Ethics* 96 (2010): 187–206, https://doi.org/10.1007/s10551-010-0458-5; James A. Waters and Frederick Bird, "The Moral Dimension of Organizational Culture," *Journal of Business Ethics* 6 (1987): 15–22, https://doi.org/10.1007/BF00382944.

35 For example, see Gregory Moorhead, Richard Ference, and Chris P. Neck, "Group Decision Fiascoes Continue: Space Shuttle Challenger and a Revised Groupthink Framework," *Human Relations* 44, no. 6 (1991): 539–50, https://journals.sagepub.com/doi/10.1177/001872679104400601; Kathy Sawyer, "Misguided 'Groupthink' Blamed in Decision to Launch Challenger," *Washington Post*, June 18, 1986, https://www.washingtonpost.com/archive/

politics/1986/06/18/misguided-group-think-blamed-in-decision-to-launch-challenger/e8cc84b9-5301-4ea0-beac-545e486db52f/.

36 Aalbers and Teo, "The American Psychological Association and the Torture Complex," 198.

37 Bryant Welch, "The American Psychological Association and Torture: How Could It Happen?," *International Journal of Applied Psychoanalytic Studies* 14, no. 2 (2017): 116–24, https://doi.org/10.1002/aps.1519.

38 Ibid., 122.

39 For further background, see Patrick Collins, "Why Does the US Spend So Much on Defense?," *Defense One*, January 26, 2020, https://www.defenseone.com/ideas/2020/01/why-does-us-spend-so-much-defense/162657/; K.K. Rebecca Lai, Troy Griggs, Max Fisher, and Audrey Carlsen, "Is America's Military Big Enough?," *New York Times*, March 22, 2017, https://www.nytimes.com/interactive/2017/03/22/us/is-americas-military-big-enough.html.

40 Dwight D. Eisenhower, "'The Chance for Peace,' Delivered before the American Society of Newspaper Editors," April 16, 1953, https://www.presidency.ucsb.edu/documents/address-the-chance-for-peace-delivered-before-the-american-society-newspaper-editors.

41 For further background, see Heidi Garrett-Peltier, "Job Opportunity Cost of War," *Watson Institute for International and Public Affairs, Brown University*, May 24, 2017, https://watson.brown.edu/costsofwar/files/cow/imce/papers/2017/Job%20Opportunity%20Cost%20of%20War%20-%20HGP%20-%20FINAL.pdf; Elliott Negin, "It's Time to Rein in Inflated Military Budgets," *Scientific American*, September 14, 2020, https://www.scientificamerican.com/article/its-time-to-rein-in-inflated-military-budgets/.

42 Examples include the following: American Psychological Association, "Resolution on Affirming Psychologists' Role in Addressing Global Climate Change," 2011, https://www.apa.org/about/policy/climate-change; American Psychological Association, "Public Policies Can Mitigate the Effects of Scarcity and Poverty," n.d., accessed May 3, 2022, https://web.archive.org/web/20210125203439/https://www.apa.org/advocacy/socioeconomic-status/index; American Psychological Association, "Civil Rights: Race, Ethnicity & Religion," 2017, https://www.apa.org/advocacy/civil-rights/diversity/index; American Psychological Association, "Resolution on Firearm Violence Research and Prevention," 2014, https://www.apa.org/about/policy/firearms; American Psychological Association, "APA Advocacy Related to Immigration," n.d., accessed May 3, 2022, https://web.archive.org/web/20220121221744/https://www.apa.org/advocacy/immigration; American Psychological Association, "Recent APA Advocacy Related to Women's Health," n.d., accessed May 3, 2022, https://www.apa.org/advocacy/health/women; American Psychological Association, "Resolution on Appropriate Affirmative Responses to Sexual Orientation Distress and Change Efforts," 2009, https://www.apa.org/about/policy/sexual-orientation; American Psychological Association, "APA COVID-19 Information

and Resources," n.d., accessed May 3, 2022, https://www.apa.org/topics/covid-19; Melissa Dittmann, "Protecting Children from Advertising," *Monitor on Psychology* 35, no. 6 (2004), https://www.apa.org/monitor/jun04/protecting.

43 Martin Luther King, Jr, "Speech: Beyond Vietnam – A Time to Break the Silence," April 4, 1967, https://www.americanrhetoric.com/speeches/mlkatimetobreaksilence.htm; see also Serdar M. Degirmencioglu, "The Psychology of Napalm: Whose Side Are Psychologists On?," *Journal of Critical Psychology, Counselling and Psychotherapy* 10, no. 4 (2010): 196–205; Jim Orford, "Turning Psychology against Militarism," *Journal of Community and Applied Social Psychology* 27, no. 4 (2017): 287–97.

44 "APA Urges Congress to Reject President's Proposed Budget," news release, American Psychological Association, March 17, 2017, https://web.archive.org/web/20190422211059/https://www.apa.org/news/press/releases/2017/03/reject-presidents-budget.

45 For example, see Heather O. Kelly, "Supporting Human-Centered Defense Research on the Hill," *Psychological Science Agenda*, July 2006; Heather O. Kelly, "APA Advocates for Psychological Research within the Department of Defense," *Psychological Science Agenda*, July 2009, http://www.apa.org/science/about/psa/2009/07/dod.aspx; Heather O. Kelly, "APA Member Presents APA's Defense Appropriations Testimony in the Senate," *Psychological Science Agenda*, July 2010, https://www.apa.org/science/about/psa/2010/07/dod; US Senate, Subcommittee of the Committee on Appropriations, Department of Defense Appropriations for Fiscal Year 2010, "Statement of Gavan O'Shea, Ph.D., on Behalf of the American Psychological Association," June 18, 2009, https://www.govinfo.gov/content/pkg/CHRG-111shrg89104348/html/CHRG-111shrg89104348.htm; see also Stephen Soldz, "The 'Black Jail,'" *Counterpunch*, May 21, 2010, https://www.counterpunch.org/2010/05/21/the-quot-black-jail-quot/.

46 Roy Eidelson and Jean Maria Arrigo, "Op-Ed: How the American Psychological Assn. Lost Its Way," *Los Angeles Times*, July 30, 2015, https://www.latimes.com/opinion/op-ed/la-oe-arrigo-psychologists-apa-report-20150729-story.html.

47 For a reprint of this letter, see Franz Boas, "Scientists as Spies," *Anthropology Today* 21, no. 3 (June 2005): 27; see also David Price, "Anthropologists as Spies," *The Nation*, November 2, 2000, https://www.thenation.com/article/world/anthropologists-spies/.

48 American Anthropological Association, "Uncensoring Franz Boas," n.d., accessed August 31, 2022, https://www.americananthro.org/ConnectWithAAA/Content.aspx?ItemNumber=2134.

49 For example, see Carolyn Fluehr-Lobban, ed., *Ethics and the Profession of Anthropology: Dialogue for Ethically Conscious Practice,* 2nd ed. (Walnut Creek, CA: AltaMira Press, 2003); David H. Price, *Cold War Anthropology: The CIA, the Pentagon, and the Growth of Dual Use Anthropology* (Durham, NC: Duke University Press, 2016).

50 Roberto Gonzalez, Hugh Gusterson, and David Price, "Introduction," in *The Counter-Counterinsurgency Manual*, ed. Network of Concerned Anthropologists (Chicago: Prickly Paradigm Press, 2009), 10.

51 David H. Price, *Weaponizing Anthropology: Social Science in the Service of the Militarized State* (Oakland, CA: AK Press/Counterpunch, 2011); Roberto J. Gonzalez, *American Counterinsurgency: Human Science and the Human Terrain* (Chicago: Prickly Paradigm Press, 2009).

52 NBC-DFW, "Plano Anthropologist Maps 'Human Terrain' of Afghanistan," March 14, 2009, https://www.nbcdfw.com/news/local/plano-antropologist-maps-human-terrain-of-afghanistan/1889282/.

53 AAA Commission on the Engagement of Anthropology with the US Security and Intelligence Communities, "Final Report on the Army's Human Terrain System Proof of Concept Program," October 14, 2009, 3, https://s3.amazonaws.com/rdcms-aaa/files/production/public/FileDownloads/pdfs/cmtes/commissions/CEAUSSIC/upload/CEAUSSIC_HTS_Final_Report.pdf.

54 For further background, see Scott Jaschik, "Embedded Conflicts," *Inside Higher Ed*, July 7, 2015, https://www.insidehighered.com/news/2015/07/07/army-shuts-down-controversial-human-terrain-system-criticized-many-anthropologists; Tom Vanden Brook, "Army Kills Controversial Social Science Program," *USA Today*, June 29, 2015, https://www.usatoday.com/story/news/nation/2015/06/29/human-terrain-system-afghanistan/29476409/.

55 For additional information, see Zara Abrams, "Serving the Armed Forces," *Monitor on Psychology* 50, no. 10 (November 2019): 58, https://www.apa.org/monitor/2019/11/serving-armed-forces; Arthur Evans, Jr, "Proud to Serve Those Who Serve," *Monitor on Psychology* 49, no. 9 (October 2018): 8, https://www.apa.org/monitor/2018/10/ceo.html; Amy Novotney, "The VA Is Hiring," *Monitor on Psychology* 49, no. 9 (October 2018): 64, https://www.apa.org/monitor/2018/10/careers-va-hiring.

56 Karen Stamm, Peggy Christidis, and Luona Lin, "How Much Federal Funding Is Directed to Research in Psychology?," *Monitor on Psychology* 48, no. 4 (April 2017): 15, https://www.apa.org/monitor/2017/04/datapoint.

57 Examples include the Human Resources Research Organization (https://www.humrro.org/corpsite/); Special Psychological Applications, Inc. (http://spasupportinc.com); and OSS Consulting (http://www.ossconsultation.com/index.html).

58 For further background, see Jean Maria Arrigo, Lawrence P. Rockwood, Jack O'Brien, Dutch Franz, David DeBatto, and John Kiriakou, "A Military/Intelligence Operational Perspective on the Weaponization of Psychology by the American Psychological Association," *History of the Human Sciences* (in press); Jean Maria Arrigo and Jancis Long, *Psicologia: Teoria e Prática* 10, no. 1 (2008): 186–99; Meredith P. Crawford, "Highlights in the Development of the Human Resources Research Organization (HumRRO)," *American Psychologist* 39, no. 11 (1984): 1267–71, https://doi.org/10.1037/0003-066X.39.11.1267; L. Rabasca, "The Architect of

APA's Financial Foundation, Meredith P. Crawford," *Monitor on Psychology* 31, no. 8 (2000); Frank Summers, "Making Sense of the APA: A History of the Relationship between Psychology and the Military," *Psychoanalytic Dialogues* 18, no. 5 (2008): 614–37, https://www.tandfonline.com/doi/abs/10.1080/10481880802297665; Bryant Welch, "The American Psychological Association and Torture: How Could It Happen?," *International Journal of Applied Psychoanalytic Studies* 14, no. 2 (2017): 116–24, https://doi.org/10.1002/aps.1519.

59 For example, see Defense Human Resources Activity, "Department of Defense Youth Poll Wave 19," 2010, https://jamrs.defense.gov/Portals/20/Documents/Youth_Poll_19.pdf; Human Resources Research Organization, "Form 990-Return of Organization Exempt from Income Tax," 2010, 2, http://990s.foundationcenter.org/990_pdf_archive/237/237029310/237029310_201109_990.pdf;Cheryl Paullin, Michael Ingerick, D.M. Trippe, and Laurie Wasko, "Identifying Best Bet Entry-Level Selection Measures for US Air Force Remotely Piloted Aircraft (RPA) Pilot and Sensor Operator (SO) Occupations (Report No. AFCAPS-FR-2011-0013)," December 2011.

60 Human Resources Research Organization, "Board of Trustees," n.d., accessed July 7, 2022, https://www.humrro.org/corpsite/who-we-are/board-trustees/.

61 Dutch Franz and Jean Maria Arrigo, "The Compromise of Military and Psychological Ethics: Subversion of the American Psychological Association by a Defense Contractor, and Government Manipulation of Vulnerable On-Line Communities," paper presented to the International Society of Military Ethics, Washington, DC, January 26, 2017.

62 Martin E.P. Seligman and Michael D. Matthews, eds., "Comprehensive Soldier Fitness (Special Issue)," *American Psychologist* 66, no. 1 (January 2011).

63 For further background, see Roy Eidelson and Stephen Soldz, Does Comprehensive Soldier Fitness Work? CSF Research Fails the Test, May 2012, http://www.ethicalpsychology.org/Eidelson-&-Soldz-CSF_Research_Fails_the_Test.pdf; Institute of Medicine, Preventing Psychological Disorders in Service Members and Their Families: An Assessment of Programs (Washington, DC: The National Academies Press, 2014), https://www.nap.edu/catalog/18597/preventing-psychological-disorders-in-service-members-and-their-families-an; Maria M. Skeenkamp, William P. Nash, and Brett T. Litz, "Post-Traumatic Stress Disorder: Review of the Comprehensive Soldier Fitness Program," *American Journal of Preventive Medicine* 44, no. 5 (2013): 507–12, https://doi.org/10.1016/j.amepre.2013.01.013; Gregg Zoroya, "Army Morale Low Despite 6-Year, $287M Optimism Program," *USA Today*, April 16, 2015, https://www.usatoday.com/story/news/nation/2015/04/16/army-survey-morale/24897455/.

64 See also Roy J. Eidelson, Marc Pilisuk, and Stephen Soldz, "The Dark Side of Comprehensive Soldier Fitness," *American Psychologist* 66, no. 7 (2011): 643–4, https://psycnet.apa.org/doiLanding?doi=10.1037%2Fa0025272; Roy Eidelson, Marc Pilisuk, and Stephen Soldz, "The Dark Side of 'Comprehensive Soldier Fitness,'" *Truthout*, April 1, 2011, https://truthout.org/articles/the-dark-side-of-

comprehensive-soldier-fitness/; Jesse Singal, *The Quick Fix: Why Fad Psychology Can't Cure Our Social Ills* (New York: Farrar, Straus and Giroux, 2021). For a response from Seligman, see Martin E.P. Seligman, "Effectiveness of Positive Psychology: Setting the Record Straight," *Chronicle of Higher Education*, June 14, 2021, https://www.chronicle.com/article/effectiveness-of-positive-psychology.

65 Forrest Church, *Life Lines: Holding On (and Letting Go)* (Boston: Beacon Press, 1996), 5.

66 The discussion that follows draws in part upon recommendations colleagues and I prepared for a meeting with APA leaders in 2016. See Psychologists for Social Responsibility, Physicians for Human Rights, & International Human Rights Clinic, Harvard Law School, "Human Rights and National Security: Select Recommendations for the American Psychological Association," March 8, 2016, https://psysr.net/wp-content/uploads/2019/02/Human-Rights-National-Security-Select-Recommendations-for-APA.pdf.

67 American Psychological Association, "Letter to APA Membership from Susan H. McDaniel and Nadine J. Kaslow," news release, July 24, 2015, https://www.apa.org/independent-review/letter-members-apology.pdf.

68 American Psychological Association, "Letter from Nadine J. Kaslow and Susan J. McDaniel to Psychology Colleagues in the International Community on Behalf of the Board and Members of APA," news release, 2015, https://www.apa.org/independent-review/international-letter.pdf.

69 For further background, see American Middle Eastern/North African (MENA) Psychological Network, "Open Letter to the American Psychological Association & the Psychological Community," August 14, 2015, https://www.apa.org/independent-review/open-letter-mena.pdf; Kenneth S. Pope, "A Human Rights and Ethics Crisis Facing the World's Largest Organization of Psychologists," *European Psychologist* 24, no. 2 (2019): 180–94, https://psycnet.apa.org/fulltext/2018-62354-001.pdf; Gómez et al., "Collusion, Torture, and Inequality."

70 For further information, see Ian Austen, "Canada Apologizes and Pays Millions to Citizen Held at Guantánamo Bay," *New York Times*, July 7, 2017, https://www.nytimes.com/2017/07/07/world/canada/omar-khadr-apology-guantanamo-bay.html; Council of Europe Commissioner for Human Rights, "Torture Survivors Have the Right to Redress and Rehabilitation," July 6, 2016, https://www.coe.int/en/web/commissioner/-/torture-survivors-have-the-right-to-redress-and-rehabilitation; Nora Sveaass, "Gross Human Rights Violations and Reparation under International Law: Approaching Rehabilitation as a Form of Reparation," *European Journal of Psychotraumatology* 4, no. 1 (2013): 17191, https://www.tandfonline.com/doi/full/10.3402/ejpt.v4io.17191; United Nations, "Basic Principles and Guidelines on the Right to a Remedy and Reparation for Victims of Gross Violations of International Human Rights Law and Serious Violations of International Humanitarian Law," December 16, 2005, https://www.ohchr.org/en/professionalinterest/pages/remedyandreparation.aspx.

71 A review of the APA's tax filings shows that the association routinely makes donations to other 501(c)(3) nonprofits whose needs and activities are consistent with the APA's own mission.

72 The statement, "Two Steps the American Psychological Association Should Take Today," is available online at https://www.ethicalpsychology.org/materials/Two-Steps-the-American-Psychological-Association-Should-Take-Today.pdf; for more information about the United Nations International Day in Support of Torture Victims and its history, see https://www.un.org/en/observances/torture-victims-day.

73 Ellen Gerrity, "Beyond Institutional Betrayal: When the Professional Is Personal," in *Witnessing Torture: Perspectives of Torture Survivors and Human Rights Workers*, eds. Alexandra S. Moore and Elizabeth Swanson (New York: Palgrave Macmillan, 2018), 135.

74 For further background on calls to close Guantanamo, see Mansoor Adayfi, Moazzam Begg, Lakhdar Boumediane, Sami Al Hajj, Ahmed Errachidi, Mohammed Ould Slahi, and Moussa Zemmouri, "An Open Letter to President Biden about Guantánamo," *New York Review of Books,* January 29, 2021, https://www.nybooks.com/daily/2021/01/29/an-open-letter-to-president-biden-about-guantanamo/; American Civil Liberties Union, "Close Guantanamo," n.d., accessed May 3, 2022, https://www.aclu.org/feature/close-guantanamo; Amnesty International, "USA: Close the Guantanamo Detention Center!," n.d., accessed May 3, 2022, https://www.amnesty.org/en/get-involved/take-action/close-guantanamo/; Center for Constitutional Rights, "4 Steps President Biden Must Take to Close Guantanamo," December 17, 2020, https://ccrjustice.org/four-steps-president-biden-must-take-close-guantanamo; Claire Finkelstein and Harvey Rishikof, *Beyond Guantanamo: Restoring the Rule of Law to the Law of War* (Philadelphia, PA: Center for Ethics and the Rule of Law and Annenberg Public Policy Center, University of Pennsylvania, 2022), https://www.penncerl.org/wp-content/uploads/2022/09/Beyond-Guantanamo-Restoring-the-Rule-of-Law-to-the-Law-of-War.pdf; Human Rights First, "Close Guantanamo," n.d., accessed May 3, 2022, https://www.humanrightsfirst.org/campaigns/close-guantanamo; Institute for Public Accuracy, "Over 100 Groups Call for Biden to Close Guantanamo," February 3, 2021, https://accuracy.org/release/over-100-groups-call-for-biden-to-close-guantanamo/; National Religious Campaign Against Torture, "Take Action – Close Guantanamo," n.d., accessed May 3, 2022, http://www.nrcat.org/national-security/close-guantanamo/act-guantanamo.

75 United Nations, "Close 'Disgraceful' Guantanamo Camp – UN Experts Urge Incoming US Administration," January 11, 2021, https://news.un.org/en/story/2021/01/1081842.

76 Ibid.

77 Matt Spetalnick, Trevor Hunnicutt, and Phil Stewart, "Biden Launches Review of Guantanamo Prison, Aims to Close It before Leaving Office," *Reuters*, February 12, 2021, https://www.reuters.com/article/us-usa-biden-guantanamo-exclusive/

biden-launches-review-of-guantanamo-prison-aims-to-close-it-before-leaving-office-idUSKBN2AC1Q4.

78 "Letter to President Biden from the APA's President and CEO," news release, American Psychological Association, May 12, 2021, https://www.apa.org/news/press/statements/guantanamo-closure-support-biden.pdf.

79 Pope, "A Human Rights and Ethics Crisis," 187; see also Adam D. Jacobson, "Back to the Dark Side: Explaining the CIA's Repeated Use of Torture," *Terrorism and Political Violence* 33, no. 2 (2021): 257–70, https://www.tandfonline.com/doi/abs/10.1080/09546553.2021.1880193.

80 American Psychological Association Commission on Ethics Processes, "Report to APA Board of Directors & Council of Representatives," August 2017, https://www.apa.org/ethics/ethics-processes-report.pdf.

81 Ibid., 1.

82 Ibid., 4, 7, 10.

83 American Psychological Association, "Frequently Asked Questions regarding the Simplification of the Rules and Procedures of the Ethics Committee," August 2018, https://www.apa.org/ethics/faqs/new-committee-rules; Ethics Committee of the American Psychological Association, "Rules and Procedures," June 15, 2018, https://www.apa.org/ethics/committee-rules-procedures-2018.pdf.

84 American Psychological Association Commission on Ethics Processes, "Report to APA," 11–17.

85 American Psychological Association, "Complaints Regarding APA Members," 2018, https://www.apa.org/ethics/complaint.

86 For example, see Kenneth S. Pope, "The American Psychological Association Outsources Adjudication of Ethics Complaints: 5 Far-Reaching Consequences," July 22, 2018, https://kspope.com/ethicsoutsourcing.php.

87 Psychologists for Social Responsibility, Physicians for Human Rights, & International Human Rights Clinic, Harvard Law School, "Human Rights and National Security."

88 Dutch Franz and Jean Maria Arrigo, "Recommendations to The American Association for the Advancement of Science Committee on Scientific Freedom and Responsibility for Constraints on Defense Contractors in the Health, Behavioral, and Social Sciences," September 2016, 3.

89 For further background, see J. Wesley Boyd, Alice LoCicero, Monica Malowney, Rajendra Aldis, and Robert P. Marlin, "Failing Ethics 101: Psychologists, the US Military Establishment, and Human Rights," *International Journal of Health Services* 44, no. 3 (2014): 615–25; Alice LoCicero, Robert P. Marlin, David Jull-Patterson, Nancy M. Sweeney, Brandon Lee Gray, and J. Wesley, "Enabling Torture: APA, Clinical Psychology Training, and the Failure to Disobey," *Peace and Conflict: Journal of Peace Psychology* 22, no. 4 (2016): 345–55.

90 Psychologists for Social Responsibility, Physicians for Human Rights, & International Human Rights Clinic, Harvard Law School, "Human Rights and National Security."

91 Philip Cushman, "The Earthquake That Is the Hoffman Report on Torture: Toward a Re-Moralization of Psychology," *Psychoanalysis, Self and Context* 13, no. 4 (2018): 311–34.

92 American Psychological Association, "Human Rights," n.d., accessed May 3, 2022, https://www.apa.org/topics/human-rights.

93 Coalition for an Ethical Psychology, "Letter to the APA Board and Council of Representatives," February 18, 2013, 3, http://www.ethicalpsychology.org/materials/Coalition-Letter-APA-Council-2-18-13.pdf.

RECOMMENDED RESOURCES
FOR FURTHER STUDY

If *Doing Harm* has spurred an interest in further exploring the issues I've examined here, there's a wide range of books and other media worthy of recommendation. That list is much longer than space allows, so here I offer only a sampling.

The so-called US war on terror, including the role of torture and the participation of health professionals, has received critical attention from scholars, journalists, and insiders. Among the books that I've found most valuable are the following:

Ackerman, Spencer. *Reign of Terror: How the 9/11 Era Destabilized America and Produced Trump*. New York: Viking Press, 2021.

Fallon, Mark. *Unjustifiable Means: The Inside Story of How the CIA, Pentagon, and US Government Conspired to Torture*. New York: Regan Arts, 2017.

Hajjar, Lisa. *The War in Court: Inside the Long Fight against Torture*. Oakland: University of California Press, 2022.

Mayer, Jane. *The Dark Side: The Inside Story of How the War on Terror Turned into a War on American Ideals*. New York: Doubleday, 2008.

Miles, Steven H. *Oath Betrayed: Torture, Medical Complicity, and the War on Terror*. New York: Random House, 2006.

Phillips, Joshua E.S. *None of Us Were Like This Before: American Soldiers and Torture*. New York: Verso, 2010.

Sands, Philippe. *Torture Team: Rumsfeld's Memo and the Betrayal of American Values*. New York: Palgrave Macmillan, 2008.

Scott-Clark, Cathy, and Adrian Levy. *The Forever Prisoner*. New York: Atlantic Monthly Press, 2022.

Siems, Larry. *The Torture Report: What the Documents Say about America's Post-9/11 Torture Program*. New York: OR Books, 2011.

There are also several valuable books that provide insights into the experience of torture, from the perspective of both academic experts and torture survivors, including released Guantanamo prisoners. Here are some examples:

Adayfi, Mansoor. *Don't Forget Us Here: Lost and Found at Guantanamo.* New York: Hachette Books, 2021.

Begg, Moazzam. *Enemy Combatant: My Imprisonment at Guantánamo, Bagram, and Kandahar.* New York: New Press, 2007.

Moore, Alexandra S., and Elizabeth Swanson, eds. *Witnessing Torture: Perspectives of Torture Survivors and Human Rights Workers.* New York: Palgrave Macmillan, 2018.

Pérez-Sales, Pau. *Psychological Torture: Definition, Evaluation and Measurement.* London: Routledge, 2017.

Rejali, Darius. *Torture and Democracy.* Princeton, NJ: Princeton University Press, 2009.

Scarry, Elaine. *The Body in Pain: The Making and Unmaking of the World.* New York: Oxford University Press, 1985.

Slahi, Mohamedou Ould. *Guantanamo Diary* (restored edition). New York: Back Bay Books, 2017.

Here are two scholarly books focused on interrogation, along with two lengthy US Senate reports that provide details about the treatment of war-on-terror prisoners in US custody:

Barela, Steven J., Mark Fallon, Gloria Gaggioli, and Jens David Ohlin, eds. *Interrogation and Torture: Integrating Efficacy with Law and Morality.* New York: Oxford University Press, 2020.

McCoy, Alfred W. *A Question of Torture: CIA Interrogation, from the Cold War to the War on Terror.* New York: Henry Holt and Company, 2006.

United States Senate Committee on Armed Services. *Inquiry into the Treatment of Detainees in U.S. Custody,* 2008. https://www.armed-services.senate.gov/imo/media/doc/Detainee-Report-Final_April-22-2009.pdf.

United States Senate Select Committee on Intelligence. *Committee Study of the Central Intelligence Agency's Detention and Interrogation Program,* 2014. https://www.intelligence.senate.gov/sites/default/files/publications/CRPT-113srpt288.pdf.

Finally, here are some excellent films from the past decade that are directly relevant to *Doing Harm*, including two documentaries by dissident psychologist Martha Davis:

Bennett, Stephen, director. *Eminent Monsters*. Hopscotch Films, 2020.

Burns, Scott Z., director. *The Report*. Amazon Studios, 2019.

Coyote, Peter, and Sherry Jones. *Torturing Democracy*. Bullfrog Films, 2008.

Davis, Martha, director. *Doctors of the Dark Side*. DODS Productions, 2013.

– *Expert Witness: Health Professionals on the Frontline against Torture*. DODS Productions, 2016.

Gibney, Alex, director. *Taxi to the Dark Side*. THINKFilm, 2007.

– *The Forever Prisoner*. HBO, 2021.

Kennedy, Rory, director. *Ghosts of Abu Ghraib*. HBO, 2007.

Kirk, Michael, director. *The Torture Question*. PBS, 2005.

MacDonald, Kevin, director. *The Mauritanian*. STXfilms, 2021.

INDEX

Office of Medical Services (CIA), 35, 102

Olson, Brad: APA member-initiated
referendum, 82; Coalition formation,
73–4; confrontation with military
psychologist, 78–9; Psychologists for
an Ethical APA, 76

O'Mara, Shane, 47

operational psychology and
psychologists: adversarial
operational psychology (AOP),
8–9, 139–52; Brookline Principles,
143–4; collaborative operational
psychology, 143, 145; defense of AOP
by operational psychologists, 147–9;
description of, 42; opposition to APA
reforms, 137, 173; practice guidelines
proposal, 149–50

Opotow, Susan, 29, 76–7, 110

O'Shaughnessy, Tiffany, 114

Parry, John, 122, 128

*Pay Any Price: Greed, Power, and
Endless War*, 8, 100, 101, 105

PENS Report. *See* Psychological Ethics
and National Security Task Force
and Report

PENS Task Force. *See* Psychological
Ethics and National Security Task
Force and Report

Pentagon. *See* Department of Defense

Phillips, Joshua, 48

Phillips Davis, Rosie, 160

Physicians for Human Rights: call for
apology and reparations from APA,
169; call for federal investigation
of APA, 102, 107; Coalition, 74–5;
experimentation on detainees, 60,
144; opposition to APA resolution
returning psychologists to
Guantanamo (2018), 132; PENS
annulment petition, 90; Senate
Intelligence Committee CIA torture
report, 103

Pipher, Mary, 82

Podber, Naomi, 110

Pope, Ken, 23, 88, 156–7, 170–1

Popowski, Deborah, 96

post-traumatic stress disorder (PTSD), 35,
40, 45, 167

Press, Eyal, 47

Price, David, 165

Project Camelot, 165

ProPublica, 63

Psychological Ethics and National
Security (PENS) Task Force and
Report: Coalition annulment
campaign, 89–93; conflict of
interest, 61–2; emergency vote, 61;
Hoffman Report critique, 104–5,
141; irregularities, 60–3; listserv, 63;
members, 55–7; Nuremberg defense,
58; research recommendations, 59–
60; "safe, legal, ethical, and effective,"
57, 63, 96, 133; Wessells resignation, 61

Psychologists for an Ethical APA, 5, 76,
82, 88

Psychologists for Social Responsibility
(PsySR), 5, 75–6, 107, 109, 135

PTSD. *See* post-traumatic stress disorder

Puig-Lugo, Hiram, 134

al-Qahtani, Mohammed, 39–40, 54, 94

Rahman, Gul, 36

RAND Corporation, 19, 20

Raymond, Nathaniel, 75, 81, 100, 105

Reese, Michael, 96

Reisner, Steven: *All the President's
Psychologists*, 105; APA convention
(2006), 68; APA convention (2007), 81;
APA convention (2015), 110; Coalition
formation, 73–4; documenting
detainee abuse, 118, 120; ethics
complaint against, 135

reprieve, 121

reputation management, 157–60